ONE WOMAN'S RECOVERY

from **Abuse** *and* **Her Fight** *to*
Change the Law

ZOE DRONFIELD

Copyright © 2022 by Zoe Dronfield. All rights reserved.

This book or any portion thereof may not be reproduced or used in
any manner whatsoever without the express written permission of the
publisher except for the use of brief quotations in a book review.

Strenuous attempts have been made to credit all copyrighted materials used in this book. All such materials and trademarks, which are referenced in this book, are the full property of their respective copyright owners. Every effort has been made to obtain copyright permission for material quoted in this book. Any omissions will be rectified in future editions. Certain individuals' names have been changed to preserve anonymity.

Cover image by: Sam Art Studio, 99 Designs
Book design by: SWATT Books Ltd

Printed in the United Kingdom
First Printing, 2022

ISBN: 978-1-7396871-0-6 (Paperback)
ISBN: 978-1-7396871-1-3 (Hardback)
ISBN: 978-1-7396871-2-0 (eBook)

Zoe Dronfield
Coventry

Reviews for *Mind Over Manipulators*

"As a victim it's important to understand that you are not to blame for the abuse, nor should you feel ashamed. The shame lies solely with the abuser."

This is a book about the courage, resilience and determination of a woman who was stalked, suffered horrendous physical and emotional domestic abuse and had to fight for custody of her children when she was at her most vulnerable. Zoe Dronfield is an extraordinary woman whose super power really is what she calls 'strength in adversity'.

At every turn, Zoe's horrific suffering was exacerbated by the police and judicial system that failed the victims of stalking and domestic abuse. Somehow she found the strength not only to survive, and keep her family together, but to relentlessly challenge the system whenever she found it to be unfair and to campaign with others to bring about vital changes in the law so that others would not have to suffer the same injustices. She used her experience to educate those who should already have been aware of the ignorant, damaging policies and practices that were being pursued. Thanks to her advocacy and her tireless campaigning, stalking laws were introduced and then strengthened, the Domestic Abuse Act has brought about many vital changes and, for the first time, there is a national strategy for the policing of women and girls which puts victims first.

This book is not only about Zoe's journey, it is a mine of invaluable information and advice. It should not only be read by all those who work with victims of domestic abuse but also by those who are still suffering at the hands of an abuser. Where the courts are concerned, her advice is clear: be prepared, be organised and understand the process.

We don't all have Zoe's inexhaustible inner strength but we can all learn from her experience.

Baroness Jan Royall, Principal, Somerville College, Oxford University

A searingly honest, harrowing and eye-opening account of male violence and abuse and how the system re-victimizes women at every turn. Zoe is a warrior and an inspiration. Read this book – it might just save a life.

Laura Richards, Producer 'The Crime Analyst' Podcast, Founder, Paladin National Stalking Advocacy Service and criminal behavioural analyst, formerly of New Scotland Yard

Zoe Dronfield's book is not an easy read but it is a hugely powerful and important one. Many readers will find it almost impossible to comprehend what she has been through. Equally hard to take in is the scale of domestic abuse and stalking going on within our society today. This, as Zoe says, "has no social class, no financial class, no ethnicity. It crosses every boundary. It can literally happen to anyone".

This is why we should all pay attention to Zoe's story: not just professionals working with DA victims or assailants, not just victims themselves or their friends and families. There are so many lessons to be learned and we need to work together – both to empower victims to seek help much sooner and to ensure that the system reacts in the right way when they do. Despite some significant steps forward in recent years, much of it due to campaigns Zoe has taken part in, we still have a long way to go.

Professor Clive Ruggles, The Alice Ruggles Trust

This is a powerful account of how a woman found herself in the middle of an abusive relationship; how she came back from the brink of death, and how she stepped up to fight the system. Zoe's story will help so many women.

Victoria Derbyshire, journalist and broadcaster

This is a terrifying account of how a strong confident woman was groomed into an abusive relationship and how agencies designed to help repeatedly let her down. This should be compulsory reading for all those involved in the criminal justice and family law system and should shame them into change. Many people would not believe that what happened to Zoe was possible in modern Britain which is why I would urge everyone to read this jaw dropping account of a nightmare that never ends – even to this day.

Rachel Horman-Brown, Head of Family & Director – Watson Ramsbottom, and Chair of Paladin National Stalking Advocacy Service

This is the best self-help book I've ever read and I will recommend it to my clients and anyone that has to deal with abusive partners, abusive frenemies or even family members.

Zoe is a true hero; she humbly writes her account but I watched and felt as her whole world fell apart at the failings of the court systems, the police failings and the obscenely weak support system for survivors. Zoe, now the leading voice on change, has charitably and tirelessly worked to support other survivors to regain their soul having had it destroyed, and this book is the intelligence learned from years of struggling, therapy and supporting others.

When you climb a mountain like Zoe has, your legs get strong, and if you can maintain your integrity and dignity in the face of the family court degradation system you truly are a saint.

Personable and showing herself laid bare in this beautifully eloquent account, Zoe has shared just a small account of her amazing recovery and so I am sure she has another few books to come.

David Kilmurry, Practice Lead at Kilmurry Life Centre

As a fellow survivor of this abusive perpetrator, I can empathise only too well with the horrific events Zoe endured at his hands. I warned the authorities many years ago that this man was capable of killing someone, and ten years later this prediction almost came to pass with the truly horrendous ordeal suffered by Zoe.

Zoe's book lifts the lid on the struggle many victims face when attempting to leave violent offenders and the challenges faced once in 'the system'. She analyses facets of her childhood and instances which set the tone for what transpired to her later in life, dealing with two abusive relationships, ultimately having to fight for her life and children through an archaic system where the victim is treated poorly.

Her account of events is heart-wrenchingly brutal and will at times have the reader in tears, however Zoe's shining warrior light is evident throughout the narrative of this book, highlighting the strength of her character, and certain phrases used will also have you chuckling at her refusal to back down. She is a force to be reckoned with.

Zoe's transformational journey from hitting rock bottom, fighting for her life and children, to speaking out, her ensuing battle for justice to force change within the system and being a champion for domestic abuse victims everywhere, is an inspiration to all.

Carmen Chicarella, Police Officer at West Midlands Police

Contents

Dedication

I dedicate this book to my children Cameron and Sofia. Without you I may not have survived. You are the reason I had to fight on; you gave me the power and drive to stay alive. I love you, always and forever.

And to my mother, my guardian angel

And to my sister Marion who spent most of her life troubled by her own experiences of male violence. You can now rest in peace (March 2022)

Acknowledgements

Writing this book was the most frustrating, infuriating and time-consuming thing I have ever done in my life, but it had to be done. It needed to be said. Anyone who knows me understands. I was not going to walk away without my side of the full story being told. This was more than just an incident, this was an ordeal that no-one should ever go through, and most of it could have been avoided had people done their jobs with integrity, joined the dots, believed, learned, and had empathy. So much has changed around domestic abuse over the years, however there is also still much to do.

I want to thank everyone who stood by me through this awful journey and in particular I want to thank:

Dad, even though our story is hard, it shaped me into who I am today. I am proud of myself and I hope you are too.

Rich, always by my side. Thank you for standing with me through the ups, downs and sideways.

Wayne and Dawn for your ongoing support and for being an amazing blended family to my children.

Auntie Debbie and Uncle Roger for picking up the pieces.

Auntie Pat, the family matriarch superseding my amazing Nan. Growing up with you both showed me what strong women are capable of and to always speak your mind.

Angela and Francesca for seeing the truth.

Joan Downie, my surrogate mother. You contributed more to my life than you will ever know.

Friends

Melissa, Jodi, Ceri, Maxine, Mel, Matt and Sarah, Charlotte, Terrie, Vicky and all of my friends from school, work, college, everyone who contacted me on social media – Facebook, Twitter, LinkedIn – thank you to you all. Every single solitary message helped me stay strong.

Mark Sugden (my former manager, at Atlantic Data and GB Group Plc) thank you for writing to the court, and Miss Duffy and Mr Machin (rest in peace) of Finham Primary School, your support meant so much.

Professionals

David Kilmurry for his clarity and support, and for dragging me back to human existence after being kicked over and over again, while already on the floor.

Laura Richards (Founder of Paladin NSAS, Criminal Profiler and The Crime Analyst) for the intelligent validation, for being a strong role model providing a shield of armour in dire times and for amplifying my voice.

My advocate from Refuge who supported me through court, you know who you are.

Staff at Women's Aid and Refuge, Polly Neate (former CEO Women's Aid), Sandra Horley (CEO Refuge), Elaine Yeates (CEO Coventry Haven), and Shonagh Dillon (CEO Aurora Dawn).

MPs & Legal

David Hawley for being my strength throughout the family court ordeal and giving me hope, drive and a clear view to see it through. For this my children and I will be forever grateful.

Barbara Caulfield, for believing me and speaking for me in court.

Jim Cunningham (former MP Coventry South) for listening to my many grumbles about the failings in our systems and how unjust the whole criminal and family justice system is.

Baroness Jan Royall, Jess Phillips (Chair VAWG All Parliamentary Group and MP for Birmingham Yardley), Peter Kyle (MP for Hove and Portslade), and John Bercow (former Speaker of the House) for being the voices of victims in the Houses of Parliament.

Rachel Horman (family solicitor) for taking on my criminal case and listening to me forever moaning about our shit family court system.

Josh Hitchens (barrister) and the rest of my legal team for seeing the police failings in my case and joining the fight for justice.

Survivors

Carmen my 'doppelganger', Dr Eleanor Aston, Claire Throssell MBE, John & Penny Clough MBE (parents of Jane Clough), Rachel Williams, Clive & Sue Ruggles (parents of Alice Ruggles), and thank you to all victims and survivors of domestic abuse and stalking. You are the strongest women I know.

Zoe's Angels (not Charlie's)

Karen Williams (The Book Mentor), Louise Lubke Cuss (Editor), Sam Pearce (SWATT Books). Without your professional support putting this together, I would not have made this book a reality, thank you.

And lastly thanks to all the haters; you made this happen and look at me now! #wrongvictimassholes

Foreword

The voices of victims of domestic abuse, sexual violence, stalking and exploitation are, without question, the most important voices in the fight to end men's violence against women. The sad truth is that they are for some reason the hardest for our institutions to hear. Every single day a new story will be reported about a woman killed, maimed, or left utterly broken after she tried again and again to report the abuse she was suffering. Politicians and police chiefs stand in front of lecterns at press conferences and encourage women to come forward and report their abuses as if women aren't doing just that. They are! Thousands of women, every single day, do exactly that, and of those thousands only a handful will receive justice or protection.

Accounts of abuse and violence like the one you are about to read should not simply be treated as a true crime thriller. It must be read as an activist's call for us to listen to the accounts of victims failed by the system again and again. Zoe is not merely a victim, nor is she a triumphant survivor, she is also an activist who has spent her life post abuse trying to ensure that the systems that failed her and millions of others are improved. We should hear her voice now, in a way that we have failed to in the past.

I meet victims of violence and abuse every day; some are still in the throes of the abuse, not yet able to escape, some are free from abuse but only slowly rebuilding their and their children's lives. Others, like Zoe, are victims who have such a clarity of purpose in their struggle that they grab politicians like me and walk firmly beside us to change things. The story of Zoe and her family is not merely an anecdote I can tell to make a speech better, it is an account that should train us all in what it is to be tortured by someone you should be able to trust, and ignored by those who you were raised to have faith and belief in. It is not presented for drama but to help us learn. Learn we must.

It has been my honour to work with Zoe for many years. It has been a privilege to listen to her fears, hopes and dreams. We should all feel like this as we read the account of her life, as if she is imparting privileged information to us, information that will have been hard to write and which she was for so many years groomed to keep to herself. As you read this, know that there is someone on your street who is not able to tell their story; there is someone at your work who has tried to tell their story but found that they couldn't be heard. Know that it is a privilege to be heard and make sure as you read you commit to be able to hear all the other women just like Zoe who need your ears. This is why Zoe writes this: she is calling you to action.

Jess Phillips
MP and Shadow Minister for Domestic Violence and Safeguarding

CHAPTER 1:

Mummy

There are key moments in life that shape the person we become in the future. These experiences have an impact on how we see the world and others. I have had several significant events in my life that have shaped the person I am today. However, the very first experience I can remember has both been my downfall and also fuelled my superpower.

I grew up without a mother.

My mother died from cancer when I was just six years old. According to attachment theory, young children need to form a strong attachment to at least one primary caregiver who can provide unconditional love and support, which allows them to develop the necessary relationship skills as they grow, so this trauma affected the rest of my life.

Have you ever watched a Disney fairytale movie? Like most fairytales around this time, they told stories of the lives of young girls who had lost this significant person in their life. Cinderella, Snow White, Belle from *Beauty and the Beast*, Ariel the Little Mermaid. These were the only stories I had to relate to at the time as a little girl myself. None of my friends had no mother. In fact, I did not know anybody who had lost their mother to death. I was unique and very alone.

These fairytales would often depict the effect of having no mother on the young girl's life and it was never positive. Wicked stepmothers and witches preying on emotionally naïve girls until they finally met their handsome prince who would save them. The stories were all the same.

Consider the most famous fairytale character, Cinderella. She was waiting for her Prince Charming to save her from her awful life as a slave to her stepmother and two ugly stepsisters. Her father remarried after her mother's death, then unfortunately he also died, leaving Cinderella a slave to her abusers and she had no-one, until her prince came along. A dangerous analogy to feed a little girl, a false narrative that a man will 'save' them.

The morning my mother died was the day I became an adult. My naïve perfect world turned inside out and upside down. Often people ask me where I get my strength from. It is as if it is obvious to others that there is an inner strength. This came from this loss. I suppose I am older and wiser than my years and peers. My parents named me 'Zoe', from the Greek meaning 'life'. This seems very poignant now, given the journey I have been on.

The day started like any other. I was at home with my mother. My father was there too which was unusual. He was not at work. He was always at work. We had recently moved to a rundown house situated on the corner of a street in a very nice, affluent area of the city. Quiet leafy suburban avenues of privately owned homes where children would play 'Kerby' (a game where you would throw a football across the street to each other, aiming to hit the street kerb to score a point). The quiet avenues meant it was safe for us to ride up and down the road on our bikes, or roller-skate down the roads, next to the manicured lawns where the neighbours all knew each other.

Dad bought this house as it needed fixing up, so he got it for a good price. It was quite dilapidated in comparison to the surrounding properties. Scruffy on the outside, a large corner plot, no heating, no double glazing, garden all overgrown, weeds everywhere, and the windows were rotting. Frosty air would come through the gaps and blow the curtains in my bedroom, and there was condensation on the window panes when it was cold.

The floorboards were rotten, and in the garden there were big mounds of earth where grass had grown over and they looked like trenches. After talking to our neighbours, we discovered the previous owner had been a bit of a hoarder. There were pots and pans, crockery and all sorts of odds and sods within the mounds. I loved it though; it was like an adventure ground for me, with so many places to hide and play.

My mum's bed was downstairs in the lounge under the bay window. She was too poorly to climb the stairs and had a commode in the lounge too, which is a posh portable toilet.

My beautiful mother, she had cancer. I heard the word mentioned now and again, but at six years old, it did not really mean much. *Mummy is poorly, and she will be better soon and can play with me again*, I would think as I played beside her bed.

She was bedridden most of the time, but this day seemed different somehow. Dad had stayed home, and my godmother Helen, an elderly lady from the church, arrived. There was a feeling of panic and hush in the air as Mum was in pain.

There was so much confusion. Everyone was standing around, whispering to each other. I couldn't hear them, but I could feel it through the tension in the air. An ambulance silently arrived outside the house, and the adults were mad that it had taken so long to arrive.

Two paramedics took my mother from the house on a stretcher. I jumped at the sound of the sirens as the ambulance sped away. My father had gone with Mum in the ambulance, and I was in a car with Helen following behind them.

I felt a knot in my tummy, like something bad was going to happen. However, I was so young, I did not know why I felt this way or was not entirely sure what was happening. When we arrived at the hospital, my mother was nowhere to be seen. Helen and I were ushered to a waiting area, and I played with my dolls that I had dragged along with me, whilst my father was with my mother.

We waited. All I wished was for us to hurry up and go back home. I was fidgety, restless; a hospital is not a place for a child to be hanging around. Hard plastic chairs and the smell of disinfectant. It was boring. Nurses and doctors walking around. Blank plain walls. No fun.

I knew my mother had been poorly for a while but, as a child, I did not understand how poorly she was. She was good at putting on a brave face. It must have been so hard for her knowing she was so ill with a six-year-old daughter.

Before moving to the new house, I had gone to a Catholic school. My mother was very religious, and I went to Sunday school each week. When we moved, she got a job at a local Catholic school and worked part time as a dinner lady.

My dad was an engineer by trade and had his own business. He worked extremely long hours. We barely saw him but when he was home, he would always be fixing something. We had a huge pile of sand in the back garden at home that I played in for hours.

I would be in a make-believe land with my Barbies. Well, they were not real Barbies. Dad would always compromise and get me a cheaper version. Anything to save a few pounds.

"It's the same, it's a doll," he would say in the shop, holding up a cheaper version. I would scrunch up my nose. "They are a bloody rip-off; this one will do." I did not want to upset him, so I just made do. I would play for hours on my own making up stories. I was a happy and content child. I was the only child at home, happy to play alone; that was my normal.

I did have a half-sister, who was 20 years older. Same mother, different fathers. She left home many years before I was born. Although she did visit us regularly with my niece who was close in age, three years younger than me, so she was like a sister.

My mum had me at 42. Quite late in age back then. I was her birthday present, born on her birthday, the 24th July. I was so proud of this and loved that we were Leos. My mother was very spiritual as well as religious.

At the hospital Dad appeared out of a side room. I stopped twirling on my tiptoes. Dad shook his head, then all eyes were on me.

No-one spoke but I knew. I just knew.

Dad was crying.

She had gone.

"Your mummy has gone, Zoe." I looked up at him blinking, not quite comprehending what I was being told. Gone where? When is she coming back? How long has she gone for?

"Can we let her say goodbye?" My dad turned to the doctor who was beside him. He took me into the room.

I remember that day so vividly. The air was cold, the room felt chilly. Sitting next to her holding her hand she looked so peaceful, rested. Like the pain was gone, her beautiful pale cold skin, her eyes closed. I realised that was the last time I was ever going to see my beautiful mother again. I kissed her goodbye. I don't recall crying; I just felt numb.

My nurturer, my main caregiver, my mummy, who I needed for everything, was gone.

When we left the hospital, we went home and I remember looking out of the car window thinking, *is this real?*

It was horrible and now it was up to me to make sure Dad was ok. I felt sorry for him. How was he going to look after me? Mummy did everything in the house, the cooking, the cleaning. Dad had work. How would we cope without her?

My mum died that day and so did the child in me. From that moment on I had this feeling of fierce independence. I felt a responsibility and instant maturity. I knew how hard he worked and I did not want to be a burden.

Mum used to sing before her untimely death. It was a big part of her life and she sang in the church choir. Dad used to say, "Your mother has the voice of an angel." They were so in love. So happy. I have pictures of them together back then, and they looked like such a trendy young couple.

"When your mother sings, she makes me cry, it's so beautiful." Mum was everything to Dad although after her passing he never really spoke of her again. Only at New Year would he get upset. He would have one too many drinks and cry, but other than that we never talked about her. This really upset me, but I could never tell Dad that, as I did not want to upset him. It was tough, as I so wanted to hear stories about her life, but I could not bring myself to ask him. I remained quiet as I felt an enormous duty to look after my dad.

I was very close to my mother; however, I had a different relationship with my father. It was somehow removed, maybe as my mother was my main caregiver, maybe due to the family dynamics back then, with my father being the breadwinner. I also often felt like he wanted his son as I had lost a younger brother who had heart problems when I was three, and maybe that was why. He never said it; it was a feeling.

Life continued, and Dad's attitude was to carry on, bury our heads.

Dad would drop me to school and collect me, then most days I would be left with our next-door neighbour Mary who would look out for me while Dad went back to the factory. Mary had three children: Gene, Rebecca, and Kimberly. I was best friends with Becky, and we would have the run of my house as my dad was not there and I had a key!

I had to grow up fast. I did this quietly; however, I was very astute. I would sit in the company of adults listening. I believe this is where my strength of character has come from. I absorbed a lot at a very young age.

I remember being sent away a lot when I was younger too, to stay with family friends and relatives, my nan, uncles, aunties, neighbours, my older sister. I even got sent off alone on a scary holiday for children with single parents. It was set up by a company called the Gingerbread Club, a charity that supported bereaved or single families with children.

The other children were not like me on the trip away. My mother had died. They were all from broken homes, parents who had divorced or separated. I was the unique one. I only had one parent now. Not a single parent. A widowed parent. I was the only one without a mother.

One evening on the 'holiday' we all queued as usual to get our snacks and a few of us headed to the dorm. We would sit around on the beds chatting. I'd got a little more confident a few days in, so I sat with the older girls.

"What happened with your mum and dad then?" one girl asked me. "Mine have split up," she continued. "They kept arguing, my dad had an affair. My mum said he's a two-timing bastard." She chomped on her crisps, shrugged her shoulders and rolled her eyes.

"My mum's dead," I said, looking at her blankly.

The girl just froze with a gaping wide mouth, crisps falling out the sides. I suppose it gave me a sense of power. I had been so powerless over everything in my life. This made me realise I could stop people in their tracks with this piece of information.

I walked over to my bed and got in. I pulled the covers over my head. And so I slowly found coping ways to deal with the sadness. I would tell myself I was special. I would exchange sad thoughts into something positive. I did not have a mother who was alive, but she was watching over me like an angel and helping me grow strong.

Dad did his best. It cannot have been easy. He worked long hours and being a single dad back then was unheard of. Sometimes Dad let me go to work with him. If I was poorly and off school, I would sit in the office and pretend I was the boss. I liked being there and not at school.

Kids can be cruel and would often say nasty things to me. "At least I've got a mum!" one boy said to me in the library at school one day. I threw a pencil at him. He started to cry, and I got told off.

I soon realised that it was better not to react to these jibes as I would get the blame. It was as if people did not know how to deal with a grieving child.

I silently got emotionally tougher. I told myself I must be strong because why would this happen to me and no-one else. This was my superpower: the ability to deal with adversity. To grow from pain. I never thought badly of myself; none of this was my fault. I learned that people were and are cruel. I programmed myself to filter out the noise I did not want, the negativity.

This internal strength is something that has grown and gives me the resilience I have today.

RED FLAGS & REFLECTION

Attachment theory explains that losing a significant person or caregiver in your life at such a young age can have a profound effect. The separation, and in my case the reluctance of my father to talk about my mother, plus my fear of upsetting him, led to my 'fixer' personality.

"The purpose of attachment figures is for us to feel comforted and secure and for us also to provide comfort. So, what happens when our early and later life attachments aren't a source of safety and security?

"When infants and children grow up with caregivers who aren't reliably able to attend and respond to their needs, their relationships with themselves and others are often negatively impacted. One of the possible consequences is the development of an insecure attachment style that continues into adulthood. Often, this will mean they are less able to navigate the normal stresses and trials of life and may have difficulty trusting and bonding with others.

"People with a preoccupied (sometimes referred to as anxious) attachment style tend to have low self-esteem, often process their experiences primarily through their emotions, and need extra reassurance and control in their relationships.

"People with a dismissing (also referred to as avoidant) attachment style tend to have an overly positive view of themselves yet avoid activities that stimulate emotion and vulnerability and may seem aloof and detached or choose not to engage in close relationships.

"People with a fearful attachment style tend to be self-critical and depressed, chronically vulnerable, and passive and exploitable in relationships. Any of these disruptions in interpersonal relationships can create additional difficulties and complications for a grieving person."

(From *Providing a Safe Haven: An attachment informed approach to grief* by Marney Thompson, January 2019)

So, ultimately your childhood life experiences really do shape the way you are in your adult life. Empowering children, showing empathy, being open and honest are all good ways to raise a healthy child with good boundaries. Start by setting a good example.

If you have children, who provides that safe place for them?

CHAPTER 2:

Making My Way

Life after losing Mum was difficult. My childhood had been ripped away, and I was soon thrown into a whole new world that, in my mind, would destroy my mother's memory, and I plummeted into loneliness and a longing to be loved and needed.

It was just Dad and I for the first year. We struggled through, however I never thought I would have to share him. But he started seeing someone. He introduced me to a woman who was to be my new stepmother, June.

At first Dad brought her to our house and I heard them talking. "She won't like me," she said. She was right. I did not. Given that I was raised on fairytales, is there any wonder?

In my mind, the wicked stepmother had arrived, my worst nightmare. I did not want a new mother and I was angry and hurt.

I was in my bedroom playing and Dad and June both peered around the door. "This is June. Say hello."

"Go away!" I shouted in response.

It was like I was betraying my mum. I was seven years old. This was the start of an internal animosity building inside. The feeling of deception that my father could bring another woman into my life to replace my mother was unbearable. I cried myself to sleep that night.

June was a Scottish lady who had three children, two girls and a boy. The older daughter was a year older than me, and my younger step-siblings were twins, who were three years younger – a boy and a girl.

To start with, Dad and I used to stay at their house. I hated going there. It was situated on a busy main road. It had a funny smell and the kids in the area were all tough. I did not stand a chance. I was an only child, mollycoddled by my mother, who went to ballet and Sunday school. The other kids were covered in dirt, out playing on the main road. And very loud and obnoxious.

Fighting each other, June's kids were confident and bolshy. I felt frightened. I never felt safe or happy when we went there. Dad and June would often go out in the evening, and we were meant to go to bed, but I did not want to be left alone with them.

The twins were young, messy and boisterous. My older stepsister was cruel to me. I was an easy target and had no idea how to fight back. She would sneer "Get out of my room" and bullied me. She would get my younger stepbrother or one of her friends to pick a fight with me over something silly. That gave her the excuse to chip in and start on me too.

I had no bedroom either, so there was no space for me. I was meant to share a bed with my older stepsister and sleep top to tail, my head at one end and her head at the other, when we stayed there. But "You're not sleeping in my bed tonight", she would say. So I would sleep on the floor next to the bed.

I hated being there. I hated their ways. Punching and kicking each other. Shouting, screaming, biting. And no-one cared or stopped the violence. It was a whole new scary world. I would try and tell June that I was being hit. I was immediately told to "Go away" or "Stop telling tales" or "You're as bad as each other". And there was no point trying to speak with Dad about it.

However, I was so far out of my comfort zone and extremely vulnerable. I still wonder today if my dad or June showed any empathy at all towards me as a child who had just lost her mother. It was only later in life that I realised June was jealous of my dead mother, which made it impossible for me to talk to Dad about Mum.

Dad was more interested in life with June, and it was not long before they moved in with us, into my family home. I was hurting so much inside and felt betrayed by my father.

I had to start fighting back. Growing up together through my teen years was difficult. I felt like they had invaded my mother's house. I had been an only child with two bedrooms to myself before they arrived. One I used as a playroom and the other was my bedroom. When they all moved in, us three girls had to share together. It was horrible. We had no boundaries; there was no personal space.

I felt I was just existing. They would go off shopping at the weekend and I would stay home alone. I slowly disengaged with the family. We also had no money. There was food on the table but nothing fancy. All I ever heard was "We can't afford it". I swore to myself that when I got older, I would have money. We lived in an affluent area however we were the poorest, or so it seemed anyway. My friends all got pocket money, whereas I got none.

We rarely had new clothes and my school uniform was often a hand-me-down from my older stepsister. Home life for me was miserable and chaotic through these years. One thing for sure, however: I built a toughness and a resilience.

It felt to me like June had landed on her feet meeting my dad. Single with three kids, and now she had the run of a lovely house. My mother's house. I felt like she just wanted me, the stepdaughter, out of the way. I did not feel a part of the family. I felt like an outsider in my own home. I would daydream about leaving and being saved by my prince. I could not wait for the day I could leave.

In my childhood I saw various types of lifestyles, and this gave me a good understanding of how different people lived. After Mum died, I was farmed out a lot, and spent a lot of time with my uncles, my dad's brothers: Keith, Roger, Chris and Ade. My dad had four brothers and one sister. My auntie lived in London about 100 miles from us, so we only saw her at family gatherings. She was always so glamorous.

I went pony trekking with my uncle Chris and Leigh his wife, visited Uncle Roger and Uncle Ade quite a bit as they had young children too, and visited Uncle Keith and Auntie Patsy who were property developers. They contributed to the drive and determination I have today. They worked hard and my uncle Keith would tell me stories of how he bought his first house and renovated it, adding value. They had done this over and over and by then lived in a huge mansion.

Their house was like a wonderland. My auntie Patsy bought and sold antiques and the house was renovated to the standard it would have been in Victorian times. Vast manicured gardens so long you could not see the end, rooms galore: a full snooker room, piano room, basement, playrooms. It was magical going there as a child. This was the type of life I wanted to lead.

I remember as a child driving through the wrought iron gates, onto the gravel drive. You would hear the stones crunch under the tyres. They would always sit in the large kitchen with its big wooden table like in an old farmhouse, and wooden dresser displaying polished crockery, the Labradors curled up in the corner in their beds.

I'd go exploring through the house like Alice in Wonderland. Their staircase was as wide as a normal suburban house; there were porcelain dogs halfway up the winding staircase and great big stained-glass windows floor to ceiling on the landing which the sun shone through, lighting up the hallway. The winding stairs led to a landing which brought you to solid doors, behind them huge bedrooms with four-poster beds, and at the very top on the fourth floor there was a small attic with a large wooden doll's house – perfect for me when I was little.

Downstairs there was a lounge. "It's just for show," Auntie Patsy would say. My auntie was very particular that nothing was moved out of place. It was so opulent. There was even a full-size lift to a granny flat in the basement. It was magical for a child, especially having the life I did, being passed around. I wished I could stay there more.

They were my family, my real family. I felt more at home there than I did in my own house now so overrun. My uncle Keith would sit me down and tell me stories and I would be mesmerised, listening intently.

"Once upon a time there was a frog, with wide WIDE eyes..." He was so animated telling me these stories.

June, however, did not like it. She thought they were snobs and could not understand why they had a show lounge. I loved it. I loved the way they lived. I loved the showiness. I loved that they were snobs; I loved that my auntie Patsy used to put a hanky to her nose when we walked by the butcher's. June and my dad smoked cigarettes; our house had overflowing ashtrays. My auntie Patsy would not have any of that. She would not even cut an onion in her kitchen because of the smell. Ok, that is maybe going a bit too far.

My other uncles lived fairly normal lives and I would go on holidays with them, but I also got to see both ends of the social spectrum growing up. My half-sister, my mother's other daughter, 20 years older than me, had a completely different life. She did not work and relied on benefits to get by. I would also stay there a lot as a child.

I loved my sister. I looked up to her, but she was angry. She was my only link left to my mother, but she was never happy. Life was hard for her. She had a lot of unresolved issues and I felt bad for her. There was no food in the cupboards, and she struggled to make ends meet although she always found the money for a bottle of some sort of cheap alcohol. She would sit writing out her list of bills and counting the coins she had. She would tell me tales of how she was so poor, and the world was so hard and tough.

Going to my sister's house was an adventure for a lot of other reasons. She was a bit crazy, lively; she would hold seances at her house, and there was always someone crying in the corner after they'd had a reading. She had three dogs, two cats and three tame rats. The dogs would be jumping around and barking, and she loved to play her rock music full blast. There would be some oily dude there with long hair, a biker.

It was not until I got older that I really started to look at the contrast between people's lives. This fascinated me. You do not really understand the social divide as a child, but I knew there was a huge difference between the lives of these people.

I realised that the reason we had very little in my childhood was due to us having no money. Too many mouths to feed and bodies to clothe. Money was always tight. This contrast in lifestyle made me realise what I did and did not want out of life, that's for sure. I had dreams and aspirations. I promised myself I would never be this way. I would make money a priority so I could have the freedom to live the way I wanted.

One positive thing I learnt from my childhood was a work ethic. My dad worked really hard, as did June. So I did any jobs I could to make money from an early age.

Around 13 I was working collecting glasses in bars. I worked on an ice cream van at Watford Gap service station. I would stand and do piles of ironing for £10. Vacuum the stairs, clean the bathroom for a fiver.

In my teen years I started counting down the days until I could get the hell out of there. As soon as I left college and got a job, June announced she wanted me to pay rent, over half of my weekly wages. I was earning £35 a week and she wanted £25. Yet her daughter who was a year older was to pay nothing. I knew I had to go.

My fierce independence and reluctance to rely on anyone kicked in, although I did build other attachments – with boyfriends. I had a long-term boyfriend all through secondary school. I think this was my safety net, looking back. I suppose it meant I was not alone.

So, I decided I needed to take the power back. I spoke to friends and found someone who was looking to rent out their two-bedroom house. I took it. I figured out the rent and got some help from the government. I was working and going to college, so they topped up my money.

I left, 17 years old and nothing but the clothes on my back and my stereo. That was it. I told June and my dad the night before and packed the few belongings I had, and left the next morning. I don't think they believed it at the time. They thought I was bluffing but I had everything in place.

I was so empowered. True independence. Now I was completely reliant on myself.

They did not as much as buy me a saucepan. I got zero support. Nothing at all. My friends at this time were all travelling the world, working in bars, taking time out of their studies, but I had to knuckle down. I had no choice.

I had my day job, went to college one day a week, and got an evening job in a restaurant/bar. Sometimes I would leave that job to work in a nightclub afterwards.

They were fun times in that house. I rented for about a year, saving like crazy, and managed to rustle up enough money to put down a deposit to buy a property. I was obsessed and utterly determined. I was putting every spare penny away. It had to be the right property too, something I could add value to like my uncle Keith had done.

Dad always said, "Invest in property, love, they double in value every seven years." It was good advice although Dad never invested himself. Instead, he would tell the story about when he was going to buy the neighbour's house but bought the factory instead, and to me that was crazy as he worked 12–18 hours a day some weeks.

I bought my first house all on my own when I was 18 years old. I was so proud of myself.

It needed completely gutting, but it was perfect even though it needed so much work. It had no heating or double glazing, and was totally run-down. There were cobwebs in the kitchen cupboards. An old man had lived there and it still had his stuff in it, even one of those old steel baths from the war time. It was a two up, two down, they call them.

The house gave me something to talk to Dad about. We had been quite distant since I left home, however he was super helpful and loved to fix things so he would help where he could, fitting new windows, laying floors. It gave him a reason to see me, which was good. There were no cuddles or declarations of love in our house as a child, but I knew that this was Dad's way of showing he cared and was proud of me, although he never said it then.

My life at this time felt perfect, albeit I was struggling financially, and the house was upside down, but I was struggling upwards. I was making moves towards a better life. I had completed my studies; I took the long route as I had to do this around jobs, however I now had a business degree. I had a great group of people around me and gosh, did we have some parties at that house, all-nighters. They were good times.

Importantly, I had my freedom, I was in control of my future and it felt good to be on the property ladder.

RED FLAGS & REFLECTION

Childhood is often not easy and even more so when you are part of a blended family. Looking back, I believe that I went through sibling abuse. If you're in this type of situation, you may find there is an older sibling who you could call the perpetrator, who may well take advantage of a younger sibling's dependence on them. That's why I believe parents should be aware of how their children are interacting. If conflict or disagreements are not dealt with calmly, or if they are ignored, not heard, or even dismissed, it gives power to the perpetrator of that abuse, so they continue, which in my case led me to rebel. It also meant that my boundaries were crossed often as a child and this was allowed by the adults in my life. This made me accept behaviour towards me that was not healthy.

As a parent you should consider how to deal with conflict. My advice is to have an open and honest relationship with your children. Let them speak freely and believe them if they tell you something is happening that they dislike. A victim of any circumstance wants their reality validated. I like to think that in today's world we have much more information about the impact of certain behaviours, and it's all at our fingertips. Understanding a situation first and foremost is key to having a healthy response. I do believe that we should do more in schools and educate not just the children but the parents too.

What is your parenting style when it comes to conflict between siblings?

CHAPTER 3:

I'm a Mummy Now

Becoming a mother was a significant milestone in my life. It was an unconditional love I never even thought existed. At 27 years old I had moved on from my party house. It was great while it lasted, but it was time to move and start trying to do something else with my life instead of working and partying every weekend. The party lifestyle had to go, alongside relationships which didn't serve me.

I bought a bigger house away from the area where I could stumble home from the pub. I was maturing and wanted to be surrounded by people who were driven like me. I got a new job in car sales, and I had made a chunk of money from the sale of my last house. My life was progressing, and I was excited for the future.

"Hi, I'm Wayne, top sales performer for used cars Ford," the guy in front of me said confidently. With his gelled jet-black hair, tan, sharp suit and cheeky smile, I remember thinking he had a kind face.

I now worked all week and every weekend, every Saturday and every other Sunday, so I lived and breathed work, but I was excelling and making money which was important. I was spending a lot of time with my work colleagues, so it was good to have a laugh and get on with them. They were different to my friends from the city where I grew up, more naïve, more driven.

Wayne was not into partying. He was sensible. He did not drink and was a hard worker, which is what had earned him his top sales ranking. We instantly got on, although he was a few years older than me. He made me belly laugh.

Selling cars was good money and there were always stories to tell at the end of the day about the obnoxious customers who would give you hell and the nice ones who never even asked for a discount, or we would count the commission we had made that day. My standard of living had massively improved as I was earning much more money and going out less, and I also got to drive numerous different cars home.

One evening a week we had to work late doing prospecting calls. We took it in turns to stay behind. We would be calling people at teatime asking if they wanted to renew their car. You know the sort of cold call when you are just about to put a mouthful of your dinner in your mouth: "Evening sir, I see you are currently paying £x for your car..." Nine times out of ten they would hang up. We all hated it, but it was part of the job. To make it more fun, we would sometimes get pizza or arrange to go for drinks after work.

One week was pretty tough. We had done several late nights as a new registration number was launched, which meant more sales. That month I had actually knocked Wayne off his top spot, so I was very pleased with myself and let him know about it.

"Who's the top of the leaderboard so far this month then, Wayne?" I said, blowing on my knuckles and shining them on my top. We laughed.

"Hey, we are all going for a drink after work if you want to come, Zoe?" Wayne responded.

"Now?" I looked around. Everyone had left already and Wayne was locking up. He was the only one management would trust.

"Yeah, I'll meet you there if you like, at the Leopard?" he said casually.

"Ok cool, see you there," I responded. I went to fix my make-up before heading off.

As I pulled into the car park, I could see Wayne sitting on a bench outside the trendy gastro pub. It was a warm summer's evening, and he was on his own.

"Where are the others? At the bar? Who came?" I was trying to look through the window to see. Wayne started laughing.

"What are you laughing at?" I could tell something was going on; it was a mischievous laugh. Then I twigged. "They aren't coming, are they?" I started laughing, quickly realising that this had been his way to get me there. I stayed anyway. I was slightly flattered and found it quite amusing. We would all go to that pub quite a bit, so it was fine. I had no reason to rush home, so we had a drink and then got some food.

A few weeks later, Wayne asked me out properly on a date. He was such a gent, holding doors, polite to everyone, tipping the staff in restaurants. He spoke with authority and confidence. He was a soft guy, not an ounce of aggression in him. Different to other lads I knew in a world that could be edgy at times.

We started dating and for the first time I felt like a grown-up and safe. It was not long before he moved into my house.

Wayne was a traditional guy. He wanted kids, marriage, the car on the drive, mowing the lawn on a Sunday. I got swept away with this 'normal' life fantasy. We soon started talking about our future and what that looked like. We would joke that we would have a son called Cameron.

However, I was not really ready for children. I had a vision of what my life would look like. I wanted freedom and to be successful, wealthy, and it's funny how life, peer pressure and of course society can steer you down a path that was not necessarily meant to be. Looking back, the wanting to please and attachment issues were forever present and impacted upon the decisions I made.

Wayne and I lived a good life. We went on luxury holidays and I was having my house extended. From the outside looking in our relationship was great, however I don't think I conformed to society's norms. As everyone else was settling down it felt like the right thing to do. Wayne wanted to settle down quite quickly and do things the 'right' way.

That year was the turn of the millennium at New Year. We had always wanted to stay at the Metropole Hotel in London, so we booked a room, hoping to go celebrity watching. Well I did anyway.

Wayne drove and we arrived at the hotel, and the valet parking took the car. I looked around. "This is the wrong hotel!" I exclaimed, trying to find my booking. I was sure we had booked the Metropole with Nobu next door to it, where Liam Gallagher from the band Oasis would often be seen falling out of the doors, causing chaos most weekends.

We had booked the wrong hotel. "Madam, this is much better than the riffraff in there, you will not be disappointed," the concierge reassured us, as there were lots of millennium celebrations happening that we could book.

Wayne booked a table in the restaurant for the evening. It was lovely and so grand. There were ice sculptures and balloons everywhere in the shape of 2000. Once we had finished our meal we moved to the bar, and then suddenly Wayne got down on one knee next to me.

What is he doing? And then it dawned on me.

"Will you marry me?" He opened a small ring box and I nearly died.

I was not ready for that; everyone started turning around and cheering and clapping.

"Yes," I said quickly. I was mortified. I had no idea. We had not discussed it. I could not believe he had done it. I wanted the ground to swallow me up. But how could I say no with all these people looking? People began coming over congratulating us. We ordered champagne and strawberries and went back to the hotel room as everyone kept looking over.

I was so overwhelmed. I was swaying between feelings of disbelief and then terror and guilt. Wayne looked so happy. I did not want to say no, but I also did not want to get married. To me it felt final. 'Till death do us part' is not really a sentence I would ever say, and marriage could not be further from where I wanted to be. I still felt young and had so many dreams.

Back in the room Wayne asked me, "Why aren't you ringing everyone?" but who was I going to ring? I didn't have a mother to give the news to. Who would I ring, my dad? I felt sad more than anything. It highlighted the gaping hole in my life.

"I will in the morning," I replied.

I know I dreamt of a prince whisking me away, but I had not thought it through properly. I was not one of those girls that dreams of their wedding day. I was driven, wanted my own money and my own career, my own house. It was like I shifted between two people. The first needing the security and attachment of a relationship, the second fighting through life alone and declaring my independence. This was a trauma response from losing my mother at such a young age. Also, marriage was about sharing. Sharing never worked for me as a child with my stepfamily so I was not about to give up my independence easily as an adult.

But I did not want to disappoint Wayne, so I went along with it, thinking my apprehension would go away. I mean, why was I not happy? Every other girl I knew was over the moon when they were getting married. They would even turn into bridezillas, meticulously arranging their big day with military precision. I really could not understand it though. I had no desire to arrange a wedding day and certainly not change my name for that matter. The guilt of my feelings kept me quiet. It was a place of safety knowing Wayne was there, I suppose.

Once we got back home from London, we shared our news with family and friends. Everyone was full of joy and sending best wishes. I got swept away with it and thought maybe it could work out but then of course came the next question on everyone's lips: children.

Wayne and I did talk about this, and we often joked about little Cameron in the back seat of the car. A few months went by; we were still making plans but I had avoided setting a date. I even said in passing to Wayne that I was not sure marriage was for me. The talk of a baby was still very much out in the open. Many friends had already had children and people were saying "You're next" or "Are you trying?" Everywhere I looked there were babies. Not the youngest of my group of friends, I felt I was getting left behind. Then there was a worry in the back of my mind: what if I can't have children? That would be awful. No-one wants that decision taken away.

After talking to Wayne, I came off the pill. I'd been on the pill since I was 14, so I did not expect that, BOOM, two weeks later I would miss my period. We went to the chemist to get a test. When we got back home I went into the toilet and...

"Oh my goddd!" I screamed from the bathroom to Wayne. He was sitting on the landing waiting to hear. "I'm PREGNANT." I didn't know whether to laugh or cry. Wow, I had a little baby inside me. I had this sudden rush of love and hormones. It felt right. I was with a safe pair of hands with Wayne. It all became quite real but we were over the moon.

I became obsessed with buying everything for the baby from that moment on. We had a new nursery decorated, and I bought everything down to little nail clippers. We were all ready to go. Even my hospital bag was packed by the front door ready and the talk of marriage quietly went away.

Quite far on in the pregnancy I had gone for a weekly check-up at the doctors. I was so swollen. "Look at my ankles, where the hell are they?" I laughed, showing the midwife. "I have put on three and a half stone, oh my god," I said, shocked after standing on the scales. I was so huge I could barely see my feet.

"So, Zoe, have you given the birth any thought, hospital birth, drugs?" the midwife asked, poised to take notes.

"I want it as natural as possible, no drugs," I said naively.

"That's a big baby in there. Shall we just note that you do not want any drugs but are happy to if required? Actually Zoe, I would suggest that to be honest." She gave me a concerned look.

"Oh, ok then," I said, happy that she had confirmed my baby was healthy. I had no idea what was ahead of me.

My due date arrived, so we had to wait for two weeks, and then if there was no sign of the baby, I would have a date to be induced. And that's what happened. The two weeks slowly passed as I got bigger and bigger. Finally, on induction day, we arrived at the hospital and the nurses got me comfy on the ward before the consultant arrived to carry out a sweep, which is an internal examination on a pregnant woman to initiate labour. We then had to wait. Contractions should start on their own. There were four ladies on the ward with their partners next to them. One by one they started screaming with the contractions and were wheeled off to the labour ward.

We were there for hours, and nothing. Wayne went home and came back the next day. I was on the induction ward for three days. I went in on the Friday and I remember the nurse saying as she clocked off her shift, "I don't want to see you here when I'm back on my shift Monday morning." But I was.

"I said that as a joke on Friday! What are you still doing here?! Have you been checked? Any obs done?" she asked, looking concerned.

"No." I started to panic. *Would this be happening if I had a mum*, I wondered. Probably not; she would be asking the right questions. I had just sat there, not wanting to make a fuss. I had no clue what I was doing and was in the hands of the hospital. Wayne was as clueless as me and utterly useless at this sort of thing.

The nurse came back with monitors and put a lead around my tummy with a computer attached. "Ok," she said as she went to get the consultant. When they both came back, the nurse explained.

"Zoe, you need to go down, Cameron's heartbeat is slowing." There was a small panic in the air. Luckily Wayne was there with me. I was wheeled down to the labour ward.

As I was pushed through the hospital corridors I heard the haunting screams of women coming through the doors on either side. I was terrified. *Oh my god, it's me next*. Shit got real.

Once in the labour room the midwife talked me though everything in between contractions but I only ever dilated by a couple of centimetres. She showed me what this looked like using a cardboard vagina opening, where the pages flipped from a small opening to a large opening. "You are here," she said, pointing to a two-centimetre gap and she flipped the card over many times to show a vagina open to 9–10 centimetres. "You should be here." I nearly passed out.

"We need to break your waters Zoe..." Oh for fuck's sake, seriously. Honestly, your dignity goes right out of the window when you have kids. There were doctors and nurses coming and going, and I was lying there, legs akimbo. I still didn't have much pain though, so it was really odd.

Then almost immediately after the breaking of my waters, the pain was excruciating. I was still hooked up to the monitor and I could see the needle on the graph monitoring the level of contractions going up and down and almost off the page. The pain was that bad it was like I was looking down at myself, having an out-of-body experience.

"GIVE ME DRUGS! What can I have?" I had tried gas and air, but it made me feel sick.

I was not dilating enough, and it was getting dangerous. The consultant popped his head in the door and said "Another five hours" to the midwife. We heard something about the budget for the evening having gone. Caesarean sections cost over £6,000.

I looked at Wayne. "I can't! Get this baby OUT!"

Wayne was furious. "Zoe is not waiting another five hours; she needs a C-section now!" They finally agreed.

They needed to numb me from the neck down, a complete spinal block. When the anaesthetist came into the ward, I knew him. He was a customer of mine. "I sold you a car?"

"Let's not worry about that now, Miss Dronfield, you need to stay very still when I put this injection into your back." He was very professional. Wayne rolled his eyes at me, laughing. "Trust you, always thinking about your deals."

Once numb, I was wheeled to the theatre and Wayne had gone to get scrubbed and dressed in a surgical gown. He started goofing around pretending to be a surgeon but when he walked into the operating room where I was lying ready for the C-section, he saw the six-foot screen in front of my tummy and went grey.

He was about to pass out. I could tell by his face he was going to be no use whatsoever. He is so squeamish. I mouthed to him, "Oh pull yourself together." We laugh about this now. I was not fazed. Well, I was completely numb so could no longer feel the contractions which was good.

Cameron was born on the 14th January by emergency caesarean section. Eight pounds twelve ounces, he was a big bundle of a boy. And God, did he make his presence known. He did not stop crying for 14 weeks. He was nocturnal. I could not wake him in the day and at night he screamed the place down.

I loved him more than anything else on the planet. *This is what love is.* I was so happy. When we took him home, we were ready, well at least I thought I was.

Having a baby put a huge pressure on our relationship. We were naïve to think a baby could paper over the cracks in our relationship. If anything, they highlighted them more. Cameron was my priority now and he came first. Wayne found this hard as Cameron took up every second of my time.

Being at home with Cameron was difficult for the first few weeks, the sleep deprivation, the lack of support. Wayne was still working long hours at the dealership. With my independence taken away from me, I felt trapped, tired and lonely. I was struggling with this new responsibility and lack of freedom.

Just going to the gym was difficult as I would need Wayne to watch Cameron and he would always ask "How long will you be?" or make comments like "Don't be long", making me feel guilty. I felt like I was tied to my new baby and Wayne did not make it easy for me to go off and have some time to myself. I did not feel like a human. I was just existing at home with this baby that would not stop crying.

I think Wayne thought I was at home chilling out with my new baby all day, but the reality was I was stressed and tired and finding it so difficult to deal with the lack of control over timings. I was totally at this baby's beck and call. To try and keep a sense of reality I was keeping a log on a spreadsheet so I could see how much time I was getting to myself. I was going insane with tiredness, although I now know using a planner is a good way to try maintain some level of control over your life when feeling overwhelmed.

I loved my baby boy Cameron so much, but I was tired. So tired.

Wayne now slept on the sofa because he said he needed sleep. I was reading book after book after book trying to figure out a way to get some bloody structure back into my life.

Dog tired and at my wits' end, I called June. I was at breaking point and had no other option.

"I can't do it anymore!" I just burst into tears down the phone. I felt like a failure and completely out of my depth. I did not feel like a natural mother. I lacked support and guidance, and even friends did not really come around. "Oh, I bet you have so many visitors, it was a nightmare when I had my little one, I had no peace," they would say to me. The reality was very different and I felt isolated. I'm sure if my mother was alive guiding me then maybe things would have been different. Another milestone without her.

To be fair to June, she stepped up in this instance. Although I did not want her as a mother when I was young, we got on much better in my teenage years, when I started to rebel and found my voice. June liked me more then. Although I had left home with my two fingers in the air, June had been there herself. She knew what it was like as she did not grow up in the best environment herself. She came from a small village in Scotland, and they were poor, really poor. Not poor like us where we were not allowed 'real' Coca Cola, I mean poor where they had no carpets, heating or hot water. June took two buses and turned up at my door. I was quite shocked, but she was there, and I was so grateful.

"Just get yourself up to bed and leave him with me, just show me where the bottles are and what he needs," June said, scooping Cameron off me.

"Right, you wee shite, let your mummy sleep and don't give me any jip," she said, bouncing Cameron in her arms. He was such a happy baby, just hungry. Hungry ALL the time; you could not fill him. Most babies root for food. Cameron just screamed without even opening his eyes.

I went straight upstairs. I lay on the bed, shut my eyes and that was it, I was gone.

I did not wake until it was dark. I opened my eyes in a panic, went downstairs and there was June, sitting on the sofa.

"Why don't you have the TV on?" I asked. She was sat in silence, Cameron asleep in his Moses basket. "He's asleep." I looked at him lying there all content. I loved him so much. The little shit. I could not believe how hard it was being a new mum.

"He's just gone off, wake him up for next feed, oh and I couldn't work the TV." She pointed towards the television that was on standby. June was never good with tech.

"You've sat here the entire time with nothing to do!" I was shocked.

"You needed sleep and it's fine. I got Cameron sorted and had some peace." June was always doing stuff for people at home so I suppose it might have been nice for her to get away for the day.

My relationship with June was better once I had Cameron. There was a reason to keep in touch and I wanted my son to have his family around him. I gave him the middle name Troy, the name of my little baby brother who died, out of respect for Dad.

Here I was, 28 with a child now, and in a relationship that just did not fit. Wayne was a good guy, however he was more bothered about work, selling cars, and not supportive of my goals – and now we had a baby. He thought I should be a housewife. Definitely not on my list of goals. With a traditional view of a relationship, he wanted me to stay at home with Cameron, work part time, get a little job. A 'we'll get by' kind of attitude. No way.

"There's absolutely no way I'm relying on you for money!" I'd argue with him. I was flabbergasted at the thought. Wayne could not understand it. "Most women want to be kept," he would say. "Well, I don't, thanks!" I would retort. I did not want to be controlled. I was already independent, however having a child made me vulnerable financially. I wanted my own money, my own life, my own career, my own path and why the hell not?

"I don't want to ask you for money if I want a night out with the girls. Are you having a laugh? I am not doing that at all. I'm going back into work the minute I can." I was adamant and it was a deal-breaker in my mind.

"I can put £1000 in your account every month so you can sort the bills," Wayne said, thinking this was the answer, but I was fuming.

"A thousand pounds," I screamed at him, "is that it? I do not want to live on a thousand pounds for fuck's sake! I do not want to ask you for money if I need it. I want to live in a big house, with a big garden, I want a detached property, a gravel drive, I do not want a poxy thousand pounds and I don't want *your* money either. I want my own." I'd lost it at this point, unable to even get my head around how he even thought I was this person. Did he not know me at all?

The pressure of this difference and Cameron's demands did not help our relationship. Things eventually became too much when I wanted to get back to work. Wayne and I mutually agreed to part and he moved out.

We were on different paths. I wanted to make my own money and Wayne's idea of life was stifling. Our differences were like an ocean between us. We remained friends and Wayne saw Cameron whenever he wanted. It was hard to begin with, but we showed a united front to Cameron and that was what was important. Positively co-parenting.

There I was with a baby of two years old. With no job, as I had been made redundant on maternity leave from my job selling cars. Having a child did not fit in with their working hours or culture. So, what was I going to do?

I started researching jobs that I could do at home while raising Cameron. Flicking through pages of jobs... nope, nope, not enough money. Right, I needed to think outside the box. I'd completed my business degree, so I thought to myself, *I'm going to set up a business*.

RED FLAGS & REFLECTION

People pleasing is usually a result of a lack of parental attunement as a child. Parents of people pleasers are often too worried about their own problems to tune in to their child. They may also misread a child's feelings. Children in this dynamic can often take on the caregiving role which ultimately leads to people pleasing behaviour into adulthood.

I often found myself caring more about my father's feelings than my own. In addition to this, having my personal boundaries crossed at a young age by the stepfamily, and having to just accept it, meant I found it difficult to say no. It was normal for me to go along with plans that I did not want or agree with. This hugely impacted decision-making in intimate relationships later in my life.

What boundaries were in place in your household as a child? And how attuned are you to your child's needs?

CHAPTER 4:

Building the Business

When one door closed, another opened. I was a single mum, however I still had dreams. I refused to be the stereotype portrayed in the press. I wanted to show the world I could be a mother and a success.

I started researching business ideas. A childcare business seemed like a good choice. I could run the office and take on qualified staff to look after the children, so I found a company I liked the look of who were selling a franchise. I met the owners, and my business was born.

I offered private exclusive childcare. I employed qualified childcare staff to look after children like mine. Mothers who, like me, wanted to work but needed help at home to give them the support to do what they wanted to do. I set up my office, and due to the nature of the business I could work from home. I got to work, networking and making connections.

I had the best of both worlds. I had my lad next to me and I could build my business from home. Cameron also spent time at nursery which allowed me the time to have meetings and build my connections in the sector. Being sales trained, the business development came easily and I was confident talking at all levels, so the business soon flourished.

The business had several arms to it. We offered babysitting services for high-profile clients and mobile crèche facilities for weddings. I managed to secure a few high-profile celebrity clients and we also supported families in need: those on the child protection register or in family court proceedings, or families with learning difficulties. The child protection register is a confidential list of all children in the area who have been identified at a child protection conference as being at significant risk of harm. This part of the business, the social care element, grew very rapidly. There was a huge demand in Coventry.

There was an urgent need for out-of-hours emergency care for children with disabilities and families who needed support before and after school, and being a young entrepreneur I started recruiting to fill these roles. Not only were we helping families, but I was building a legacy for my son. I was in my element as one of my skills is seeking opportunities and now I was a managing director of my own business. I was absolutely thrilled the day I bought my first prestige car, a lovely black Audi Estate top of the range S-line. I loved that car. It felt like a turning point.

What a change; the shackles had come off. You can have it all. A far cry from the 17-year-old who left home with nothing but the clothes on her back or almost being a kept wife with an income ceiling of £1000 a month, needing to ask if I needed more money. Ha, no chance! You do not have to follow the norms or do what society pressurises you to. This is one thing I have always done, buck the trend. I go my own way and if you don't like the bus I'm on, then get off.

As the business built up traction, I started diversifying and the social care element was growing rapidly, much quicker than I anticipated. I gained contracts with the local councils to support them with families in need of support with children with special needs or going through the family court. This was my first but was not going to be my last experience in our family judiciary in the UK.

We supported families for many reasons. Initially I would carry out a home visit with the family and have a meeting with the social worker to understand what was required from that referral. Sometimes it was help at home for the parents who struggled due to disability, or their children had needs and they needed extra support before and after school. However, the family court-supervised sessions we had to cover were the most upsetting.

Families were in court proceedings for many reasons, but my business was mostly involved in care proceedings where children were about to be removed from their parents for neglect or some sort of abuse. We covered supervised contacts with those families who were on their last chance; my supervisors took notes that would be presented in court. These notes contained information on interactions in supervised visits with the child or children's family. The person being supervised was the one under scrutiny. It was often a very sad situation.

We had various cases, and all were very different. One case was a father who was a convicted paedophile that wanted contact with his child. By law he was allowed this even though he was a child abuser. These were the most upsetting of cases. Who in their right mind allows a convicted paedophile near children?! It was very stressful on my staff who would have to supervise the criminal's visit with their child. It was sickening to all of us that this was even allowed, but at least we were keeping the children safe. My fear was what happened if the courts allowed unsupervised access. I spoke to social workers about this, and it was common practice. Just because someone is convicted of abusing a child it does not mean they cannot have access to their own child. This is horrific and something I campaign about today.

We would regularly get these referrals to supervise convicted paedophiles with children. A fax would arrive with the details, and I would turn to Jodie, my assistant. "We've got another one." We both felt constantly upset when reading what these children had been through. How does a court find it acceptable to allow a child to have ANY contact with anyone with such risks?

Another case was a mother of three beautiful girls of mixed race. This is poignant as I believe there was a stigma against her because of her colour. The mother was a feisty young woman. I covered one of her supervised contact visits as I had one of my supervisors call in sick and I did not want to let them down. It was hard not to get emotionally involved; you felt for these families.

I turned up at the social care office, and there was a frosty reception even to me as a professional attending the office. I was let in by a plump red-faced woman, and the social worker who came to the front desk was rude, abrupt and very stern looking. I put this down to the stress of having to deal with the hardships affecting these children daily.

"I'm here to supervise family X," I said, showing her the referral form. "I'm from Safehands." "You know the background to this family, do you?" she asked, looking at me without even breaking a smile.

"Yes, the mother has had her children removed, a domestic abuse victim, and the father is in prison according to the referral we received," I replied, looking sadly at the woman, pursing my lips and tilting my head to the side in empathy. She made no attempt to even reciprocate my emotion. Quite frankly she looked annoyed.

"Yes well, get ready. She kicks off every time, she is a handful, no wonder she can't get her kids back and if she carries on, she'll never see them again. Make sure you get everything in those notes as we are in family court next week and they will be presented to the judge."

I was absolutely astounded at how this social worker was talking about a mother and her children. She had never harmed the children according to the referral, in fact this mother was a victim of abuse herself.

"Ok, has she harmed the children before? It doesn't say Mum is a danger," I asked, querying the social worker's attitude. She did not even flinch or respond.

She ushered me into another room where the contact would take place. It looked better than other rooms I had been into; at least this one had pictures on the walls, sofas to sit on and a low, long coffee table. Some are just bare grey rooms bar a few chairs. Not really an appropriate setting for a child to have contact with a family member.

"No but she's a nightmare, like I said," she snapped back at me as she left me in the room. I thought she was judgemental and found her behaviour and attitude quite unprofessional. The woman had had her children removed because her boyfriend was violent; how was that her fault? *The mother is angry, I'm sure she is*, I thought to myself.

I waited in the room for the children to arrive first and then the mum was scheduled shortly after. I did not know what to expect but as a mother myself now I could not even begin to fathom having your children removed and dealing with social care. That social worker quite frankly was a bitch but held power over her kids. It did not bear thinking about. I suppose in a way you must try and keep that emotion in check and be as professional as you can, however these types of referrals were hard and emotive.

The three young girls were led into the room by the social worker, all under six. Beautiful, bronze skin, curly hair, dressed in lovely clothes. They were so lovely, such happy little souls. You could see in their eyes they were excited to be seeing their mum. It broke my heart they were in the care system. While running my business this was my first encounter with the misconception that a victim of violence is somehow to blame for the violence they have received. It did not make sense. No-one enters a relationship knowing they will be abused or wishing to be, for that matter.

The next thing I heard was the main door open and I could hear someone shouting, "I'm getting my girls back you know, you fuckers!" She was banging on the front desk. It was the girls' mum (who I will call Miss X). She was in her early twenties. She was dressed in jeans and a black t-shirt and had curly black hair like her girls. She was angry. I don't scare easily so it didn't faze me, but she pushed open the door quickly, chewing gum, and swung her bags onto the floor.

Her girls looked up at me. "Mummy's here!" I said, smiling at them and they all smiled back, excited.

She scooped them all together, hugging them tightly. The bags were full of fruit, juice, colouring books and dolls. She immediately got down on the floor and started getting all of the things out. "This is for you; this is for you." She was giving them each a gift of something they liked. They were so happy, jumping up and down.

"Mummy loves you, you know; I love you so much. You will be home soon. I'll get you back."

"You're new," she snapped at me, giving me a sideways glance.

"Yes, social services have asked my company to supervise the visits with your girls. They are beautiful, by the way. We are not social services; we are an independent organisation," I said. I knew she did not have a great relationship with the office, so I was trying to set our visit apart. I wanted her to feel comfortable, not threatened.

Suddenly my phone rang. My ringtone was Rihanna's 'Umbrella', and I quickly jumped up to get my bag which I had put down on the other side of the room. "I'm so sorry, that should be on silent." I don't know why but this seemed to put the woman at ease with me.

"You're sound, aren't you? Those fuckers in there, I swear I'll do something one day."

"Yes, actually, can I get on the level with you, don't give them that," I said, empathising with her. I pulled her to one side. "You, coming in kicking off, banging the desk, swearing. You are playing into their hands; that's all being noted down and will be used against you. I am sorry you are in the system, and I can see your girls love you to bits and you are a good mum. I have supervised some visits where the parents have clearly been drinking or are not even paying attention to their children and definitely haven't brought two huge bags of gifts and fruit. You ignored me when you walked in and they were your priority. I can see you are a good mum."

"Will you write that?" She looked at me and in that second, I felt her vulnerability.

Her and the children's lives could easily be destroyed by being separated, all because of a violent man. This is victim blaming. Surely there is another way. She was a victim of violence and then had her three beautiful girls thrust into the social care system.

"Of course I will, I will write the truth. I'll just sit over here. Try and pretend I'm not here. I know it's hard."

I moved to the other side of the room and smiled at her. She looked more relaxed. As a mother myself, if I thought for one second that she was in some way a danger to those children I would have put that in my notes, however that could not have been further from the truth from that session with the woman and her beautiful girls. She was quite young herself and I just felt for her. It's hard being a mummy, and she was a victim of abuse so I could imagine having to deal with that too. As women we are so vulnerable as new mothers. I empathised with her. I did not blame her or want to shame her. I wanted to help.

I saw so many different variations on this. I visited one house of a mother and father with learning disabilities where there were 20-plus carrier bags full of soiled nappies just sitting in their front room. It stank; I was retching the minute I walked in. There was no food in the cupboards, four children at home, all dirty faces and barefooted, walking on a dirty floor, dog hairs all over the highchair, no carpets. Yet their social worker said that was fine even though they were bringing a newborn baby home that day. The differences in social workers' opinions and standards were extremely shocking.

I sent my most experienced worker into that job; she could not do it and to be honest I did not blame her. She called at the address and was so concerned and alarmed by the extent of what she saw that she left after the first 30 minutes. I called the social worker who did not seem to see anything wrong.

There was such a disparity between different social workers; it felt like if your face did not fit then they would have your kids. How is that even a possibility?

This process had become such a huge part of my business that I took my eye off the other areas as all my carers were out at full capacity most of the time at unsociable hours, dealing with the most difficult of situations: suicide watch, supervising paedophiles with contact, travellers who threatened my staff, and drunk, aggressive parents. They were not all bad, but these were some of the cases my carers dealt with, often very difficult and sometimes dangerous. They dealt with them well, and I was so proud of my small business and the help we were providing. All the staff were qualified higher than any of the usual agency staff.

The family court stuff was the worst. This seemed such a cold and unbelievable process; some parents had lost their children and they were placed in the care of the system. Some families just should not have been there, and it was soul destroying to watch how the system picks up these families and systematically destroys them due to procedures not fit for purpose.

The family court, I was later to realise, is a dark institution a bit like social care itself. They hold judgement against families without proof. Most of the attitudes are based on bias and everything in court is dealt with on a balance of probability as opposed to actual evidence. The evidence to sway the balance could have been our contact notes, so this made me question whether social workers were trying to plant bias in the minds of my workers. It did not seem like justice to me when you have a biased social worker looking to sway the decision. In fact, you would expect this to be a criminal offence because imagine the damage this power could do in the wrong hands.

Some information that was used in the courts was altered to suit the social worker's narrative. For example, in relation to Miss X's family, I found out from an internal resource much later that there was a multi-disciplinary meeting held and I was not invited which was extremely suspicious given my business was involved in the contact with the children.

I subsequently discovered that the social worker had disregarded our contact notes and apparently made a comment that I (the managing director of the organisation) must have got too friendly with Miss X and apparently she said she thought we were 'painting nails together'. It was the most preposterous thing I have ever heard and a complete lie. The social worker clearly had it in for Miss X and now she was making up stories about me to keep my notes from the court. I was flabbergasted. I had my ear to the ground and people were reporting these things back to me.

It all became very tiring and was not at all a happy work life, if I'm honest.

I complained to her superior and asked for our contact notes to be included in the file for court, as it would otherwise be withholding evidence. How would they justify not adding the notes and why were they hell-bent on taking her children? It made no sense. From what I saw over the contacts we covered, she was a good mum, and there was no evidence to show otherwise apart from her being a victim of domestic violence. By now I had seen the bias again and again. They blamed Miss X for her perpetrator's actions.

I found out much later that Miss X got all three children back. I never did see her again, but I have always thought about her and hope they are safe and ok. One of her girls gave me a rainbow sticker which is still stuck on my calculator to this day. It makes me smile and I really hope they went on to live a happy life.

I found it disgusting that many of the social workers had aggressive views towards those mothers, the mothers who had suffered abuse themselves. How can you be blamed for being a victim? They were being blamed for staying with violent men, but these men would not leave them alone. How were they meant to keep the men away? This is where the system fails.

Not once were the actions of aggressors questioned. Surely the perpetrator should be held to account!

Many of the social workers had the view that "They should just leave them" or would say "Why do they stay with these violent men?" I would often be left in complete shock at the attitude of these social workers who quite frankly did not exactly lead the best lives themselves and were holding judgement on others. The power they had over a family was concerning given that this could affect the lives of many people including innocent children.

I was yet to find out the inside extent of this prejudice against women, especially victims of domestic abuse, and the catastrophic outcomes that follow family court proceedings. The service we delivered provided the notes for court, that was it. We were not involved in proceedings nor did we ever attend court.

I had one social worker complain about our notes as they wanted us to make the mothers sound bad. If my carers (who were all highly trained) wrote fondly of the mothers they would say "Are you sure that happened, you know she's done x and y?" like with Miss X. It felt like they wanted to destroy these families. It also felt like a social class bias too, because these families were often the most vulnerable who might have flourished, had they been offered support.

Social care uses a sledgehammer to crack an egg. Don't get me wrong, they aren't all bad, some were lovely, and the families relied on their support, however there were a few as I've described whose motives I questioned.

My understanding of social care was that you went there if you wanted help. Yet it seemed to me at every opportunity that some of the social workers wanted the families to fail so they could say I told you so. They would put them on parenting courses. I sat in on one once and it was so condescending. How did they expect to get the best from people when they treated them like second class citizens?

One mother had lost custody of her children due to her drinking. She too had been in a relationship with an abuser, and she had not had the most stable upbringing, having been through the care system herself. This meant there was even more of a stigma against her.

Though she was an alcoholic, she was not violent to her kids, and she was self-medicating for a reason. I covered some of her contact visits with her daughter who was around 11. She loved her mum and wanted to go home but as the mother was drinking the daughter was made to stay in the care system. This was so damaging. The daughter would scream at the end of contact, and I felt like the system stunted her emotional progression. Mum really would have benefitted from structure, support and guidance. Not prejudice and punishment. This process was not only destroying the mum, but the daughter's life would inevitably be ruined too.

It was not the same for the families in need due to disabilities; it was where there was violence against the mother. There was a definite bias against them.

I ponder, why is it that we do not support these families more at home? Why, if the mother is struggling because her ex is a complete maniac, do we not support her to be the best mother she can be and get the arsehole put in prison and remove him from the equation? Why do we expect the mum to run away from everything she knows?

I ran that business for five years without a holiday and in that time, we only ever had mothers in this situation. There was never a father who was violently abused by a mother or blamed in the whole five years of running that business. It seemed clear to me there is a stigma attached to victims of domestic abuse. It made my heart sink.

The system is open to abuse and is currently patriarchal. Mothers just seem to get a bad rap and these decisions are life altering for both mothers and their children. I did not see it with both eyes open then, but I would soon. People making decisions around children's lives and destroying their future only for their own agendas.

Anyway, I knew we were helping many of these families, however building a business on misery is soul destroying. Every time the fax machine went it was a new referral from social services for a child in need of support, or a contact to be supervised between a known convicted criminal and a child. It was extremely difficult. A double-edged sword. I was burnt out but compelled to help these poor families.

It was utterly exhausting. The only saving grace was that I was able to spend time working from home with Cameron. He was such a happy baby after we got over the first 14 weeks of crying and I had settled into motherhood. Working with all these families every day made me so grateful for my life and I could really see how far I had come. That could have been me, when I was just six years old at home alone, with the neighbour just looking out for me. Had social services got wind of that, would I have been in care?

Cameron was such a good boy although he hated me leaving him and would scream and cry when I dropped him off at nursery. I used to feel so guilty. I'd call the nursery worried, thinking he was sitting there just crying for me. "It's Cameron's mummy, is he ok?"

"He's fine as soon as you are gone, he gets on with it," they would say. There was me thinking he had separation anxiety. He was playing me.

Even though I was super busy with the business and juggling being a single mum it felt like there was still something missing. I was nearly 30 now and felt I had kind of lost my identity with all the hours I was ploughing into the business. I also worried I might never have another child. I did not want Cameron to be an only child or lonely like me.

I needed something else.

RED FLAGS & REFLECTION

Victim blaming, when the victim of a crime is held fully or partially to blame for the harm that took place – what is the reason for this? Why do we look at the victim of a crime or incident to try and understand what happened? I personally found this time and time again after my ordeal and even professionals would ponder on the thought of what the victim had done to 'deserve' the crime against them. Have we been programmed as a culture to look for and find blame in the victim?

Is this easier?

Why do we not look at the perpetrators of a crime and ask, "Why do they break the law?" Should we accommodate the bad people in this world by changing our behaviour to reduce crime? Surely the focus should be on those doing wrong.

Victim blaming can come in many forms; there is the downright obvious or it may be that when hearing about a victim of a crime we think how we would have behaved differently so that the crime did not happen. This is victim blaming.

Some examples of how we victim blame:

- Someone was pick pocketed – "Why did they have their purse/wallet on show?"
- A woman is raped – "What was she wearing?"
- A mother who has been domestically abused stays with her abuser – "Why doesn't she just leave?"

Why is it we think that there is a simple answer to reducing these crimes, by somehow changing the victim's behaviour? Many criminals can be opportunists and some are hell-bent on committing the crime. A victim changing their behaviour will not stop them. A victim's actions did not cause their behaviour either. The person doing wrong is solely responsible.

The focus must fully be on a perpetrator's actions and their reasons as to why they behave the way they do. Not the victim.

What are the thoughts that come into your head when you hear of a crime?

CHAPTER 5:

The Taker

I had been single for a while. It was tough being a single mum and a businesswoman. It can be a lonely place and being busy with the business meant that I did not get out much. As a single mum without family to support me I struggled with childcare in the evening, so I was at home most evenings alone. As soon as I tucked Cameron into bed that was my night done too.

One Saturday afternoon, when Cameron was with his dad, I met one of my oldest friends Jodi for lunch in a local bar. A few of my old male friends walked in and they were with this guy I'd never seen or met before. He was very handsome. A few years younger than me. Good looking, Italian. He was tanned, with short, shaved jet-black hair, well dressed and well groomed.

"Alright Zoe," one of the lads said, nodding. I invited them to join us.

"Wow, who are you?" Jodi blurted out to the Italian guy. Jodi is the loudest of my friends; she has always been forward like this.

"How fit is he?!" Jodi whispered when we walked to the bar. She made me take a second glance in that kind of way. I probably wouldn't even have noticed otherwise.

"I suppose," I said, and she elbowed me as we stood at the side of the bar waiting to be served.

"Ask him on a date! I wonder if he's single. I'm going to ask him if he's single." Here she goes... "He is nice looking though, isn't he?"

I looked back at him again from the bar. There was something about him that was kind of mysterious. "I've never seen him before, maybe we can ask the others about him?" Jodi whispered to me. It was kind of awkward. I get embarrassed in these situations. Not in a shy way, but I'd rather play it cool. I'm not really a flirty girl; I'm quite serious. Whereas Jodi would blurt things out in front of everyone.

She didn't this time, thank goodness. We spent the next couple of hours in the bar, as the lads had joined us, so we were all chatting, having banter. I found out his name was Moran and he was a DJ.

As he was a DJ, I thought we must have a lot in common. I loved my music, house music, and I missed the days when I went partying into the small hours and everyone would come back to my house so we could play more tunes. I never allowed anyone else to touch the stereo, my pride and joy.

I tried speaking with Moran. He seemed shy. He failed to hold eye contact when we talked, and kept looking down or away or trying to bring someone else into the conversation, like he was nervous. It was kind of cute and the opposite to Wayne who was confident and owned the room. Moran seemed mysterious, intriguing. Stand-offish, nonchalant.

I could not quite work him out. He seemed uncomfortable talking to a girl as he was not like that when speaking with the lads – then he would get his confidence. I just thought maybe he was painfully shy with girls. From the moment we shared eye contact there was definitely something going on between us, an attraction, an energy. I could feel it.

I had just been to London on a DJ course for the weekend. I'd booked it as a bit of fun and stayed in London. I needed to get away from work, escape from all the harsh stuff I dealt with daily with the business and meet up with complete strangers. I like doing new things and meeting new people. I was telling Moran about it.

"The DJ teacher guy taught to mix vinyl. It was hard trying to blend the music. Not sure I'll pick it up. I want to dance too much," I joked, trying to make him laugh.

"Oh yeah I DJ a bit," he said, laughing. "I think I'll be too busy enjoying and dancing to the music and forget to mix the next tune in, that would be a disaster." I'm quite a joker, so kept dropping in one liners. He seemed nice.

"Well, I can give you a few lessons if you like." Moran suddenly spoke really quickly at me.

"Ok, that sounds good. I've just bought some decks too actually, well CDJs rather than vinyl decks because that's the way the music tech is going. I'll let you know when I've got them. I'm waiting on delivery." CDJs are DJing decks, but they play CDs instead of records. I had treated myself as I needed a release. Stuck in the house with Cameron, I thought I would start a little hobby.

After meeting at the bar, we started chatting on MySpace, the social media platform for music sharing. I was following some DJs already and listening to their music; it was a good place to connect with likeminded people, although there were a few freaks on there too. I'd often get the odd creepy message from some random pervert.

Moran and I often chatted about music and where we'd like to go on nights out. We started contacting each other regularly, and soon Moran asked me if I wanted to meet him for a drink. I agreed and we arranged to just go to a local pub for a drink and I said I'd pick him up.

I picked him up from his house in my new Audi; I suppose it was me being a bit of a show-off. I wanted him to see I was a successful woman, and I didn't need him for anything. Lots of my girlfriends were obsessed with finding someone with money, someone who would pay for their meals out, new bags, new shoes. I just wanted to meet someone for me. He walked out of his door wearing a big white coat with fur trim which set off his olive skin. He looked fit!

I noticed a blonde girl looking out of the door as he hopped in the car. "Hi, who's that?" I nodded towards the door where I could see the girl peeping. I was laughing.

"Oh, it's my sister," he responded. "Let's get out of here." He didn't seem to laugh. "She's annoying, she's just being nosey."

"Ahh that's cute she cares." He responded with a "Huh" in reply.

We went to the local pub and played pool. It was all quite flirty; he was still really shy or playing it cool, I could not quite make it out. I liked that about him. I could tell he liked that I was independent; he was intrigued about my business, owning my own house and how I raised Cameron. He said he loved kids.

Moran was from a big Italian family who I expected to be close, as I suppose that's how you think of Italian culture. This was attractive and really interesting to me as I had always wanted to be part of my own big family, especially as I felt like such an outsider growing up.

Our relationship started out quite casual. Moran would come to my house. We didn't live far from each other, incidentally, which turned out to be handy. He would turn up with a bottle of wine and we'd play music while having a drink. It was nice and I was glad of the company. I would ask him to come once Cameron was fast asleep in bed and he never stayed too late.

We had been seeing each other for a few weeks before we kissed for the first time. Although he was shy and awkward, he made me happy, and I liked his company.

Moran was very family orientated. He often spoke of the kids in his family. One evening he asked, "Do you think it would be ok if I meet Cameron?" I was a bit shocked he asked, but in a way I thought it was nice he wanted to meet my son, and I thought he must want to get serious if he was asking.

"Maybe I can meet him next time and say 'hi'." It was so sweet that he was taking an interest. Cameron is my world and whoever I'm with must absolutely understand Cameron comes first. I was quite shocked that it never bothered him I had a son, as he did not have any children.

"Why don't you come tomorrow then, and I'll make dinner," I responded.

The next night Moran came to the house. He had brought a bottle of wine. "You're a proper mum hey, not like other girls. You make dinners." I laughed and looked at him and said "Of course."

I was not sure what he expected. It was an odd thing to say. I was in the kitchen being a mum and cooking dinner for my lad. He had only seen the fun 'out' side of me, I suppose. "Cooking a proper dinner and all this," he said, nodding around the kitchen. My kitchen was open plan with a breakfast bar. My DJ decks sat at the end of the kitchen under the skylights but now I had pans on the hobs cooking dinner and Cameron's toys were out on the side, his plastic cutlery, plates, and a little table small enough for him to sit at and eat.

"It's not all partying you know, I'm a mummy first and I like a clean house. There is a place for everything. I put all of Cameron's things out the way in the evening or if he's at his dad's, then I can be Zoe again." House proud; I could tell this impressed him.

"Fancy going to the Ministry of Sound next week?" he asked. This is a super club in London which is often on all through the night and has amazing DJs playing. I was over the moon – I had not been out clubbing since before having Cameron. It was going to be amazing.

"Yes definitely, I'll book a hotel." I said this with butterflies; it was like I was living three lives. On one hand a single mummy, the other a businesswoman and then I'd now found a release and someone who I seemed to have a lot in common with.

"Well, I was going to say we could get the train down and then get the first one back, probably won't spend much time in the hotel," he said.

"I'd rather have a hotel, I'll drive down," I responded as I like to make sure I know how I'm getting somewhere, where I'm staying and how I'm getting back.

"Up to you," he said, pulling me into him and kissing me. He seemed perfect. I was really starting to fall for him.

"Cameron, come and meet Mummy's friend Moran." He was in the garden playing with his cars. He had hundreds of them, all stacked in a lorry that opened on either side. Running in, he looked up at me with his big brown eyes, and instantly hid behind my legs.

"Hello little fella," Moran said, putting his arms out. Cameron looked at me innocently, I smiled, and he lifted him up. "You're a big boy, how old are you?"

"Three," he responded.

"I've got a nephew who's three, shall I bring him round so you can play together?" Moran was a natural with him. Just looking at the way he was with Cameron made my heart melt. I had no idea how this was going to go or if Cameron would accept someone else in his life. I had a lot of apprehension around this due to my childhood. I never wanted Cameron to feel second best or pushed out, ever.

Things gradually started to get more serious and before long Moran moved in. We spent so much time together anyway, that it just felt like the natural next step. He was an electrician by day, so he would be up and out of the house at 6am. He was quite strict with his routine. He did not really drink in the week, whereas I liked to have a glass of wine to unwind in the evening. He would be up, showered and gone in the morning.

We got on with our own lives and we would save the weekends when Cameron was with his dad to have party fun. We would go out or have friends over. Life was much easier having Moran around. He was so good with Cameron, and his family would often pop around too. His mum would come over if she was in town.

I liked his mum; she was a little naïve and not the woman I expected as the matriarch of an Italian family. I expected a very strong woman but she was quite soft; Moran ran rings around her, and she definitely preferred her sons. Moran had a younger brother and two sisters. He was estranged from his older sister and had a tumultuous relationship with his younger sister, a very attractive young girl who had a son the same age as Cameron. She was well manicured and looked after herself, but she was extremely fiery. Moran and she would openly fight and scream expletives at each other but then the next day it would be all over as if it had never happened. I did not particularly like that side of his family. The fighting reminded me of the toxic relationship I had had with my step-siblings. However, I had no educational knowledge then on toxic families or how to deal with them. Having this knowledge is important.

By now my business was expanding and we were busier than ever. This meant sometimes I had to work weekends or cover a shift if a carer could not make it. However, as I had quickly become part of the family, his sister would help, so I would often take Cameron there to play with Moran's nephew.

Looking back, the relationship with Moran was great from a traditional perspective, however it lacked any passion. I could not quite put my finger on it. Moran would often seem nonchalant with me, but not like in the early days. Now he seemed bored and his lack of passion was not something I expected when dating an Italian. I wanted him, I fancied him, but it was becoming clear this was very one sided.

I was charmed by his good looks, the music, the hedonistic lifestyle we had together at the weekends. When I could be myself, be free, go dancing, forget my stresses and be the old Zoe again but still there was something missing, something he was not giving me, even though I felt I gave him everything. I felt like I was constantly trying to please him. The sex when we did have it was not sweaty, steamy passion. It was awkward as if he wanted it to be over. Or he would make comments to make me feel dirty. Over time it became non-existent as he was never the instigator of any passion and seemed disgusted with anything to do with a woman's anatomy.

"Errrrr I'm not doing that, it's disgusting," he would say. I have to say I was pretty shocked; most men definitely don't have that same thought. I put this down to him being so particular and fussy about things. It had to be his way. It was as if he did not want to give me pleasure or it made him feel weak, or maybe he had a sense of power saying no.

I would talk to the girls about it when we'd have one of our wine nights.

"That's weird," they'd say.

"What the fuck, I'd fuck him off straight away Zoe."

We'd all fall over laughing but it was not funny; it made me feel unattractive and worthless.

"I know right, he never ever pesters me for sex, in fact I'm the one chasing it. What the fuck is that!" I'd say, laughing along.

Moran was very blasé; he never fussed if I was doing anything, like going out with the girls or popping around my friend's house, which was good because I could finally get back out with the girls or pop round theirs for a wine in the week.

"I'm going out this weekend with the girls."

"Ok," he'd say, not even glancing over or questioning who with, where I was going, or when I'd be back.

Although I found it to be refreshing that he did not question my every move and we did not live in each other's pockets, unlike my relationship with Wayne, who was worried when I went out without him when we were in a relationship, the opposite was happening with Moran. I felt like I was chasing him. He would go out and not answer his phone all night. He would also disappear for hours on end.

When he finally answered the phone, it would go something like...

"Where are you?" I'd ask.

"Out," he would reply, drunk, no emotion, no care.

"Oh, who with?"

"You don't know them, Zoe. I'll be back soon." It was like I craved him when he wasn't there. Or maybe it was my gut trying to tell me something. I often brushed it off.

I'm an independent person, I'd think to myself. He's just out having fun with his mates. Once Moran was back at home, he would be all over Cameron, playing with him, making him laugh hard at his silliness. It made me think I was being selfish. *Am I just thinking of myself all the time? Why do I need to know where he is, for god's sake? If he kept asking me where I was, I would get annoyed*, I'd think.

"So, where did you go?" I'd ask him.

"I was just out with mates Zoe, drop it."

"Yeah, but who, I probably know them," I'd say but he wasn't giving me anything.

Moran would often show his frustration that I had my own business. He hated his job and wanted a shop, something to do with music. So, me being me, a fixer, I started looking into helping him set up a shop. I told him how to get stock, helped with a business plan, helped him get funding from the Prince's Trust and before long we opened a record and designer menswear shop in Coventry. He got what he wanted.

'Renegade' had been a small independent store in the city, a hangout from my heyday, so I was so pleased when we secured it. Alongside keeping the store as a record shop and selling designer menswear, we decided to also sell DJ equipment and eventually event tickets. We spent the next few months getting the business sorted. Moran was loving it. I was running around like a lunatic making sure we had everything we needed – in addition to running my own business and looking after Cameron, plus trying to keep the house in some sort of order.

As Moran had given up his job as an electrician, I bought all the stock on my credit card. The idea was we would clear this debt once we got the sales. Moran was going around bragging to his friends, however I noticed how when he talked about it, it was as if he had done everything himself. He did not give me any credit, and I had a nagging feeling that Moran was in it for himself.

Having the shop had given him an ego boost. His confidence or arrogance was starting to grow, although underneath I knew he was a complete nervous wreck when the reality of running a business kicked in.

We spent the last few days before the opening getting everything ready. The clothes were steamed, the records out, posters up, and the shop looked amazing, really funky. I was so impressed. I could tell Moran was happy, and I was happy he was happy. I just wanted us to be successful.

Looking out the door waiting for our first customer, Moran was shaking. "What's the matter with you?" I asked him. He was fidgeting and getting all agitated.

"I don't know, I'm nervous," he said, looking at the till and throwing his hands in the air. "I don't even know how to use this." This made me laugh. He was such a worrier and got dramatic if under any pressure. If there was a problem with anything, he would find it.

"Just relax, they are only people." I had worked with the public for years so this was not new territory for me, but Moran was Mr Awkward. I thought, *he will grow through this*. It made me proud, and I couldn't have been happier.

The first day at the shop was a success. It was a good day and that evening we discussed having a baby.

Moran was raising Cameron anyway and I could see he would be a good dad; it made sense. It was the natural next step. I never wanted Cameron to be an only child, so we agreed that I should come off the pill. True to form, within a few weeks I was pregnant.

“I must be the most fertile person in the world!” I exclaimed. I was so happy. I felt like my world was coming together. Business was good, the shop was open, I was pregnant, and Cameron was thriving. There was a lot going on.

The relationship was Moran was ok on the surface. I just had a feeling that he wasn’t really there for me. Most things were about him. I had to help him with the business. He was not really contributing financially, a couple of hundred pounds here and there, and he was distant from me in the relationship. And sometimes he made me feel unlovable. But I convinced myself to be grateful.

It was like I needed his validation on things. I craved it. I would do my best to help him so I could get that praise, that attention from him. I wanted love but then he’d piss me off with his disappearing acts at the weekend and it was worse now I was pregnant. It was like a swinging pendulum between me feeling lonely, to angry, to wanting his attention.

He realised he did not need to try anymore, at all. I, on the other hand, was going around and around in circles. I was pregnant. He had me now so there was no need to try. Not that he really tried anyway. How had I got so carried away with the whole Italian family thing, when incidentally it turned out they were not so close, and it was in fact toxic and full of tensions.

I would question myself. *What am I doing? This is not life*. It was like an emotional rollercoaster. He would make me feel so utterly disgusting, calling me fat when I was pregnant, and turning his nose up to me in disgust. Then one small comment of praise or attention and I’d be putty.

On my birthday I’d arranged to go out with friends and their partners for the evening. I was huge, a big pregnant stomach, seven months pregnant.

“You’re not wearing that, are you?” Moran looked at my maternity dress, at the huge bump that I was proud of. He always knocked my self-esteem. If I felt good, he would find something to say that would chip away at my self-worth.

We met my friends at the restaurant, then after dinner Moran and my friend’s boyfriend disappeared. He did this a lot; he would drag other people along with him. When they came back a few hours later, my friends ended up having a big argument and went home. On the way home I told Moran that he should not have disappeared, and why did he feel the need to always drag the evening down? He got mad. Suddenly, he pulled on the handbrake of the car, we lurched forward, and I hit my stomach on the steering wheel. I screamed in shock.

I was so upset; I could not fathom what had just happened. He was acting like an idiot.

This was the start of things to come.

RED FLAGS & REFLECTION

Putting someone else's needs before your own can be a dangerous game, especially if you are not clear on their intentions. Be conscious of this. One thing for sure, I was very naïve in personal relationships. I did not realise this at the time. I thought I was a tough cookie, that I was wise, I could handle shit. Hindsight is a great thing. I did not know it at the time, but I was vulnerable for many reasons and in the wrong circumstances and with the wrong person this could be a disaster. This is why education around healthy and unhealthy relationships is so important.

Takers never stop taking, so givers need to set boundaries, and when someone shows you their true colours with their actions believe that this is them. There are certain actions that should not be tolerated in a relationship and disrespect should never be ignored.

One thing I have learned is to be conscious in my decision making around other people's motives.

Do you blindly walk into relationships, like I did?

CHAPTER 6:
It's a Girl

Making the best of a bad situation felt like the story of my life. It had always seemed to be a rollercoaster of ups and downs since my childhood. However, forever the optimist, I'd get through anything. That's what I would tell myself. Although Moran was still acting like a super plonker most weekends I thought he would be different once we had a child of our own. I thought he would respect me again. I was wrong.

It's a girl! I was so happy. We found out the baby's gender before the birth, as I had kept all of Cameron's old baby things just in case it was a boy. I was over the moon. No-one can explain that feeling you get after giving birth and looking at your newborn child. It's an unconditional love.

My family life was complete now, with one of each. I felt like Moran was going to be a good dad, so I forgot about the stupidity; I was just elated.

"A boy and girl, one of each, how nice," people would say.

Sofia was amazing. From the moment she was born, she slept through the night, unlike Cameron. She was born with a full head of jet-black hair like her dad, and another boomer, at 8lbs 7oz. I elected for a caesarean section with Sofia, so this time around the birth was so much better. I was prepared. I knew what to expect and I had all the drugs!

There was no agony in the labour ward. I even had a spray tan done before I went in. I did not put on as much weight with Sofia either. Probably good, as Moran often told me how disgusting I was when I was pregnant.

The children are 4.5 years apart. A great gap. Cameron was so happy when Sofia came along, and Moran brought him to the hospital to meet his new sister. I had bought him a doctor's set as a present so he could pretend to be one of the doctors. I didn't want him to feel left out, so I made that moment a special one.

"When can she play, Mummy?" he would say when peering into her Moses basket. He would often sit on the floor next to her, waiting. Then he would get frustrated.

"She's boring, when can she play? How long will she take to walk?" He would look at her, screwing up his face. He would make us laugh at how attentive he was with her. Moran was a hands-on dad; I knew he would be. He was good with both the children, and doted on them. It was me he seemed to neglect. I just got on with it, as I always do.

However, the cracks in my relationship with Moran were widening and as the children were my priority, I had less tolerance of Moran's bad behaviour and his critical attitude towards me. Everything I did was wrong. I was walking on eggshells all the time trying to please him.

He made me feel like I was left out. It was like I did not even exist at times. I could not remember the last time we were even intimate at this point. I felt I should be grateful, but I just wanted to be held, cuddled, told I was beautiful. I felt lonely and unattractive. My self-worth was low.

Of course, when we were out or around other people, Moran acted differently. It would be great. He would show what a good dad he was. It was often better when we had friends over but as soon as they left, he would lie on the sofa and fall asleep and leave me to clear up.

One evening, after both children were bathed and fast asleep in bed, Moran went to bed. I thought I'd try again; maybe he would show me some affection. I had a bath, put on a little sexy slip and slid into the bed next to him. I started to stroke his back.

"Don't Zoe, I've got work." I just had that hollow feeling again, like my heart had been ripped out. The rejection was horrific. Why was he so nice to me in the day and then the evenings would be hard? It was lonely.

He continued speaking to me in a derogatory way. It would escalate when he was drunk but by now he did not hide his bad attitude; it was an everyday thing. I was starting to get sick of his shit, quite frankly. If we were with other people he would ignore me and be all over everyone else. It was a game, I'm sure of it.

By this point he'd go out with his friends at the weekend and not even come home at all. If he did text, he would just call me names, swear at me. It was of course my fault he was feeling like shit because he was acting like a lowlife scumbag, drinking too much. He would take it out on me because he had no self-control.

I'd text: `[Where are you?]`

`[Fuck off you cunt]` was Moran's response.

I'd just look at the phone in disgust. Who is he talking to?! He can fuck off. What am I doing with this loser? By this point I wanted the relationship to be over. He had zero respect for me at all. I'd been through enough. I wished he would never come back.

`[Who speaks like this, you're a loser!]` I'd text back, then get a load of abuse. Then nothing.

The animosity was building between us. It was horrible.

One evening when he came back home, he came up the stairs into the bedroom and woke me up, then drunkenly stumbled back downstairs. I heard the music go on; he did not even care that Sofia was in bed. Cameron was at his dad's, thankfully. I had to get up to tell him to turn off the music. He was being a drunken idiot. I was furious.

Sofia never woke up, bless her. As soon as her head hit the pillow, she'd be fast asleep. I used to say a bomb could go off and it would not wake her.

As I approached him, I could smell the alcohol seeping through his pores. It made me sick when he was like this, but I would also be shaking with anger and anxiety at what was coming next. There was nothing worse than being woken from sleep to a drunk, aggressive Moran. I could not reason with him like this.

"Get out of my face Moran, you've just woken me up." He was Mr Brave when he'd had a drink.

He came right up to my face. "Get out of my face Moran, I'm warning you!" I was not scared of him; I was angry, but so tired. Tired of this shit every goddamn weekend. I pushed my head forwards to move his face away from mine and as I did, I caught him on the nose, because he had his face almost pressed up against mine. His nose started bleeding.

I was scared at this point. From being in bed to up having a row, now there was blood and Sofia was asleep in bed. I was worried what he would do next. His face changed.

I ran through the doors of the lounge and into the hallway whilst calling the police. He just stood there for a minute, stunned.

"I've had an argument with my boyfriend, he's drunk and he's shouting in my face. My baby is in bed. I need him to get out."

The next minute there were police at the door. I opened the door and explained what had happened.

"I want him to go, look at the state of him." Moran was swaying drunk, barely able to stand. I felt terrible. It was the right thing to do. Moran didn't care the police were there; it did not faze him one bit.

"Where's the blood from?" The police officer was trying to get sense out of Moran.

"We clashed heads when he was shouting in my face."

"Let's go you, he can sleep it off at the station. Night in the cells, son." Moran did not even flinch and just left with the police.

My heart was broken that I had to call the police. It was just no good. What the hell was I going to do now? I couldn't raise the kids on my own.

I would find myself excusing his behaviour though, hoping he would see sense. *It's the drink*, I'd think to myself, justifying his actions. *If only he didn't drink*. I knew full well deep down it was disrespect, but I was trapped.

Moran come home the next morning, tail between his legs as usual. He was sorry; he said it would not happen again. He felt terrible. Was Sofia ok? The usual...

"I need to stop drinking Zo, it's the root of all evil. I'm not like that when I'm not drinking."

"Why are you such an arsehole Moran! You are so disgusting to me."

"I don't mean it. It won't happen again; I'm giving up drink."

I desperately wanted our relationship to work for the kids and I still looked at him fondly when he was being nice, as much as he made me mad. I wanted us to work out. I did not want more upheaval, especially for Cameron. Cameron had got used to Moran. But really and truly, what kind of existence was this? I just existed to be the mother of my children. Women are more than mothers. I still had dreams. Having children never stopped that, although having Moran did. His dreams became my problem.

Sofia was now at nursery and both children were doing well. My relationship however just went from bad to worse. Moran was still going out at the weekends partying while I was at home alone with the children. Then he would even bring people back to the house in the early hours and play music really loudly while we were in bed. I often got up, going crazy. It was the same shit, different day. I even tried to level with him at times and get up and join in. It was useless. I would be exhausted the next day and it was not fair on the kids.

One evening he came back with a friend. I was furious at having to go downstairs and yet again kick him and his friends out of the house. It was embarrassing. I just looked like a complete walkover.

"Get out, you loser! Who frickin' lives like this?!"

"We are going alright!" Moran was spitting at me.

I went back to bed, and while I was lying there, I heard the front door go. I thought he had let his friends out and was coming to bed.

Then I heard a car engine outside. *That sounds like my Audi*. I got out of bed, looked out of the window and I saw my car door being shut. I ran to the top of the stairs to tell Moran my car was being stolen and then I realised it was him.

He had 'stolen' my car. Not insured and drunk! What was I doing with this guy? I had to find a way out.

The following Monday morning I put on the news as normal as I like to know what is going on in the world. There was a story about a small boy, named in the press named as Baby P (we now know his name was Peter Connolly), who had been abused and murdered by his parents. He was on the child protection register and under child social services, so when news of his murder surfaced, it horrified the nation. Coventry Council made a knee-jerk reaction to freeze any social care contracts using outside agencies to do their due diligence.

This meant my childcare business would be affected. I was horrified. I had no idea what the impact would be. The very next morning the council arranged an emergency meeting with me. A woman and man came to the office. Jodie let them in and slipped out to grab coffees.

"We have to freeze your contracts," the woman said, looking at me sternly. She went on to explain about Baby P.

"Why freeze the contracts? That doesn't make sense. What about all of the families we support? What about my staff? Who will take care of the children we look after?" I replied. This was a typical local authority knee-jerk response, not thinking of the consequences or the knock-on effects.

"We need to do our due diligence," she said, looking at her paperwork.

"You are already doing due diligence. I am registered! So, you are closing all agencies? All of them? How is that helpful? What about all the families that rely on our support? When is this happening?" I responded fearfully.

With no emotion, she replied sternly: "Immediately."

I burst into tears. How could they do this? We did great work with families and now who would support them? Had they even thought this through? There were families struggling with daily life, and my carers would go in every day. The kids! My mind was whirling.

"TODAY! We are registered with the Commission for Social Care, what bloody due diligence do you need to do? We are already inspected. I don't understand!" At this point I had to find some tissues.

"So, when can we start delivering the support again? How long will our contract be frozen for?" I was looking around at the filing cabinets I had in the office, each one with the family surname on the side, running through my head the type of support we were providing to each and every family, the support they would no longer receive. I was appalled at this decision. It was unbelievable.

"Once we have done our due diligence you can start supporting again but we cannot give you a timeline, I'm afraid," said the woman.

"It's not just your company." The male council worker finally spoke. Tears were pouring down my face. This was terrible.

"We'll have to close. We can't sustain a freeze in work. We just don't have the funds; we are a small business."

"I'm sorry Zoe," they said in unison. "We can see you care." They left. That was it. Just like that. The end of an era.

I had to close the business. It was no longer financially viable; we didn't have enough reserves in the bank to keep all the staff in shifts. We could not withstand a freeze. We had got so busy with the social care side of the business, and I hadn't nurtured the private babysitting services or mobile crèche arm of the business. A big lesson learned. Spread your risk. I had put far too much focus on the social care business and had never even envisaged a freeze in contracts. It was unprecedented.

I had around 40 carers on my books and many regular families we supported. I now had to tell them there was no work. They had their own families to feed and this was the hardest decision of my life so far.

Jodie and I had to advise the staff one by one. It was the worst thing I have ever done. Jodie was a real trooper through this and really supportive. She had become a good friend. A lot of the staff blamed me. Some were empathic, and some were quite cruel, getting angry at me. It was an awful situation.

I hadn't stopped to think about me. After spending all my energy telling the staff we had to close it dawned on me. I had no income and I was the breadwinner. How the hell was I going to pay the mortgage? And my home was at risk as I had put it up as collateral to set the business up. The shop we opened in the city was not even breaking even yet, and certainly was not bringing in enough money to pay the mortgage and keep the children.

When I got home, I spoke to Moran. He did not flinch or show an ounce of care. I was closing my business I had worked so hard on for the past five years. He did not give a shit. No offer of help. No words of advice. It was, "Oh, what are you going to do now?"

Although Moran had agreed to pay his way when he moved in to mine, he did not. Was he really not going to stand with me and help after me setting up the shop? I knew the answer. He was happy my life had gone to shit. This made him feel more superior.

I had to speak to my dad. He was my only option and at least he would care. Dad had been living in the house I grew up in alone now for a few years. My stepmother had died a couple of years before and this was hard on him. She had loved the grandkids. She had been on so many meds towards the end and often out of it. It was heartbreaking to watch such a strong woman disintegrate in front of your eyes and I knew only too well how precious life is.

My dad was rattling around the big old-fashioned house – 'the house that Jack built' was the expression we often used. He was not utilising all the space and had let it go. Overflowing ashtrays, a half-drunk bottle of whisky on the floor in the 'lounge', half-finished crosswords strewn on the floor. His hairbrush, toothbrush, razor and one of those plastic mirrors sat on the kitchen windowsill. He only had the heating turned on in two rooms.

When I told him what had happened, he said, "Just come home, love!" So matter of fact.

"Rent your house out" and that was that. This was the best decision I made. There was some organising to do to get the house to a standard for the kids. Sofia was crawling so the house needed a good scrub. We needed to finish the half-finished loft, put in some skylights so that Cameron could have my old bedroom, and decorate throughout. Then we all moved in with my dad.

This worked out great all round. Dad was no longer on his own and he could see his grandkids every day. It gave him a new lease of life and I felt secure again.

He would pick Cameron up from school and take him for dinner at the supermarket. It allowed me to start planning again for the future and get back on my feet. I took a training job to fill the gap while I found something better. Life soon settled. The children were in a good routine and they loved living with Grandad.

Moran did not want to live with my dad, though. He would often question this, although if he had been prepared to cover the bills at the old house, we would have still been there. I did not care what he wanted. He chose to stand back and let my world collapse. It was obvious we were not a team. He had made that quite clear when I lost the business and he didn't even give me a hug to say sorry.

We still had the shop, the business I had built, however Moran kept me at arm's length even though I had set this up. We did have staff at the stage too, so he basked in my misery and now used to disappear for whole weekends at a time, as he obviously could not bring people home to my dad's house. At least that stopped that behaviour and we could sleep in peace. Now when he came home after disappearing, he would invariably stink of alcohol and stale cigarettes. He would slide in the door thinking no-one would notice. I would just let him get upstairs out of the way of the children. Then I would go and speak to him. The contempt and anger were building; we had pure animosity towards each other. I wanted him gone. I no longer wanted to be in this relationship.

It made me sick how he could behave this way. He was no role model for the children. When he was sober he was ok, but still he had an air of rudeness. 'Taker' became my new nickname for him. He was there for what he could get and to live for the smallest amount of money possible. He barely contributed to anything. It felt hopeless.

One Saturday evening Moran came back, his usual argumentative self. I was already in bed. He was drunk and being mouthy. I'd just had enough. I'd been here, time and time before, but now we were in my dad's house. This time it was getting really heated. We were in the loft bedroom and our voices started to get raised. My dad was in the bedroom below.

"Why have you bothered coming back like that, look at the fucking state of you, you are such a fucking loser!" He was wobbling around, eyes glazed over, couldn't even speak.

"Cunt!" he spat at me.

"Oh you are just lovely aren't you, why don't you fuck off. What an embarrassment."

"I'll do what I want to do alright, and I couldn't give a fuck, ok." Then he pushed me.

"Get off... Dad!" I called out. Dad hates conflict. He came running up the loft stairs.

"Don't hit her." I felt so bad for my dad having to be involved. This was a point of no return.

"Do you have no shame? This is my dad's house and you come back like that!" I was now shouting.

"Shut up Zoe." Dad did not want things to escalate but I was so angry. Was I supposed to let this fucking arsehole get away with it?

The next thing I knew, Moran lunged for my dad's throat.

"What are you doing!" I screamed. Moran obviously shocked himself because he immediately stopped and stumbled as he left the room.

I went down the stairs after him. He was swaying all over the place and wobbling around, still not even coherent. "I'll go," he said.

"Yes, I think you should." He left by the side door, and I locked it behind him.

I got some black bin bags, went back upstairs and filled them with all his clothes. Looking out of the side window, I saw him sitting on the wall outside on his phone. I shouted out the window "You are not coming back!" and chucked the bags out of the window.

My dad had gone back into his bedroom and slammed the door. And that was that. It was over. Moran picked up the bags and walked off up the road.

After a few months, I was finally getting myself back on my feet. I was in a new job, now working in IT in criminal background screening, which my previous business had given me the experience to do. People with these skills were hard to find, which was good news for me!

In the UK they had introduced a new law where all people working with vulnerable groups had to have a Criminal Background Check. The government had overhauled the criminal screening process by introducing a new piece of legislation.

This followed the murder of the two schoolgirls, Holly Wells and Jessica Chapman, by Ian Huntley. Dubbed the Soham murderer, Huntley was the residential caretaker at Soham Village College. The Soham case exposed serious failings within the vetting system which is designed to prevent people who may pose a threat to children from getting jobs in schools.

Though Ian Huntley had no convictions for sex offences, he had been reported to police in his native Humberside on six occasions for sexual assaults with underage girls. In addition, social services in the north east had investigated four relationships between Huntley and schoolgirls, one only 13, and an alleged indecent assault on an 11-year-old girl.

But checks made by the police on Huntley when he was appointed caretaker of Soham Village College failed to unearth these details of his past because the system did not join the dots and, at that time, checks were not cross referenced with other police forces, so if an offender moved, they'd slip under the radar.

The changes to the law relating to background checks also made changes around previous name history. Huntley used his mother's maiden name for the position at the college. The checks at the time on Huntley did not consider this intelligence collected on an individual. This was very important given that often abuse cases do not make it through the justice system.

The software we used in my new job reduced the processing time from 14 weeks to five days, which was obviously a huge benefit for companies who had to have staff cleared before they could employ them, especially in the NHS. The 14 weeks would cost NHS trusts hundreds of thousands of pounds.

I loved this job; I was so passionate about it. It gave me the stability I craved. It was a fresh start. It was also an hour's commute to a city near London, so it was great to be away from Coventry.

I had a new group of colleagues, so I could be someone else at work. No-one had to know about my history with men. I never made it common knowledge I had two children with two fathers, as I felt that people would judge me.

I excelled in that position, and I could feel my confidence rising again. I was starting to feel like the old me with the tenacity to succeed. Within the first three months I had signed hundreds of new accounts. I was smashing it and I was soon promoted so I could work from home.

Dad helped a lot with the school run to and from nursery when I was in the office, and being able to work from home made life so much easier and much more enjoyable.

Financially stable again, I knew it was probably time to move out and move back into my old house, although I was earning a small cashflow from the rent, so I did not really want to. I thought maybe I should buy another rental. It was a good stream of income and was fairly hassle-free as my tenants were a lovely family.

"Now I'm sorted, Dad, I can move out if you like." Dad looked sad. He had grown used to having us around. He didn't want us to leave; he liked having the kids around and it was helpful for me too as they were still so young. So, we came to an agreement. I would buy the house off him. I made the arrangements to get a mortgage and the deal was he could live with me for free forever. That meant he could go off travelling as he was about to retire from his work. He deserved it as he had worked hard all his life.

I bought the house and gave Dad the money we agreed. It was a win-win. The perfect solution and everything seemed to be working out just fine.

RED FLAGS & REFLECTION

You get one life, so live the life you want and be happy. Moran was toxic in my opinion. The relationship could not continue; it was destroying me and it was not healthy.

I don't believe that you should stay together 'for the sake of the children'. If there is abuse, constant arguments, misery and one person in a relationship is hell-bent on destroying the other, it is toxic and not a good environment to raise children. It also sends out the wrong message to children of what is acceptable in a relationship. The destructive language, the derogatory way I was being spoken to, was emotional abuse. I had to remove myself and the children from that.

One word of warning: co-parenting with someone displaying the traits of a sociopath is exhausting. It is more like counter-parenting. It is not a decision anyone will make lightly but for me it was the right thing to do, and I had a sense of relief when Moran and I ended. That told me everything. However, a very important piece of advice: end it safely. If you are leaving a toxic partner, have a plan. It's at this time that things can escalate, therefore it is very important to have support. In my view staying for the sake of the children is more damaging, because you cannot parent successfully in a toxic environment. This was something I was not prepared to do.

Are you drained after interactions with your partner? Do you feel like you are walking on eggshells?

CHAPTER 7:

The Illusion

Without realising it we can unconsciously walk into something that may well have been avoided with education and some degree of confidence. By now my self-worth had been successfully eroded by Moran. Even though he was no longer living with us, there was constant conflict and he wanted to make my life a living hell. I threw myself into work, which I enjoyed. Life was pretty good apart from that, so I vowed to stay single for a while.

By then, Moran and I had been split up for six months. He was having Sofia when he could. He had moved in with his dad and his girlfriend, so Sofia could not stay overnight but he would pick her up most weekends and in the week. He was a good dad, but it was me he hated. However, I was free of his incessant bad behaviour and disruption. It was now just his verbal abuse I had to endure while trying to co-parent with him. That was difficult.

Dad had gone on his travels for a month, so it was me and the children. It was nice, and apart from dealing with the regular draining communication with Moran, things were good. At least I could manage the amount of airtime Moran got in my life.

One evening after tucking the children into bed, I poured a glass of wine, put on some music, and sat in my newly refurbished kitchen. I'd had it done not long after buying the house from my dad. I looked around and finally felt a sense of relief.

I was sitting at the breakfast island flicking through the newsfeed on Facebook when I saw a post by one of my Facebook friends, Smith.

`[Black Porsche, full black leather, fully loaded]` 'Fully loaded' meant it was a high spec.

I made a comment: `[How much?]`

I love cars; since selling them I have always had a passion for nice ones, like the Audi that I treated myself to when I set up Safehands and the company cars that I had used whilst working at Ford.

Maybe I could get a little sporty car to use when I don't have the kids, I thought, scrolling through the pictures. It looked like a nice car. I wondered if I could afford it.

`[What's the mileage?]` I added.

`[It's my friend's car, he's not selling it]` Smith answered. While he was on my friends list and his face looked familiar, I didn't think I'd actually met him. Maybe he'd been a customer in the shop, as I had used my Facebook profile to promote the shop I had with Moran. I had over a hundred mutual friends with Smith, so I never thought anything of it.

That was our first communication. I never really paid much attention to his profile as I was looking at the car.

`[Oh I thought it was for sale]` I replied to his comment.

`[No but it's nice isn't it?]`

`[Lovely, I'll have to keep looking lol]`

From that time onwards Smith would often pop up and say hi when I was online. I had a look through our mutual friends. He seemed to know everyone. He looked friendly and seemed lovely, polite. I never really thought much of it.

He would sometimes try to make more conversation. It was nice given that once the kids were in bed, I'd often just be alone at home. It was also nice to have some attention too, given my self-esteem was low.

`[Hey, you]` It was Smith. I had butterflies in my stomach.

`[So have you got children?]` he asked. *Oh god, the question I was waiting for. Now watch him run a mile.*

`[Yes two, little girl Sofia is three years old, she is a feisty little madam and my lad Cameron who's six. He is a good boy, very calm. Who's the little girl in your pic?]` I asked Smith.

`[My daughter Bella, she's part Italian. She's five years old, right in the middle of your two, we'd make a good family hey?! Ha ha]`

Ha gosh he's cheeky, I thought. I was shocked. He wasn't scared off, quite the opposite.

`[Oh wow, so is Sofia. She is a quarter Italian. They look very similar, don't they?]`

I checked out his profile. Smith had blonde hair and blue eyes, which I never normally go for, so I wasn't attracted to him initially but there was something about him. He had a cheeky smile. He was confident.

I clicked on a picture of him sitting in a Ferrari. *He likes nice things*, I thought to myself.

`[What do you do for work?]` I messaged him.

`[Car sales for Mercedes]` *Oh nice*, I thought, *well he obviously earns good money*. We had something in common to talk about and I was happy he was working and settled in a job.

Profile status `[single]`, well that does not mean anything; mine had said single for years even though I was with Moran, and he did not change his relationship status either. Said it all really.

`[How was your day?]` Smith always asked about me. Unlike Moran he was interested in ME. He always asked how I was. He was genuinely interested in my life.

`[Good, how about you, sold any cars today?]` I was impressed he worked at a prestige dealership; they are quite hard to get a job at.

`[Not today, hey I was thinking do you fancy going for a drink sometime?]`

I wasn't sure, and to be honest I was scared to meet someone else with Moran still in the background being a disruption. I did try to date someone when my dad was still home. We went on a few dates; he was lovely and came from a wealthy family with goals, boundaries and ambition. However, when Moran found out he got his whole family involved, threatening me and the guy. It was really embarrassing and became too much hassle. The guy did not want to deal with the drama. I did not blame him, to be honest. Moran was right, who would want me now. Moran had threatened him, and so had Moran's brother. It was mortifying and cruel. Why was I not allowed to move on?

So, Smith asking me for a date sounded like a nice idea but realistically it was not going to happen. I couldn't put someone else in that position. Who wants to have a relationship with a woman who has two children, now lives back at home with her father and has a complete arsehole of an ex to deal with?

I just told Smith I couldn't, I was too busy.

I'd just got the kids off to bed and the phone rang. It was Dad. He had been in Tenerife and was having the time of his life.

"Hey love, I'm flying back tomorrow, do you think you could pick me up from the airport?"

"Yes, sure Dad, what time?"

"Flight gets in at 1pm."

"Ok I'll be there."

Dad had been gone for around a month. It would be good to have him home again. The kids had missed him. He'd be home by the time they got back from school.

That evening, after putting the kids to bed, I logged in to my Facebook while sitting in the kitchen. I'd had a message off Smith, which I hadn't seen. I was kind of ignoring them. I did not want him to ask me out again. I could not be bothered with all the stress. It was easier to just be single. Then suddenly, my laptop started ringing.

I jumped off my stool at the kitchen island. Feeling confused, with my hand to my mouth, I realised Smith was calling me through Facebook.

What is happening?! I was staring down at the laptop, scared to touch anything. I had no idea how he was doing that. I was looking at the laptop in disbelief and smiling at the same time. I was mortified. Was he calling me?! I was scared to hear his voice.

He had rung me using a new Facebook feature where you can call friends you are connected to. I was in total shock. I found it very cheeky; my heart was racing.

As I clicked 'answer' I started laughing, saying, "How did you do that?"

"I wanted to see if you would answer, I bet you wondered what was happening," he said, laughing. "You can make calls on Facebook now, so you don't need people's numbers, good hey?"

"I suppose, although I was a bit shocked," I said, half laughing, half nearly dying.

"So?" His voice sounded kind. He was wanting an answer.

"So what?" I knew what he was going to ask but I was kind of making him ask the question. I didn't want to presume and then look like a total dork.

"When do you want to go out for a date?"

"Um."

"Next week? Come on."

"Well, we could maybe meet up next week. My dad is back from his holidays this week so he could watch the children. I'll think about it and let you know."

I was warming to the idea of a date. At least with Dad home I could meet him in the week and Moran would not need to know. It was actually quite exciting. *Why shouldn't I just meet him for a drink, there's no bloody harm in that.*

Over the next few days, I couldn't stop thinking about going on a date. Smith would send the odd message.

I kept going over and over it in my mind. *Why not go on a date with this guy?!*

I was doing my usual, going through the pros and cons. He is from Coventry so he's local. We have hundreds of mutual friends on Facebook. I have probably met him in the shop or out some time. He clearly knows people I do too. He is single and a father. He looks nice.

He's been polite. He's not like awkward like Moran; he's confident. He is nothing to do with my past. None of my close girlfriends or normal circle know him; I can just keep it on the low.

I kept going over and over it. He kept sending sweet messages `[Hey, you decided yet? Would love to meet up]`.

It was exciting. It was new. And no-one knew about him as I had not told my friends I was chatting to him.

The next day I collected Dad from the airport. He had had a great time. Loads of stories. My dad loves the sun too. He was nicely tanned and looked healthy. It was nice to see him so happy for a change. Now Dad was back home, it felt more feasible to go on the date with Smith as I could leave the children with him while I popped out. If I got them to bed first, Dad would be there to babysit.

`[Tonight?]` Another message from Smith.

`[Ok]` I replied.

`[Really? ... Really? Where do you want to go?]`

`[I've got work tomorrow so we could meet at my local, I don't want to go too far as I need to get back. My dad is back from his travels so he can look after the kids]`

`[Sounds good to me, I'll meet you there at 7pm.]`

I remember getting ready with knots in my stomach. I walked up to the pub; it was only a five-minute walk from my house so I got to the bar first. I wanted to find a seat and be sitting with a drink when he arrived. He walked in. Tall, big build, a big presence in the room. He walked straight up the bar, looked around and then spotted me. "Do you want a drink?" he shouted over. He was not shy at all. In fact, he was super confident. I liked that. He loudly ordered drinks at the bar, talking to the barman and making jokes.

"Hey, how are you? How have you been?" It was like we had known each other for years. He was so easy to talk to that I immediately felt at ease. I could not stop looking at him, he was so bubbly and had such kind eyes. He looked different in person. Nicer. He sat opposite me; I was sitting against the back wall facing the door so I could see him when he walked in. When he sat down, he pulled his chair around to the side of me.

I could feel an energy between us; it was electric immediately. When he spoke, he looked directly into my eyes and held my gaze. I had goosebumps.

"What have you been up to today?" He took a drink of his red wine. He had nice lips. He was quite casually dressed in jeans and a t-shirt, like he had not really tried. That felt more comfortable.

"Working as usual, not much else. My dad is back from his travels," I answered.

"Does he go away a lot?"

"I've not long bought the house off him, so he has the money to travel now. That was the idea when I bought it, so he could travel in his retirement."

"Must help you out when he's back with the kids. You're here so that's good." He winked.

We both smiled.

"Do you want to sit outside? It's nice out there, I just had a look when I walked in."

"Yeah, sure." I liked that he was leading, in control.

We took our drinks outside. He walked ahead opening the doors. He was such a gent. He switched on the heater on the outdoor light and sat down. We talked and laughed and talked. We connected. He was attentive to my every word, asking me questions about my life, the children, their dads, my work, my family. We talked for hours.

What was a guy like him doing single?

"Why are you single then?" I squinted my eyes at him, smiling.

"I haven't met the right one." He winked.

At the end of the night, he dropped me home in a taxi and I was on cloud nine. I never expected it to go that well. I did not really have any expectations but that was the best time I'd had in a long time and there was not one bit of stress. Mainly because no-one knew about it. Especially Moran.

He got out of the taxi to open my door. As I got out, he was standing in front of me. He put his big hands around the side of my neck and held my face. "I had a great night."

"Me..." but before I could finish, he bent down and his lips met mine. I felt his body move closer; the heat between us was palpable. I had yearned for a moment like this for years, the feeling of being swept up, the pull like gravity towards him. He slid his arm around my waist, almost lifting me off the floor as his tongue swept my mouth like the perfect wave lapping the shore.

My body was shaking. I could feel my heart racing, the tart taste of red wine on his tongue and lips as he pulled my head closer, pressing us together. I realised this is what I had been missing, passion.

As he pulled away, "... too" I said, laughing and touching my lips with my fingertips.

He winked again, got back in the taxi. *Oh god, the taxi driver,* I thought, snapping back into the reality of the moment. *What the hell just happened?*

"See you soon, beautiful."

"Night." I floated to my front door, trying to find my keys in my bag then fumbling with them in the lock. *Wow, I was not expecting that.*

That was the best night out I had had in years, and we had just sat in a pub talking. He had tagged me in a post on Facebook while we were out. I did not realise until I got home as we had not stopped talking all night. He had been so interested in everything I had to say, asking me about everything. It was so refreshing to have someone want to hear about me for a change.

`[Smith checked in to the Burnt Post having drinks with Zoe Dronfield]`

My friends had all messaged me. Who's that guy who tagged you on Facebook, Zoe? Where are you? Are you with him? Where did you meet him? The rumour mill had started. I had liked that no-one knew him, or that I was meeting him. I just wanted it to be private. I didn't want Moran to get any hint of what was going on, as he would no doubt find a way to try and sabotage it.

I woke the next morning with butterflies. I was still walking on air. I could not believe how well the date had gone and that Smith was a complete contrast to Moran. He was so confident and self-assured. It was attractive.

Getting the children ready for school, I could not stop smiling. I'd remember the kiss at the taxi and smile. I just kept thinking about how confident he was; the kiss! Wow, the kiss. I was in a daydream. I remembered telling Smith I worked from home and would be working from home the next day. In fact, it all came out, LOL. I had not stopped talking all night. I felt so comfortable with him.

It was a good day. The sun was beaming down, and I remember feeling so happy. *Right, must get on with some work.* I was in my office at home; however, you know that buzz you get when you fancy someone new. I kept daydreaming.

[Morning Beautiful] Smith messaged me on Facebook.

[Hi]

[Did you have a good night?]

[Yes, lovely thank you]

[You working hard?]

[Of course]

It had been a fantastic night and it made a change from having to deal with the constant shit from Moran. I was excited. Smiling. My happy was back.

As the day went on, I could barely concentrate on work. It was lunchtime when my phone started to ring [Smith calling].

I answered. "Hello."

"Look out of your window."

"Do what? Why?" *Oh my god, he isn't here is he?* And yes, there he was, pulled up outside my house. He was in a new BMW, probably one of his work cars.

Oh my god. What is he doing here? My heart was racing.

Shit, what do I look like? I had that panic – yes, all girls do this – when you think, oh my god, I'm not ready. What am I wearing ... shit! I look like shit, I look like shit, and I ran to grab some lip gloss.

"Come out and say hi." I checked my face in the mirror, straightened myself out and went outside.

"What are you doing here? I'm working," I said, shocked but flattered. I walked out of my garden and over to the car. I was embarrassed. I did not have the comfort of a few glasses of wine.

I thought it was a bit forward, but I was excited to see him. I did not expect to see him the next day. I thought he would probably call in a few days or play it cool.

He had pulled over on the side of the road, engine running, and lowered his window so he could speak through the passenger's side. I walked over to the car from my garden.

"I just thought I'd drop by and say hi and that I had an amazing time last night." He looked so good. I could smell his aftershave through the open window as I got nearer. I liked that he was so goddamn confident. There was just something about the way he was so carefree, not at all awkward or embarrassed. He was self-assured and very charming, and it was very alluring.

"Work car?"

"Yeah, look, I've got to go back to work now, just thought I'd drop by. I'll call you later," he said as he got set to pull away.

I lifted my head as if to give a knowing nod and turned to walk back into the garden as my dad came out the side gate. Smith was watching me walk back to the garden. I started hand gesturing to Dad to get back in the garden. *Don't embarrass me.*

"Was that the guy you went on a date with?" he said, trying to look out of the gate.

"Yes Dad ... get inside," I said, slightly embarrassed and trying to push my dad back inside so Smith would not see him.

"He's keen isn't he?!" he said, laughing and raising his eyebrows.

I turned and waved at Smith.

"I know," I said, still in shock that he showed up at my house the day after our first date. Who does that?! My heart was pounding still. He made me feel so excited. *Oh my god, he really is keen*, I thought. I was literally buzzing for the rest of the day. I was hooked.

Every day felt amazing waiting to spend time with Smith. He was always so open about everything. Not a negative thing to say ever. He would constantly post amazing flattering things on Facebook. He immediately acted like we were together from that moment on. I did not question it; it felt right. He made me feel on top of the world. Honestly, I don't think I had ever been this happy in my life.

My friends knew it too; they could see the constant gushing. Smith was not afraid to shout from the rooftops what he thought of me.

"My princess." "Beautiful." "Spending time with my amazing girlfriend."... *Ha ha I'm his girlfriend now.* I honestly thought I'd never meet anyone after splitting up with Moran. I was genuinely happy to be able to move on. Smith made me feel attractive again.

On our first date I had told Smith how Moran made me feel. I don't know why; we just seemed to talk and talk and talk. He was so lovely about it.

"I think you are beautiful. It doesn't make a difference you have two children with different dads, it's you I'm here for and why would it anyway, don't be silly." He made me realise that it was actually normal and to stop being so hard on myself.

I had told him how bad things were in the relationship with Moran and how he made me feel so ugly about myself. The drinking and disappearing acts he would pull. How Moran had zero respect for me and would openly verbally abuse me.

"I'll look after you baby; you don't need to worry about him anymore." Smith made me feel so safe and I started to feel like I really had a future with this guy.

Is this even real? I would think to myself.

"I know a place I want to take you," Smith said. He was always coming up with ideas. I loved the way he took the lead.

Whenever I met Smith he would pick me up, take me somewhere. He often took me to a lovely country pub about 15 miles from my home, gorgeous interior, open kitchen, log fires. It was fine dining, and he had huge attention to detail. It really was a lovely place, and it became our regular date night there.

The first time we went I remember pulling into the gravel car park; you could hear the crunch of the stones under the tyres. It was a nostalgic feeling I remembered from my childhood when going to my uncle Keith's for the weekend. My life felt perfect. Smith was perfect.

"Do you want to eat outside or in?" He always asked what I wanted.

"In." The children were at their dads'. I felt so close to him.

"Let's sit by the window until we go to our table." It was a lavish place. As soon as we sat the waiter came over immediately. "Would you like to order a drink?"

Before I could say anything, Smith ordered for me. "Can I get a large glass of pinot white, and I'll have a Magners please. It looks quiet in here tonight. How's it going?" Smith chatted to the staff. The manager came over. I couldn't work out if Smith knew the manager or was just being very friendly. They had a conversation. I felt so proud to be with him.

Smith took my hand; he would talk while looking directly into my eyes. No wavering. Always asking how I was, how the children were, how was my day, where had I been, where was I going, plans for next week. It was such a contrast to Moran who could not give two hoots where I was when we were together. If I fell off the face of the earth, he wouldn't have flinched. Moran had been in it for what he could get from me. He was a user.

"Your table is ready, sir." The waiter walked us over to a cosy small table at the back.

"Can I order, I know what you'll like? The food is amazing here," Smith said, and before I could answer he was ordering the food.

I loved how he led. I felt like he genuinely wanted to make sure we had a good night. Oh and he loved to check us in on Facebook to let the world know what we were up to.

After dinner Smith wanted to move from the table. There was a small snug outside where they would put the heater on. It was really romantic, quite the seductive environment. Smith would get the blankets the venue provided, and we would sit cuddling up. A far cry from the cold few years I'd had. I'd forgotten how to love or be loved.

Is this what I have been missing?

Smith would stroke my face. "You're beautiful, you know."

He made me feel shy, small and feminine. It was nice. He made me feel sexy. I would be yearning for him. I wanted more. Every time he touched my skin, I wanted him to rip my clothes off. I felt so close to him, like no-one ever before. I felt connected to him.

"I love your big brown eyes, Zoe." I squirmed at his compliments; they just kept coming but I loved it. Oh my god, it felt utterly amazing. He was everything. Self-sufficient, confident, totally into me and had no issues with the fact that I have children. It was just like a dream come true.

"We are like soulmates Zoe; how can this be so perfect. We are meant for each other." I didn't know how to respond to his grand gestures. I had been belittled by Moran for so long that I just melted at his kindness. It felt bewildering, the awe he had in me.

"You are amazing, I'm so glad I met you," he would say. It felt weird, nice weird, but it felt over the top. I just lapped it up. I had not had any positive interactions with Moran, no compliments, no love, no passion. This was so completely different.

Smith and I would often stay in amazing hotels, go to fancy restaurants, trips out, buy each other gifts. Finally, I had met someone on a par with me. He had his own money; I didn't have to pay for everything like when I was with Moran. He would stroke me, caress me, and we would have sex for hours. Moran had made me feel like I was being a slut for even wanting sex; it had been quite odd.

One weekend he had arranged for us to stay at Coombe Abbey Hotel in Warwickshire, a historic luxury country house in 500 acres of stunning grounds with formal gardens and a lake. The hotel was filled with antiques and offered fine dining. It really was an experience. Smith had booked us into an amazing room with a four-poster bed and arranged for us to have dinner in the orangery.

He was his usual self, making me feel on top of the world. He was posting this all on Facebook again. I was a bit embarrassed by it if I'm honest, but I was flattered all the same that he felt he could be so open about everything and the things he would say.

`[Having dinner with my beautiful girlfriend]` he posts and tags me in.

My friends would always be like... `[God you've got a good one there Zoe]`, `[He's a keeper]` and `[Oh, keep us posted]`. Yeah well, he was sure going to do that.

Finally, I had met someone who was like me. He wanted to do fun stuff, understood that making money was important to having a good life. Moran would not even acknowledge our relationship on Facebook yet here was Smith making me feel like I was the most important person in the world. Smith made me feel special, something I had not had for years.

"Can we get some champagne and strawberries sent to our suite please, we will be heading there in around half an hour." We were just finishing off our drinks at the table. Smith just knew how to make the night amazing. The cherry on top. *Champagne and strawberries in the room, how amazing.* I was already tipsy from the wine at the table. I felt free when I was with him.

When we got back to the room I went into the bathroom. I heard a knock at the door and Smith spoke to someone; it was the champagne and strawberries. I then heard a POP and fizz. I felt excited; what was coming next? I freshened myself up. I wanted him. I couldn't get enough of him. He was like a magnet. I wanted to feel his presence next to me. I wanted to taste his mouth, feel his weight on me.

I sprayed a mist of perfume, brushed my teeth. I knew what I was going to do as I went back into the room. Smith was sat on the chair, a flute of champagne in his hand, looking at his phone. My heart was pounding. I needed him inside of me. My glass was on the antique drawers next to the bottle. I slugged a mouthful of champagne and walked over to Smith. I straddled him. Shocked, he almost dropped his phone, then gathered himself, placing it on the table in front of him.

I was being very forward. For so long Moran had made me feel undesirable, but Smith made me feel different. He lit something in me; he was like a drug. Straddling him I thought, *How brazen am I being? Oh my god. Who am I?*

I shook off my own questions. I was in nirvana. It was frantic, hot, sweaty. He finished and we both collapsed down on the bed. He pulled me into him. Stroking my hair, he kissed me on the forehead. "You are so beautiful. I love you, princess."

I was hooked.

He walked over to the champagne naked, and refilled our glasses. He passed me a robe from a hook. "Shall we finish these?"

What an end to a perfect night.

Well, it always was with Smith.

Mr Amazing.

RED FLAGS & REFLECTION

Love-bombing is a term used when affection crosses a dangerous line. In the throes of a new relationship, obviously there are compliments, maybe small gifts, however it should be a red flag when from the get-go your boundaries are being crossed or your gut feeling is saying something just doesn't feel right. Maybe the affection or attention seems unwarranted or maybe it's unrelenting. It was certainly this way with Smith. It made me wince whenever he posted on Facebook about where we were and what we were doing, but on the other hand I felt so flattered by this as Moran had broken me down so much.

Sex can also be used as weapon; either by it being withdrawn or giving pleasure, it's a form of emotional control. Smith knew this was something Moran used against me.

Something I wish I could have told my younger self back then: "Things are not always what they seem. Don't be blindsided by someone's overt affection! What's the rush?" I ignored all the feelings of 'this is too much' and just went along with it, ignoring my gut feeling. I was living out my real life fairytale, and little did I know this was going to come crashing down.

Have you ever felt uncomfortable when grand gestures have been made? Did they ring true?

CHAPTER 8:

Open Door

Circumstances can render you vulnerable. They can throw you off guard and this can work as the perfect decoy for someone looking to infiltrate your life.

Are you conscious in your decision making at a time of high stress and worry? Probably not.

Note to self. Do not make life decisions that are difficult to reverse.

One morning started like any other, however I had a meeting in Milton Keynes about an hour's drive from where I live so I was rushing around trying to get the children ready for school and nursery so Dad could take them.

"LOVE, I can't feel my legs." My dad was shouting down the stairs.

"What do you mean, Dad? The kids are ready," I shouted back while putting on my coat and falling over trying to get my shoes on at the bottom of the stairs with the front door ajar.

"I need to go Dad; I have a meeting. See you later. Love you. Please make sure the kids get into school," I shouted, and I ran out of the door.

Dad always took the kids to school when I had a meeting away from the house. The kids loved it and they were good as gold for him.

Within an hour, my dad had called my uncle and said it was serious. He literally could not feel his legs. My uncle dropped the kids into school and called an ambulance. Within 24 hours my dad was on a tracheotomy and induced into a coma.

This was a bolt out of the blue. I was in complete shock.

Within 24 hours everything changed. My life was in turmoil. I had no idea how long Dad would be in hospital or if he would even recover. It was terrifying.

I did not even find out until later. I was in a meeting all day and so over an hour away. My auntie had texted to say that she had the kids and Dad was in hospital. I felt terrible. We were waiting for news from the hospital. How could this even be? He was fit as a fiddle, not long come back from Tenerife. Nowhere exotic.

My auntie watched the children so I could go to the hospital alone.

As I entered the intensive care department, I spoke to a passing nurse: "I'm looking for Colin Dronfield, I'm his daughter." I felt queasy. I could hear the machines bleeping.

"Ok, oh yes, please wait there. I'll get someone to come." She scurried off.

My chest was feeling tight, and I could feel my heart pounding. What the hell had happened to him? I was thinking a heart attack. I was so angry; he has only just retired, for fuck's sake, why!

"Hi, are you Colin's daughter?" Another nurse appeared next to me.

"Yes. I'm Zoe." She took me to the next ward.

"Do you want to come through, Zoe. It's not nice and I want you to be ready as your dad is in a bad way and he's on breathing apparatus which is helping him breathe."

I walked onto the ward. There were four beds. All of the patients were unconscious and hooked up to numerous machines, all bleeping. So much bleeping. It was frightening.

It was so warm too. I felt hot. So hot.

The nurse pointed to the bed where my dad was lying. He had tubes coming from everywhere.

"Is he awake?" I asked.

"No, we have had to heavily sedate him. He can hear you though, so you can talk to him." She smiled at me.

I felt spaced out, like I was in a dream. The nurse's words were echoing and the noises around me were winding in and out, making me feel dizzy and hot.

"Zoe, are you ok?" the nurse said. I was just standing there in a daze.

"Yes, I'm just shocked. He has only just come back from holiday; do you think he caught something there?"

"Well, we have run some tests and we think it's Guillain-Barré."

My head spun and I almost fell. The nurse quickly pulled over a chair. I just sat there.

"Is he going to be ok?" The machine next to him was bleeping, and his chest was going up and down artificially.

"He's in good hands Zoe, we'll do our best," she responded.

"How did this happen?"

"Most people make a full recovery. We have seen a few cases recently in Coventry."

"Really? Did you hear that Dad, you are going to be ok so just stop messing about now." Such a Dronfield thing to do, try to crack a joke when things should be serious. I could not even hold his hand or really go near him, there were so many wires.

Guillain-Barré is a condition that attacks your nerve endings. I have since found out there is some evidence in America that it's connected to the flu jab, which funnily enough Dad had just had before his month-long trip to Tenerife.

The syndrome is a rare disorder where your body's immune system attacks your nerves. Weakness and tingling in your arms and legs are usually the first symptoms. This is what Dad had described to my uncle. Like pins and needles. Then these sensations can quickly spread, eventually paralysing your whole body.

As the nurse explained, it made no sense. His body was attacking itself. It was horrible. How cruel life can be. He had worked his fingers to the bone all his life to finally retire and this happened.

I left there in a haze. I got back to the car and just sat there, staring out at the car park. *Give us a break!* I started banging the steering wheel.

The next day was hard and made even worse by Moran. I texted him to say what had happened to my dad. I stupidly thought I would get some help or support from him.

Did I get sympathy? Support? Empathy? Oh no. True to his zero conscience, zero care for anyone or anything other than himself.

`[How are going to look after Sofia now, you may as well give her to me. You can't look after her properly with your dad in hospital]` he texted me back.

What a low blow. Using my dad's horrific situation to have a swipe at me. This proved he would stop at nothing. He was nasty about me and towards me. I would often stupidly spend my time arguing with him, trying to make him see sense, explaining normal human interactions. Moran always thought he was superior in every way.

He would find a way to blame me for everything, even if it meant making something up. He would thrive on making a situation worse. He loved this. He was high conflict and every situation circled back to him positioning himself as some sort of saviour. Even the business collapsed with him running it. When we split up, I withdrew my money out of the account after speaking to the accountant who told me I had been resigned as a director. Moran had fraudulently removed me from the business. I sought legal advice, however the business was not worth anything, so I walked away. Since I had started researching abusive behaviours often books would use the word 'sociopath', something I had never come across before.

I wished I had never told Moran about my dad. I was far too open, far too honest and this left me vulnerable. I did not realise this at the time. I thought Moran would show care. I did not realise he was incapable; I was extremely naïve back then. Watch out for this lack of empathy. Watch how the people close to you act in times of hardship. Their interactions with each other. Moran had a total lack of conscience. His response to my dad having almost died was no emotion and to attack. This is not normal human behaviour. He never even asked if my dad was ok. Zero care that my dad had almost died and was in a coma in intensive care.

With Dad poorly, I needed to get some plans in place. My job was an hour's commute each way. I had a lot of things to organise. However, one thing for sure, I knew I could rely on myself.

My mind was in overdrive, however whenever I am in a situation like this I just have to work it out. There is nothing else like pressure in life to make you up your game. I did not have any family nearby, apart from my auntie and uncle, but they worked and could not help all the time. I also hated to be a burden on anyone.

At least I was now working from home most days, then working it out when I had meetings. It was not going to be easy. I spoke to work the next day, and they were so understanding. They really stood by me. My boss was a great guy. Full of empathy and a great leader. At least work was being supportive which was a huge weight off my shoulders. My income was safe and I could work from home and be flexible.

I called Smith and told him. "Baby! That is terrible, how is your dad? How long will he be in hospital? Who will help with the kids?" He was so sweet and caring. I could not quite believe the contrast between him and Moran. Moran used the situation against me. Wayne was also very supportive, having Cameron when he could. Most normal people wanted to try and help in any way they could.

Smith was the closest person to me at that time. Yes, I had friends, however they all had their own families to worry about. I could never ask friends for help. I saw dependency as weakness. A trauma response from a child. I wish I had asked, been honest, I wish I had the skill to be able to lean on people. I was fiercely independent, which can be a good thing but often means you deal with a lot of shit by yourself.

At home lying in bed, I couldn't sleep. The children were tucked up. I'd look up out of my skylight windows at the night sky, the brightest star. *I wish you were here, Mum.*

Her picture was next to my bed. A black and white picture of her wearing a ball gown. She looked beautiful. An angel watching over me. Every day I looked at her and wondered what she would have been like, how she would have loved the children and sung to them. I was grieving all over again. *For fuck's sake Dad, get better!*

The pain of grief for me is like a shortness of breath, a deep hollow sadness and a feeling of utter abandonment and loneliness. It is a solitude so great, and my pride stopped me from telling anyone, from crying out loud. *Be strong, Zoe. She is watching over you, it'll work out*, I would tell myself.

Smith called me the next day.

"Baby, please don't worry. I'll help you. My job is flexible. I will help with the kids, if you like. I can help get them to school or collect them when you have meetings, it's no problem at all babe. I'm here for you."

"Really?" He was like my bloody saviour. I felt awful but what choice did I have? I could not believe he wanted to be so involved. It was nice. He had met the kids and his daughter had come over a few times. I knew the kids would love that too.

"Really, are you sure?" I was so worried about Dad and looking after the kids, while working, trying to hold everything together.

"The kids love me Zoe, we can be a proper family. I want to help you."

We had been dating a few months. Things were great. They were moving at the speed of light, but Smith was amazing and given I was having to deal with the abuse from Moran, he made me strong. My life had turned upside down but here was my prince to save the day. Smith made everything great.

"Whatever you need me to do, beautiful, I'll pick the kids up, make the dinner. I'm here. You are my baby, I love you."

"Thank you so much, I don't actually know what I would do without you."

So Smith stepped in when I had meetings. He would collect Cameron from school. I would try arranging most of my business meetings on a Monday as Moran dropped Sofia into school on a Monday after having her at the weekend. I had arranged it this way so there was only a crossover on a Saturday afternoon when Moran collected her. I would collect her from school on the Monday. I arranged for her to go to after-school club, so it worked out great. Sofia was going to her dad's every weekend at the time unless we had plans to do something as a family.

Smith had really stepped up, and this was a dramatic change in my relationship with him. Our relationship was now cemented. It was a big step really; we went from dating, passion, excitement, freedom to being parents of three kids between us. We started to have his daughter more at the weekends. It was lovely; we would get the paddling pool out, the toy ride-on cars in the garden. The children played well together. The ages were perfect: 3, 5 and 7. The giggles, screams of joy and laughter in the garden were a million miles away from how I had to live my life with Moran. He was always so serious, moody even. Smith was so much fun. He didn't care; he would roll around on the floor with the kids. The girls would put hair clips in his hair, and he would play football with Cameron. He would blow up the great big paddling pool himself.

Bella did not stay over, though. Smith always had to take her back to her grandma and grandad's house, which was how I got to meet Smith's parents. Another big step, however it felt like a natural progression, although looking back on timelines we were moving fast. I had not been with Smith that long really; it was all a bit of a whirlwind.

Smith's parents lived in a modest house. They were doting grandparents who loved their granddaughter, and their kitchen was covered in her toys. When we dropped Smith's daughter off, we would only stay for an hour and have a cup of tea. Smith's dad was quite sarcastic, but his mum seemed nice. Smith's parents had been together since they were kids, childhood sweethearts.

They were a normal family, dad a builder, mum a teaching assistant at the local school. Dad was a bit of a cheeky chappie.

Smith seemed to have a close bond with his mum; they would always go out of the room whispering to each other, then I would hear his mum say, "Don't tell your dad". Smith also had a sister, but she lived in London for work, and we only met once or twice.

We popped round to his parents one evening, as Smith had to collect some more things. Smith was temporarily living with his parents when we met. He had not 'officially' moved in with me, so he was still bringing a bag. While Smith went upstairs to grab some things his dad said to me, "You're not like the other nutters, are you?" I was not quite sure what he meant and was a little taken aback by the comment.

I laughed. "What other nutters?"

"Oh, you haven't told her about the other nutters. His ex-girlfriends." I felt a bit uneasy; it was a strange thing to say.

"Oh don't listen to him." Smith walked back into the lounge and it was brushed off. When we got in the car, I asked Smith, "What did your dad mean when he said not like all the other nutters?"

"Oh, I went out with some crazy woman before, she stalked me."

"Oh gosh, really? That's awful. What do you mean?"

"Well, she'd turn up at my house unannounced. I had to get my mum and dad involved, they don't like her."

"That's terrible."

Smith was now spending more and more time at mine, helping with the children, taking us all for dinner, picking them up from school if I had to work late. He was totally embroiled in my life. He was really sweet with Sofia and would sit and help Cameron with his homework.

So, when the summer came Smith, the children and I booked a week away in Spain. Smith was so amazing with the kids when we were away. He would take Sofia down to the sea and swim with Cameron far out while Sofia was back on the beach with me. Cameron had just learned to swim, and Smith was a strong swimmer so he was teaching him how to be stronger.

"Let's take the kids to the funfair tonight." Smith was like me. I'm always 100 miles an hour. I live a pretty fast-paced life; if I'm not at work I'm doing something or other. It was great he was so energetic. He always wanted to do something. It was a really fun time. Laughing, ice creams, looking for fish, buying watermelon off the 'looky looky' guys who sell them on the beach.

Sofia loves fruit, I mean loves it. She would eat fruit over sweets all day long. "Listen to the man, Sofia," Smith said, pointing at the man walking along with a big machete.

"GET YOUR FRESH WATERMELON! WATER MEEEELLOOOOO..." He was almost rapping it into a song, and Sofia and Smith started doing the same. They had such a lovely, sweet relationship. I thought it was a shame we had not taken Smith's daughter away with us but Smith said he was not allowed.

I thought it was odd that he used the term 'not allowed'. It didn't cross my mind as to why; some mothers are protective. I know my mum was. I had met Smith's daughter's mum too. She was a quiet young girl. I asked Smith why they split up. It seemed pretty much like Wayne and I. They had a baby too soon and the relationship was strained. He admitted he was immature at the time.

We went to the funfair one evening, and Smith took the kids on the trampolines. He was funny. A big 15 stone, 6 foot guy bouncing away on the trampoline. The kids were squealing with delight.

Life was good and Smith felt like part of the family; although Dad was still in hospital and that was hard, he was so supportive. He would watch the kids when I went to the hospital. I had taken them up there a couple of times, but they were upset seeing Grandad in hospital and poorly.

Dad was really struggling with adapting to no longer having use of his legs, but he was out of the coma, breathing for himself and on a ward. The nurses said they needed to get his strength up as he should be getting physio to learn to walk again. But he had lost so much muscle mass being in intensive care for six weeks that it was looking unlikely. Most people make a full recovery from Guillain-Barré but I wasn't hopeful for Dad. He was so weak. It was heartbreaking to see him like that.

When I spoke to my friends, they could not believe how supportive Smith had been considering we had only been dating a few months. He had stepped up and they were so supportive of him.

My friends would always say "Oh my goodness what would you do without Smith, he literally turned up like an angel to help you out." I'd agree: "I know, he's amazing isn't he." I felt so lucky to have him. We still went out for meals together for date nights when the kids went to their dads. It really felt like we had a strong future.

Dad was trying to talk now. It had taken a while for him to get over having the tracheotomy down his throat, so often when I visited he would try and sign; he can't sign by the way so he would get totally infuriated trying to tell me things. I could see the frustration in his eyes.

He would make a hand gesture. "What do you need, Dad? The nurse?"

He was shaking his head as if to say no.

"A drink? Some water? Food? Are you hungry?"

Furiously shaking his head, eyes rolling. I could see his irritation.

"Are you in pain?"

Nodding over and over, he was almost crying. Sheer panic in his eyes.

"NURSE!" I shouted. "Dad says he's in pain, can you give him something?"

"He's not long had something, but I can check. Colin, are you ok?" Dad was shaking his head. He looked so frustrated, so scared and in so much pain. He was clearly very traumatised by the experience of being in the intensive care unit.

Before Dad went into hospital, he was a fit and able man. However, now he was unable to speak; he was confused. He was not going to be able to walk again and he was uncontrollably shaking. It was just soul destroying to watch him deteriorate so dramatically.

As the weeks went by Dad started to get his voice back and told me about his experience in intensive care. It sounded utterly horrifying. He'd look at me with what I can only describe as utter fear in his eyes; he would be nodding and doing a screaming face, but with no sound coming out. He was looking towards the ceiling. Dad told me when he was doing that he was hallucinating. He told me afterwards that he thought there were bugs crawling on the ceiling.

He was having all sorts of nightmares; he thought that Sofia had caught Guillain-Barré and she was dead, so when I was going to the hospital that look in his eyes was guilt, fear, trauma, thinking he had passed the disease to his granddaughter. It's not contagious but clearly he was on some mind-bending drugs.

Smith would look after the children. "You go and see your dad." He was so unbelievably helpful. When I returned dinner would be sorted. Working a full-time pressurised job, with two children, a dysfunctional and disruptive ex and now Dad in hospital, Smith was a godsend.

RED FLAGS & REFLECTION

Often when you think of grooming you think of children, however adults are vulnerable too. Looking back over this chapter of my life, it was an open door. My guard was down and of course my father was very ill and I had no-one to turn to. My relationship with Smith was still new. We had only been seeing each other for a matter of months and although his offers of help were gratefully received, it felt like a big step at this stage in our relationship, however he insisted and quickly made himself my saviour. He made dinner, collected the kids, took me out; he could not do enough. In fact no-one could fault him. Red flag. All of this was to lull me into a false sense of security and make me more vulnerable.

Being with someone who is overtly attentive, positive, has (false) empathy, when on the receiving end of this and especially when vulnerable, can make you feel special, meaning your usual natural defences are down. You can easily be coerced and manipulated to the point that you ignore or overlook the red flags.

Anyone can be groomed. Remember this is an offence and if you feel you are being manipulated you can get support from professionals. See the list of organisations at the end of the book.

CHAPTER 9:

Nothing Is As It Seems

Sometimes things that are presented to us in life are an illusion. They are what someone wants to show us, as opposed to the truth. They are wearing a mask and unless you are educated and understand what red flags to look out for, this manipulation is very subtle and can go completely unnoticed in the throes of a new relationship, until eventually realisation starts to set in and by then it can often be too late.

My dad was starting to get better, though he was still in hospital and still in a wheelchair. While he would probably never walk again he was now on a normal ward. It was good to see him sitting up. He was still struggling to talk as the tracheotomy had damaged his throat and he was very traumatised by the ordeal, however at least he was getting out of bed and managing to move.

He started physiotherapy. Although this was not going well I was trying to keep his spirits high, but it was hard. I'd take the kids to see him, but it was hard for them to see their granddad in such a fragile state. Children struggle to understand when things change, and Grandad had been such a big part in their life, and he was now trapped in hospital looking like half the man he was before.

"When is Grandad coming home, Mummy?" they'd say with their innocent little faces looking up at me.

"Soon, he just needs to get stronger and learn to walk again." But I knew that was unlikely. Dad was beaten emotionally and physically most days. He was in his late sixties and had lost so much muscle mass from lying in a hospital bed.

Smith was stopping at mine most nights now too so he could help out. He would pop back to his parents', only to pick up some more clothes or take his washing back to his mum. He now had a key to my house as he would often collect the children from school for me while I was still at work.

Normal life had begun to take over at this stage. There were many stresses with Dad and my job, but Smith helping took some pressure off although now home life was becoming strained. Smith seemed irritated with normal everyday life. It was still early in our relationship; we should have still been dating and having fun. However, my commitments had to become my priority and I'd have felt guilty going off and having fun with Dad still poorly. I still needed to be there for the children. I was working every day so spending time with Smith was becoming more of a challenge. It was hard trying to please everyone.

I wanted to try and break the monotony of work, school, kids, hospital. I decided I should make more of an effort to please Smith as he had been quite down lately, and he had done so much to help me. "Shall we stay somewhere this weekend?" I said cheerily to him. "Let's get away from it all."

"Hmm maybe." This was not like him. He did not seem happy. He would often sit on his phone for hours on end and would seem distant and annoyed.

I decided to book a long weekend Ibiza trip as a surprise for Smith. I arranged for the kids to be looked after by my uncle and auntie, so Moran did not need to know. I had started to get wise to what would trigger his high conflict ways.

It turned out to be a really good idea as Smith was on top of the world again. I loved to see him happy; he had done so much for me.

"This is what we need, babe, I'm totally different when I'm on holiday." Smith was excited, the kids were sorted, and Dad was getting there. It felt like good timing to get away.

We went for tapas, walked around the harbour, danced on the beach. I love Ibiza; it's one of my favourite places in the entire world to go. Everyone is so happy and carefree. It has a really magical feel about it, however on the last day when we were due to come home Smith seemed to go back into a dark mood. We had to check out of our room and our flight was not until the evening. He was annoyed.

"Let's just check in somewhere." He was getting agitated.

"Have you got money? I've spent enough. There's no point in spending money on a room for a few hours," I replied. I'd paid for the trip to cheer Smith up and did not really have the money to splash on a hotel for just the five or six hours before we needed to leave. I'd have happily sat at the beach bar, but Smith was adamant he wanted a room.

"Look, just put it on your credit card and I'll give you the money when we get back." I did not really want to, but I felt I had no choice. He had done so much for me and we'd had such a nice time, it was a shame to ruin it on the last day. We also could not walk around for the rest of the day with him in this mood. He should have been happy that we'd just had a lovely break. I thought he was being a bit selfish.

We walked past a five-star spa hotel. "Here! Let's see if they have rooms Zoe, I'm not walking around with these cases." I saw his point that it was annoying but seriously, we could have planned this better and spent some time having fun on the beach and put our cases behind the hotel reception but he had wanted to check out and leave.

Smith went to reception and asked. I waited by the doors with the cases. He looked back at me after speaking to reception and waved me over. "They've got a room," he said, smiling, showing me the key card.

The hotel was amazing, spa pools, Jacuzzis, dip pools, saunas. We went up to the room and dropped the bags in.

"Let's have a look around, we could get our swimming stuff on and go in the Jacuzzi," I said, trying to lighten the mood. The hotel had private glass cubes each with its own Jacuzzi in the middle of a courtyard. It was amazing.

Smith was still grumpy. "I'm going down to the front for a walk."

"Ok, shall I come?" He looked as if he wanted to be on his own. Not happy. "Ok then I'll wait here," I said, just rolling my eyes.

No point in going down to the Jacuzzi on my own. I lay on the sofa in the lounge and fell asleep waiting for Smith to return. It was a waste of money and typical of Smith's unpredictable behaviour. I was a bit annoyed but decided not to say anything. It would only irritate him. As usual I brushed this off.

The break was lovely but when we got back to Coventry, Smith seemed to slip into this dark mood again. He would go off upstairs on his own and sit in the bedroom or be sitting on his phone, not present. He seemed fed up.

Over the next few weeks his mood was becoming increasingly erratic, and I was getting really bloody annoyed with it. He didn't have the responsibilities I had. It was me working full time, sorting the kids as I was trying to rely on him less due to his moods. It was selfish. He knew how much pressure I was under.

Smith started to get frustrated with the things he was previously happy to help with.

"I have a meeting tomorrow morning, Smith..."

"I can't take the kids; you'll have to sort it," he said before I even had a chance to ask him.

I was juggling. It was hard. I could not expect any more from Smith anyway. I was more than aware they were not his children. I felt I had to accept it really. How could I complain, especially to Smith?

"Can you lend me some money? I'll give it you back tomorrow." Smith had started to buy and sell phones. He said he was not getting on at work and needed to do something else.

"Ok, why?"

"I need to get phones Zoe; I haven't got money and I need money. If you lend me £300, I will give it back, you know I will. I just need to get some phones so I can sell them."

I trusted Smith implicitly. It was not like him. He had always had his own money before.

As Smith had let me down a couple of times, I knew I had to find a way to sort this situation with the children so I was not relying on him so much. I spoke to work, and they said they could help with childcare vouchers for a childminder.

I managed to find a childminder with a space so that was sorted. At least now I could arrange meetings and if I was late the children would be able to stay there until I got back. That was a huge pressure off my mind.

I told Smith about the childminder, and he seemed frustrated by it. "I can pick up the kids, what do you need a childminder for?" he asked me.

"Well, it's sorted now and at least I don't have to bother you; I know you have your own stuff to do."

I now felt so much more relaxed about the children and the childminder was brilliant. The kids loved it there; they got to play with other kids and the childminder would sit and play with the children for hours one-to-one, and Sofia loved that. She needed lots of attention at four; a right little character she was then. Cameron was so grown up for his age. He was in primary school and was such a confident lad.

As Dad was getting better and the kids were sorted, I had arranged for Cameron to go to Wayne's on the same weekends that Sofia went to Moran's. There was always juggling to do. Moran was still being his usual awkward self, changing times and weekends. Most likely to disrupt my life with Smith. Wayne was not like that, luckily. He would happily move his weekend so it would at least give me some time to myself without the children. That's what co-parenting is about, sharing the load.

I needed a girls' night out. I hadn't been out for ages, what with everything, so I thought I'd arrange a get-together. I had spoken to Smith about it briefly, but I wanted to remind him, so he knew I was going out at the weekend.

"Remember I'm out with the girls this weekend," I said.

"Oh babe you're not, I've booked us in at this lovely hotel in the country. I thought we'd go and have dinner, you can get dressed up. We can get some drinks in the room, but you know, just go out with the girls, it's ok." He looked let down.

I felt so guilty, after everything he'd done for me with Dad being ill. I'd be really selfish to go out with the girls. I had this constant feeling that I owed him, after all he had done in the first few months for me and my family.

"Oh ok, I'll just tell them you have made plans." So I changed my plans to go out with him instead.

I called the girls. "Hey, Smith is taking me away, sorry will have to do it another time."

"Whattt really, we have not seen you for ages!"

"I know, maybe we should all go out one night with the boys too."

The girls knew I'd had a hard time. They understood; I think they were happy for me. They knew all the shit Moran had, and was, still putting me through too. He was always there in the background, although since things had got serious with Smith, he had seemed to back off a bit.

I wanted to spend time with Smith. Why would I not want to; we were a family now. I was happy or at least that's what I kept telling myself. Behind closed doors was a different picture; Smith's moods were hard to deal with but I kept reminiscing about the good times. I thought I could help him, make him happy again.

It became quite a regular thing, Smith blowing hot and cold. I didn't know if I was coming or going with him some days. I was swinging between guilt and wanting to make him happy, to feeling quite smothered as I had not done anything other than try and please Smith for a long time.

If I tried to make other plans without him, Smith would not like it, not in a 'telling me what to do' kind of way but a needy way, like I could not leave him. It was easier not to make my own plans but just wait to see what he wanted to do. This I now realise was a subtle manipulation and one I was very happy to abide by, given that I should be grateful for all his help.

However from the outside we had the perfect life. Smith played our life out on social media. Every time we stayed in a hotel or went to a restaurant, he would check us in. People would comment on Facebook, "Wow where are you guys now?"

But it was all show. Often, we would just go to a hotel for the sake of it. Smith used to like staying away. Then we would sit in the hotel room and not even go out. He would sit on his phone and be distracted and distant.

Another evening we stayed in another really nice hotel in the middle of Birmingham. The children were at their dads'. We stopped at the off-licence on the way, so we had some drinks for the room after we had dinner. We were meant to be having a 'date night'.

I spent a couple of hours getting ready in the room, drinking champagne. Smith said, "Get yourself dressed up and we'll go down to the bar and then decide what to do." I was excited. I thought we'd maybe end up in a nice restaurant or out in a bar or go dancing. That I would have loved. A night of drinks flowing, hedonistic music pumping, a complete release, dancing and laughter. I loved meeting new people too. As Smith was so friendly, we would always end up talking to people. I was looking forward to the night.

However, Smith was not really bothered. He didn't even get dressed up. "Are you wearing a t-shirt?" I asked, looking at his t-shirt and jeans.

"You won't get in anywhere without collars, will you?" I said, starting to feel that sinking feeling again.

"It'll be fine. Are you ready? Let's just go to the hotel bar, Zoe." He seemed snappy. Not a good start.

"Ok." We walked down to the hotel bar. I was all done up, little black dress, high shoes, feeling amazing. He wanted the usual selfie before we left. I was looking forward to having a lovely meal and drink in the bar.

Hopefully this will be just the tonic to get us back on track, I thought to myself. Can you notice the subtle regulation I was doing to myself, to appease Smith? This is quite apparent to me now, but not then.

The hotel bar was sleek and sharp, neon lights across the bar, dim lighting and mirrored bar. There was a real vibe in there, lots of good-looking people, a buzzing atmosphere, the music loud enough to have to raise your voice when talking. People were sitting around in the lounge chairs and at the bar, eating food. A really funky place. Groups of elegant girls chatting, nice looking guys, couples sat together chatting.

I need this, I thought. *We need this.* Although something was niggling Smith. He was not himself. *Hopefully we can have a good night and I can get the old Smith back, happy and fun.*

We sat down waiting to be served. No-one came over immediately. "Shall I go to the bar?" I asked him.

"Let's go back to the room, I don't want to sit down here." Smith looked agitated and was constantly fidgeting in his chair. He just seemed really irritated, distant and moody. I couldn't put my finger on why he had been so off lately. What had changed?

"Why? We've got all ready, let's sit down here and have a few drinks," I said, trying to persuade him.

"I don't want to sit down here Zoe." He wasn't having it; he wanted to go back to the room. He was just irritated and seemed angry, so I agreed and that was it. The night ended.

Fed up, we just went back to the room.

Was he bored of my company now? It seemed that way.

The tables had completely turned from Smith being my supporter to me having to support him. Emotionally he just seemed distant. He was often borrowing money from me, so it was a drain financially. He seemed needy, but I could not put my finger on why or what was going on. He never really said anything, or told me what he was up to most days. I assumed he was busy at work. He would either be in one of his super happy moods, or totally dark and sombre.

I felt hyper-alert to his needs and constantly felt the need to appease him. Smith seemed agitated, frustrated, and would often act paranoid. He wanted and needed extra attention from me, especially in the times where I was struggling to offer him that, when I needed to see my dad or see to the kids.

Each weekend when the children went to their dads, I'd try to keep my diary busy because if I had no plans, I often felt lost. This annoyed Smith especially if my plans did not include him. He wanted to know where I was and why I was there and who I was with. This was his paranoia. I would try to talk him down and appease him, telling him everything was fine. I still loved him; I was just going out with my friends.

One Saturday night I had gone out with one of my best friends. Part way through the evening we went back to a mutual friend's house for drinks before we decided what to do next. Smith rang me.

"What are you doing in Binley?" He sounded really angry, like he was talking through gritted teeth.

"How do you know I'm in Binley?" I was confused how he even knew where I was.

"I can see where you are on your Facebook location, get back now or I'm sending a taxi!" He was sounding really pissed off.

How could he see my location on Facebook? Well at that time if you were friends with someone, they could somehow find your location. Scary, right? Check your privacy settings!

"Don't be so silly, what do you mean?!" I was trying to sound blasé, but I could tell he was not happy, and I did not want him turning up where I was. I was shocked he was acting this way. I had not seen this jealous side.

I was not about to be told what to do. I could not understand why Smith was acting this way; it was odd. Jealousy is one thing I will not accept. It is an ugly emotion and there is no need. I knew I was 100% loyal so there was no need for him to be like that at all. I was not hiding, and I was not sneaking around.

I could not really speak as my friends were in earshot. "Look, I'll be back shortly. Are you ok?" I said to appease him.

He doesn't own me! I thought. Plus, I was embarrassed in front of my friends, and I felt I had to placate him. "Babe don't be silly ok, I'm with my friends, we are having a couple of drinks with old friends, what's wrong with that?!"

"Just get back Zoe!" He was not happy; his voice was strained.

Once I put the phone down, I sat with my friends but Smith kept ringing and ringing.

My friends were laughing. We'd all had a drink so they were of the opinion "What's his problem!" but I could tell by his voice he was not happy.

"Just stay, Zoe." My friends wanted me to ignore him, but I felt bad.

"Oh he tells you what to do, does he?" "What's he being a knob for?"

It didn't really matter what they said, the night was ruined and I should probably go back anyway. In the end it just wasn't worth it so I left.

Smith's behaviour over the next few weeks became even more erratic and outwardly disrespectful. He had lost his job. He still had work buying and selling phones but it was much harder for him to earn money. I did not know much about it; I just let him get on with it. I had enough on my plate. I preferred it when he was out, otherwise I felt like my time was totally consumed with keeping him happy, explaining myself, where I was going, who with, how long. I had a sense of relief if it was a good day. I was never sure which Smith I would get. One minute he was the most amazing guy then the next he was in a really dark mood, snappy and irritated.

One midweek day I was sat in the kitchen working on my laptop and Smith came in. He'd been out 'sorting phones' as he would call it. He came over, started cuddling me, and held my face by cupping it in both his hands. "You're mine now, baby." I felt a bit confused by this statement.

It was weird; it was a bit too much. Like it was a misplaced statement, out of the blue. I was taken back. What do you say to that? This was an ownership statement.

Just lately I had seen this possessive and jealous side rear its head. I had posted a picture of David Beckham on my Facebook page, as a laugh. He had just done a Calvin Klein advert for boxer shorts where he looked pretty fit posing in just boxers. It was a laugh, and I tagged my friends. I was at my friend Jodi's house. Smith immediately rang me. "Get that down now!" he snarled down the phone.

"What are you talking about?" Then I twigged that he meant the David Beckham picture I had posted.

"You know what you just posted, Zoe." He normally calls me babe or baby, so he was mad.

"Seriously Smith are you talking about the David Beckham picture, babe don't be silly and seriously you'll look a bit daft getting bothered by a celeb, it's not like I'm going to meet him. Don't be silly,

I've got my man." I talked him down. I could not believe he was actually being serious. It was a bit daft. "Whoa that was Smith, he did not like that!" We laughed it off.

His behaviour started to become odd at home. He would come to mine in the evening, not happy to see me, just in a foul mood, and one time he came in and went straight to the upstairs bathroom.

He was in there for an hour. "Smith, are you ok? What are you doing in there?"

"I'll be out in a minute."

"Have you been drinking? What are you doing?"

He opened the door slightly. He was sat on the toilet. "Seriously!" I covered my eyes. "Are you coming down, you have been in there an hour, what the hell are you doing?"

"I've got a bad stomach." I felt like he was lying. Something did not feel right. I shrugged it off. His behaviour seemed sneaky and he had been acting paranoid. I couldn't put my finger on it.

It was now the middle of winter. We were locked into dark cold nights, and Smith was down. In a way I was grateful when the children went to their dads so they did not have to see him being so moody and moping around the house. There was a constant tension around him which made me feel on edge.

I returned home from work one evening, after collecting the children from the childminder. I was making dinner and the kids were playing tig, where they chase each other and tap the person who is the next 'it'. "Stop it! Someone's going to get hurt," I said, smiling and watching them play together. They were always a bundle of fun. So active and happy and loved each other's company. They were so close. Cameron loved to look after his little sister and absolutely doted on her. Then I wondered where Smith was.

It was strange; Smith had been quiet that day. I hadn't really heard much from him. That wasn't like him at all; normally he was on the phone every minute: "Where are you? What are you doing? Who are you with?"

He should have turned up at mine by now. I had already dished up the children's dinners. While they ate, I still hadn't heard from him. I tried calling Smith, no answer.

So, I decided to message his friend and hairdresser Becky on Facebook messenger. I could see she was online. I had met her a couple of times. They were friends and sometimes he would meet up with her for a drink after she finished work. Becky would probably have seen him or spoken to him.

`[Have you seen Smith today Bec]` I typed the Facebook message.

`[No I haven't seen him today]`

At that moment Smith rang me. He sounded out of it. "Hello baaaaby." He was slurring.

"Where are you?!" I replied, slightly irritated that he was that drunk.

"I'm with Becky having a drink." He was now lying to me!

"Oh really?!! Well I've literally just spoken to her and she said she hasn't seen you today ... so you are lying to me now are you?!" There is one thing I will not tolerate and that is lies. "Why lie?! Why are you lying to me Smith? Where are you? What are you doing? Why are you so drunk in the week? If you want go out and get drunk, do it but don't lie!"

I could not even make out what he was saying. He was mumbling something; he was so drunk his words just sounded like noise.

"Pardon! Smith!"

"Oh no I'm going to meet her now (mumble), yeah that's it, I'm meeting her now." Did he seriously think I believed this shit now?

"You are going to meet her now, are you?" So, I typed a message to Becky `[Any plans to meet up?]` I knew I was about to catch him out. I could feel it in my gut.

"No, I'm going to meet friends after work." I just caught him bang to rights, the LIAR!

"Ok you just lied Smith. Why are you lying to me? Where are you? I'm not happy and actually I will not tolerate this you know." My voice had lowered. I was now getting angry at the disrespect.

Smith carried on the lies. "I am meeting her, I'm going now... (mumble)" He was not even making sense. He was slurring and sounded totally high. I couldn't hear anything in the background. It definitely did not sound like a bar.

"Don't fucking lie Smith! If there is one thing I don't like that's liars!" I raised my voice down the phone to him. That was probably the first time that I had got so annoyed with him and remotely showed annoyance, like that anyway. He had taken it to another level by calling me drunk. This triggered me as this is how Moran would act.

He drivelled on, something about where he was with his friend, a pub in town. So I decided to play detective; I thought, *I'm going to see with my own eyes if he's there*. He ended the call.

"Right kids get your coats on; we are going for a drive." I put the kids in the car and drove to the pub where he said he was. Deep down, I knew he was not going to be there, but I had to see for myself. I had to have the proof so I could say for certain to Smith that he was not there. And of course, he wasn't there.

This was crazy-making behaviour. He was gaslighting me. I was questioning my own sanity. I was wanting to prove his lies. I felt like I was back in the same situation again with Smith as I had been with Moran. What was I thinking, dragging the kids in the car after their dinner just to prove his lie? What reactive behaviour, but it was like I was compelled to prove the lie.

He had just broken a fundamental rule, something that has been instilled in me from childhood by my stepmother. My children both have this instilled in them. There is no point lying; it just creates more lies and more pain.

I was furious. At that point I wanted distance between us. I had to try and unravel this relationship.

Smith called me later that evening sounding sober. "Hi babe, I'm so sorry about earlier. I don't know what I was doing. I'll come and see you tomorrow. Are you ok?"

"Yes, I'm fine but what on earth was going on? You lied, Smith."

"I'm sorry, I went to an old friend's house, we got wasted. I feel shit. I'm sorry. It won't happen again. I did not want to upset you. I realise I have. I love you baby. You're my baby."

After his numerous apologies, begging for forgiveness, I backed down. Or I rationalised it. Either way, I just let it go. I couldn't be bothered to argue and go over it. It was done. *He probably needed a blowout*. I excused it.

Smith was still not working in car sales. Normally you would breeze straight into another car sales job, as it's normal to move about in that industry, but it was the wrong time of year coming up to Christmas. Dealerships do not really recruit then, as car sales slow in the winter.

I've already mentioned that Smith had been making money buying and selling phones. He had hundreds of the damn things. He would always call me from different numbers. He often needed money up front to buy the phones, so would borrow money off me, which was happening more frequently now. Smith liked to live the high life, so having no money was not an option. He would get so stressed.

I'd get it back in the next couple of days, so I suppose it didn't really matter, well that's how it was excused although he was leaving me short of spare cash and then I'd be chasing him and having to ask for my money to be returned. I didn't like it but felt I had no choice. It was getting tedious, but I just hoped that things would change once he was working again and things settled down, as he was so up and down.

Thing is, I'd been here before with Moran when I bought all the stock for the shop on my credit card, plus paying for all the bills and almost losing everything. So it was another trigger which I did not like. I didn't want to be in that vulnerable position again, yet here I was.

As Smith had lost his job, that meant he also lost his company car. This made it hard to help when I needed support collecting the kids. This was not that often now but there were still days I would need help. My dad's car was sat outside the house. Smith asked me why we couldn't use it if he needed to collect the children. He always made it sound like it would help me out. He said he would clean it, fuel it, look after it. I said I would ask my dad first.

I asked Dad if it was ok for Smith to use his car to help with the kids. My dad is reasonable, so he agreed as long as we got Smith insured. The car was parked outside the house doing nothing, so it made sense, however the deal was he did not use the car every day. It was my dad's car, and he did not want loads of extra miles on it.

As the days went by Smith started to act more and more entitled to everything, including the car. Now he was just turning up at mine, letting himself in and taking the car even though he was not collecting the children. Then I would find out there was parking ticket after parking ticket. Not just one or two; there were many.

Here I was back on a merry-go-round. My boundaries being corroded. It was exhausting.

RED FLAGS & REFLECTION

Narcissists, sociopaths and psychopaths are masters of disguise; they create smokescreens to divert attention from their abusive behaviour and gaslight their victims. This can be extremely subtle and very manipulative. These personality types lose interest very quickly in their target and become bored. This is when the games begin.

So many red flags in this chapter: gaslighting, blatant lying. Smith was trying to change the narrative of reality with his crazy-making behaviour. I was second guessing myself. It was exhausting. There was financial control; Smith was borrowing sums of money from me but making ME feel like I was being unreasonable if I tried to say no.

He was controlling what I did, very subtly. He would make plans for us, knowing I had made plans with friends. He had an extreme sense of entitlement. He would take my dad's car and be so blasé as if it was me with the problem. He was extremely grandiose; he once said to me "What Smith wants, Smith gets". He was a spoiled child in a man's body.

This crazy-making behaviour made me feel uneasy and on edge. I would doubt myself and then justify or excuse his behaviour. I felt embarrassment, anger and shame that he was behaving in this way.

His mask had dropped, and the person that I considered to be 'down and stressed' because things had been 'tough' was actually showing me his true self.

All of this is a way for the abuser to control you, your thoughts, your feelings, your reality. It's exhausting and confusing. Had I understood all this behaviour was to throw me off track or a way to control me, I would have acted differently. Distance and time away from the person causing the abuse is the key to thinking clearly.

Have you ever had been in a relationship with someone who you know is blatantly lying? How did you deal with it?

CHAPTER 10:

No More

There's no smoke without fire.

Feelings of emptiness began to surface again. Smith was my Mr Amazing. My saviour. My soulmate. But something had shifted. A dark force. I could not understand what was happening.

I plodded on regardless, making the best of it. It was the run-up to Christmas. I love Christmas time and am super busy at this time of year, getting everything ready for the children. It was a welcome distraction. I also had a work Christmas do coming up, so I had a night away to look forward to. My dad was coming to the house for Christmas dinner too and having a day out of the home he was now living in so the children were excited that Grandad would be home, and this meant I wanted it to be super special and magical.

My dad had been stuck on the hospital ward for almost a year. We had finally managed to get Dad a place in social care sheltered housing, which meant he had a warden on duty in case of emergencies as he was not fully able to do everything himself. They also had communal facilities such as a laundry, lounge and garden, as well as offering social activities and events. It was not ideal for Dad and he wasn't happy there. He was furious he was with all old people. My dad has always seemed young for his age and did not feel like he should be there. He was fit and healthy before being struck by Guillain-Barré. He was compos mentis, so being in a home with the elderly who mostly had Alzheimer's was hard. He was institutionalised.

Smith was still up and down. One minute ok, his usual bubbly self, then at others he would say he was going to bed, and he would just sleep all day in a darkened room. He was short tempered. I just took each day as it came. It was hard and the relationship was not what it had been. When his mood went dark, those days were difficult. I tried to keep things upbeat and normal, but he'd be moping about the place.

One afternoon while sitting at my office desk in the kitchen I opened up Facebook messenger and could see I had mail.

`[Hi Zoe, you don't know me, but your boyfriend has been messaging my mum]`

What was this? I screwed up my face and read the message in disbelief.

[He has been pretending he is a police officer and then threatening her, saying all sorts of nasty things to her. I thought you should know.]

I looked at her page. She was a young girl, late teens, early twenties, and her mum was in her fifties, maybe. Seriously! Is she for real? Who the fuck messages someone and says that?

As if he is doing that! I did not believe her. Stupid girl, and what's her mum playing at saying this? How weird.

Smith came into the room. "I've just had the weirdest message off some girl saying you are abusing her mum."

Smith started high-pitched laughing. "Oh yeah ok, why would I do that?"

"Well, she lives over your parents' way by the look of her profile. Why would she just come out with that?"

"I don't know babe, there's some weirdos out there. Maybe she fancies me." He winked.

"How strange, why on earth would you message her mum? I've just looked on her mum's page. Seriously, why would she? And she said you are impersonating a police officer then threatening her. She's in her fifties, what the fuck!"

"Don't know babe, don't worry about it. I've got to go out and get some phones. You got that money?" he said nonchalantly.

"Yeah, it's on the side." He kissed my head and left.

I blocked her. Weird. Why would someone do that?

Smith was in and out these days, still collecting phones, selling them. He'd have stacks of cash, then none. Needing to borrow more. I was still working from home, in my usual spot, my office desk positioned opposite the S-shaped island in the kitchen. I had now moved to a larger company so my job was mostly working from home which was much better so I could organise the children's schedules easier. Smith was so unpredictable these days, it was easier not to ask him anymore.

Christmas is such a magical time especially with young children. I was making my usual plans for the kids. Putting up the Christmas tree is a big event in our house each year. I used to make a big deal about it every year as one year I had a small eight-inch pretend tree and Jodi my friend said, "Is that your idea of Christmas, Zoe?" Ha! So I made a point after that of having a 'Christmas tree erection party' as I cheekily called it.

The girls would come around and we'd get drinks and nibbles, dance around my lounge. It became a tradition and I have kept up the tradition albeit slightly different once I had the children, although each year I would send Wayne a picture of the tree too, so he was involved.

Both Cameron and Sofia have a special decoration each that they put on the tree once it's decorated.

"Can I put my mouse on the tree, Mummy?" Cameron has a little plastic white mouse sat in a plane which has a piece of plastic holly on it, a funny little decoration which was his dad's from when he was a lad, so it was sentimental and goes on every year.

"Ok let's get the tree dressed first and then we will put both of your decorations on and take a picture."

"Where's mine, Mummy?" Sofia started screeching, rummaging through the decorations, baubles flying everywhere. She could never wait, head first in the box, squashing every other decoration in the process.

"Hang on, hang on Sofia!" She's such a feisty madam, whereas Cameron is calm and listens to instructions. Nope. Not Sofia.

"Put mine on now!" she demanded, hanging her little elf that says Sofia on the front of the bare tree.

"Hang on."

"Now this, now this..." She started hanging more decs on, not in any order... Arrrgh I was laughing at her haste.

"Hold on ... hold on Sofia..." I'm quite particular how my tree is done; there is no tinsel ever to be seen in my house. No thank you! We colour co-ordinate and everything is done symmetrically, which is a slight challenge with an excited four-year-old who is hell-bent on trashing the tree.

"Who's putting the star on?"

"Meeeeeeeee!" Sofia had already shoved Cameron out of the way. I looked at him and rolled my eyes. He gave me an endearing smile. He would always step aside for his sister, bless him.

I had to re-do the tree, of course. The children ran upstairs to write their letters to Santa, and nothing was going to ruin my Christmas, although I was not sure what Smith was up to. He was on the phone checking in with me throughout the day but mostly he would be out, doing his thing. Whatever that was.

Some days he would come home buzzing, jumping through the doors, his old bouncy self. Picking Sofia up and twirling her around. "Hey little madam!" She would screech in delight. She's a little daredevil whereas Cameron is more reserved. Smith would sit on the floor doing jigsaws with him. He was good with the kids. I would look at them fondly when they played together. He always made time for them.

One cold evening, I was sorting the children and just getting them tucked up when Smith came through the front door, bumping his way through the hall.

"Night night, see you in the morning."

Is he drunk? I thought to myself as I tucked the kids into bed, shut their doors and went downstairs.

"What have you been up to today?" I could tell he had been drinking, red eyes, slurring. I had been here before.

"Just out, babe." He went off upstairs.

Smith was drinking more regularly, daily. And now if I tried to make plans, he was getting irritated. Irritated about my friends. He used to want to meet up with my friends too so we could all go out, but now he did not want me to make any plans. If I arranged anything, or if I went anywhere, he would constantly be calling me. It was so distracting and exhausting. He needed constant reassurance and would need to know my every move, where I was, who I was with. He was acting really paranoid, even more so than before.

He came downstairs. "I'm sorry babe, I don't know why I'm being like this. I'll make it up to you."

"I'm going to bed. I have work in the morning. Don't wake me up when you come up if you stay up late." I went to bed.

"Ok baby, I love you."

"I love you too."

I felt sad. I really did not want us to become this couple.

The next day Smith got up early and left.

It was on my mind all day. I dropped the kids to school. *How can I get through to him that he needs to stop being so erratic? Why can't he see the damage it causes?* I just wished his moods were consistent.

I started looking up information about addiction, as I thought that maybe his issues stemmed from having no 'off button'. Whenever he went out lately, he was coming back drunk or I could smell alcohol on his breath.

I did not hear from him all day but when he came home later it was like he had had a personality transplant. He came bowling in the door like his usual smiley happy-go-lucky self.

"Baby I'm ok, I get it you're worried about me." He grabbed my face, kissing me off my feet.

I loved it when he was in this mood. This was the old Smith. Why couldn't he just stay this person?

"Are you sure? You are drinking every day. I don't really want the kids around it, Smith. You act different. I don't like it. You know what Moran was like. I do not want a repeat of that shitty relationship, it's destructive, you see what he's like even now."

As I said this to Smith, a text came through from Moran with his usual shitty attitude.

[I'm picking up Sofia early this weekend and don't try and argue with me about it], he texted me. I had not even replied, and the conflict had clearly already started in his head.

Oh, why doesn't he just fuck off. He created arguments that did not even exist. I would not ever have stopped Sofia going to her dad's; I would not hurt my daughter like that. She liked seeing her daddy and it also gave me a break. It is clear to me now that this was Moran's way of goading me. I did not see this at the time and would literally be fuming. This is exactly what he wanted.

[That's fine] I texted back. He does not like it to be fine though, he wants a fight. He wants conflict.

[Yes, I know it is] Jesus he's such a prick, who talks to people like that?

[Seriously why be such a dick about it, I just said it was fine]

[Just make sure she's ready and pack her bag] What an arsehole, full of fucking orders. Did he get a sense of power talking to me like that?

I showed Smith the text. "Fuck him Zoe, he's a pathetic loser. You don't need him anyway... I've got you baby!"

Had he? Had he got me though?

I could see the same pattern which happened with Moran playing out with Smith. Although he did not call me names. In fact, he never said anything nasty directly to me. Smith was amazing in comparison.

It was Christmas Eve. I finished work at lunchtime and all the Christmas shopping was done. Smith had popped out to see his friends; he'd gone for a drink. I am always super busy Christmas Eve anyway as I have the dinner to prepare. I like to get all my veg peeled and prepared, and set the table. I also always leave all the wrapping until Christmas Eve too... Once the children are in bed, I wrap the presents downstairs in the lounge ready to be put into piles before the morning.

"Can we put the carrot out for Rudolf now, Mummy?" "What is Santa having this year? Mince pies?"

"Yes, we've got mince pies for Santa, a carrot for Rudolf and we need to sprinkle magic reindeer dust on the path outside so Santa knows which house to come to."

"Shall we sprinkle it now?"

They screech in delight. It makes my heart warm, and I feel so happy. I do look up and wonder if Mum can see them. I smile.

"Where is he, where is he?" Sofia was shouting, looking up at the sky as I ushered them back into the house.

"He doesn't start delivering the presents yet, he waits for all the children to be fast asleep. Then he will put the presents in his sack and deliver them down all the good boys and girls' chimneys."

"He's got a fat belly, how does he get through the chimney, Mummy?"

"Well, he has magic dust."

"No, he doesn't!" Cameron shouts knowingly.

"Oh yes he does," I say, smiling and nodding at them both.

They both look at the chimney, then at each other, then at the chimney.

"I'm going to sleep now." Cameron ran up the stairs. I felt so blessed; they are such good kids.

"Right come on you." I pat Sofia on the bum, and she shuffles up the stairs to bed. Both of the children are tucked up. They both have a soft blanket they take to bed. Cameron has what he calls his 'best bit' he strokes, and Sofia rubs hers on her face while sucking her thumb.

"Night night and remember Santa won't come if you don't go to sleep."

"Ok Mummy," they say in unison.

"Night, Cameron," Sofia whistles as she has her thumb in her mouth.

"Night Sofia, see you on Christmas Day."

I didn't really think much of Smith drinking. I let him get on with it.

I spent the next couple of hours wrapping the presents, preparing everything for the next day, dinner with all the trimmings, dessert, cheese board, snacks for after, food galore.

Drinks set up. Dress the table. Wine for the table.

I looked around the kitchen. Everything was ready. The table was dressed. Kids fast asleep. Wrapping done. Smith came home in a good mood. He'd had a few drinks out and I'd had a glass or two of wine while getting the house prepared.

"Shall we put some music on?" It felt relaxed, like the old days.

"Fancy a Jack Daniel's?" Smith asked.

"Ok, why not." Smith and I often sat in the kitchen with the music on at the weekends but it was Christmas Eve, so I did not want a late one really.

"Another," Smith said, pouring more.

"Whoa, remember it's Christmas Day tomorrow and we've got wine to drink tomorrow, you don't want to feel ill."

The time seemed to just tick around and before we knew it, it was about 4am and we were still drinking.

"I think we should go to bed now. The kids will literally be up at 6am, I'm turning off."

"Babe, I'll come up in a bit."

"Seriously? Don't stay up too much later, it's really late, well early already." I knew I needed to get some sleep.

I went to bed... I shut my eyes for what felt like two minutes and then I could hear faint shouting from the kids' rooms.

"Mummy, Mummy is it Christmas? Can we get up now?" the kids called out. I stumbled, barely awake, into Sofia's room.

"Looooooook!" Sofia was shouting, pointing at her stocking. "Look at all the presents Mummy, have you got one Cameron, let's go see." She climbed out of bed.

I was literally slumped over the side of the bed. "Mummy, mummy, look, look."

"I know chicken, lucky girl." Cameron came through, dragging his huge stocking behind him.

"Look at mine," he said proudly.

First, we do stockings. The children love their stockings. They were so innocent; they would always think that was it.

"I love all my presents, Mummy," they would say, so chuffed with their stockings stuffed with goodies. "Ok, just wait there a minute children, just play with your presents a moment please."

Smith was still up. He had not come to bed. I was fuming. *It's Christmas Day!* What was he playing at! I needed to get downstairs and get him out of the way.

He was still in the kitchen sitting on his phone.

"What are you doing? It's Christmas bloody day, you'd better get up to the loft, the kids are up." I looked at him, furious. His eyes were glazed over. It was as if he was not there.

I could not fucking believe it; how dare he ruin this magical day! It was bad enough I had stayed up drinking until 4am on Christmas Eve but he was still up and still drinking. He went up to our bedroom in the loft. He was not even coherent at this point. I got him past the kids, who were too engrossed in their new toys.

Fuck him. I'll deal with that later, I thought to myself. I was so angry. This was a deal breaker, Christmas Day of all days! I dusted myself down and put on my happy, albeit extremely tired face.

"Come on you two, let's go downstairs." I felt exhausted, but their little faces brightened up my life. They made me so happy; their little screeches of joy meant the world to me.

As they walked into the lounge, more screeches: "THERE'S MORE MUMMY, SANTA'S BEEN!" I'd let them walk in the room first, so they could see their mountain of presents. Sleep, no sleep, it was worth it to see their faces.

"Ok, which one do you want to open first?" The kids ripped at the paper, and within a matter of minutes there was a sea of rustling paper and toys everywhere, and laughter and squeals of delight. In the back of my mind I was furious at Smith, upstairs still drinking, still drunk. Christmas morning! I was fucking livid. Why? Today of all days and my dad was coming over.

I left the children downstairs and went up to the loft to get dressed. Smith was lying on the bed. He looked terrible.

"Are you getting up and getting dressed? It's Christmas fucking day," I whispered loudly to him. He was hammered. Because he had stayed up all night, he was in one of his dark moods. "It's Christmas Day! Are you seriously going to carry on drinking, what the fuck?!"

"I'm not getting out of bed. Have we got any more alcohol?" I could not believe it; he wanted more.

"My dad is on his way! You had better sort yourself out!" I said.

I was in utter shock that he would even think this was ok. This was a new low.

Another level.

Who acts likes this?!

Who wants to lie in bed and drink? On fucking Christmas day of all days.

I was so angry, I did not want to be with him anymore. I did not need to put up with this behaviour. From that moment on I knew I had to end this relationship, somehow.

What had I got myself into again? I needed him to go. But I couldn't do it that day. I would have to bide my time.

I heard the taxi pull up outside. "Grandad's here!" the children shouted. I had to help Dad get into the house; he was in a wheelchair which meant I had to move a heavy ramp over the door frame so he could get inside. I could have done with Smith's help. I was worried Dad would fall.

"Hi Dad, do you want a drink? Dinner will be ready soon."

"Where's Smith, love?" I knew he'd ask.

"He's in bed, he's got the flu," I lied.

Dad did not really have an opinion on Smith, well not that he told me. He had enough on his plate with his own recovery so I never burdened him with any issues we were having. He'd had quite enough of that with Moran. Also, Dad was happy that Smith kept Moran away from me.

However, my relationship with Smith was unravelling too. I had to admit it to myself. Christmas was a point of no return. Something had to change. It was not acceptable one bit. The children had no idea, and Dad must have thought it was odd although he never said anything at the time.

I cooked the dinner. We had turkey, we played games, we pulled crackers. The kids had fun but once we had eaten Dad seemed tired. I was tired, sick and bloody tired of dealing with men who just seemed to drain me.

What the fuck is happening? I went to the bathroom and splashed my face, took a deep breath and went back out to the kitchen and sat at the dining table.

I was hollow.

Empty.

Numb.

The kids were sat playing games with Dad. They were happy. They were my only joy.

I poured a large glass of wine. Slug.

"Do you want some dessert, Dad?"

"Yeah, ok love, then I'll probably head back. I'm feeling tired."

"Ok, sure." I had a sense of relief and fear at the same time. I did not want to face Smith drunk upstairs. I could not forgive this.

Aimlessly serving the dessert, deep in my thoughts, at this point I think I was switching between denial and anger. I was missing the old Smith. I was thinking about all the nice things he had done. The nice words he had said. So many nice things. I was his baby, his princess, but they meant nothing really.

Then a wave of anger and disappointment would roll over me like a wave slapping me in the chest. How had I got it so wrong, again?!

Where was the Prince Charming that was fed to me as a little girl? The fairytale is a dangerous story.

Sofia was collected by her dad later on Christmas evening and I tucked Cameron in bed as he would be up early on Boxing Day morning to also spend time with his dad. Smith was in bed asleep by then. I just crept in exhausted and went to sleep.

A couple of days into the Christmas break – you know that lull after Christmas and before New Year – Smith and I had arranged to have Bella stay over at the weekend. Sofia was excited. The girls got on so well. It was always fun having them together. It was lovely tucking them up in bed. Sofia had a little portable DVD player; they chose a movie and we got them all cosy in Sofia's bed. Cameron was still at his dad's.

In the morning, I got up, made the girls breakfast and then Smith came downstairs into the kitchen. "Right, I'm off out." That was a bolt out of the blue.

I looked at him, shocked. "What about Bella?" I asked.

"You can take her back," he demanded. His tone was off.

He started looking around the kitchen. I knew what he was thinking; he was going to use my dad's car.

"You can't take my dad's car, Smith. You need to stop using it as and when you like to run around town. It's my dad's. He only said we could use it to help with the kids. He won't be pleased if you are running about using it picking up your mates and whatnot." Smith was openly irritated and continued searching.

"Where are the keys, Zoe?" He seemed in one of his moods again.

I had hidden the car keys. I was so mad that he just felt entitled to take the car, so I had put them in my dressing table drawer in the bedroom. *It's not his fucking car*, I thought angrily to myself.

I walked upstairs to get dressed. Bella and Sofia were playing downstairs, and Smith followed me.

"Where are the keys Zoe, I need to go out," he said, looking around the bedroom trying to find them.

"Bella's here! Don't you think you should get her home first?"

"I need to go out, where are the keys?"

"Smith, you can't just take Dad's car to run your own errands. Are you taking Bella?"

"You drop her back. I just need to use the car." I could not believe he was being this way about Bella. I was shocked he would just leave me to take her. That was not the plan.

He was pacing the room, looking in bags, rummaging through things, lifting stuff and not putting things back. Then he marched over to me. I was stood by the wooden dressing table and he started trying to look behind me, over my shoulder.

"Get out of the way, Zoe, don't make me angry, you don't want to see me angry." He gave me a sideways glance. I was taken aback.

Did he just threaten me? What did he mean by that?

Well, you don't want to see me fucking angry either, I thought to myself. *You'll be gone, mate.* My anger took over and I brushed the comment off however his comment was crucial, its leakage...

I was so shocked at his erratic behaviour; he was fine the day before while we had the girls, but he had turned again, a complete mood swing, and Bella was there. I was so over it. Fine one minute then something must have triggered him, this urgency to go somewhere. For what?

I was adamant he wasn't going to take the car.

Smith was trying to push past me and then shove me out of the way. This made me mad.

I stood my ground.

"Stop! You'll break something, stop it!" I was shaking with anger. He seemed to just look through me.

"The bloody girls are downstairs, stop it." *What is he playing at?*

His face was furious. My heart was pounding but I was not giving in.

Smith was getting mad; he looked straight at me. "Zoe!" His eyes glazed over.

BANG!

As we tussled, Smith trying to open drawers and me trying to stop him, I 'fell' onto the dressing table. All of sudden I could feel a searing pain through my ribs as they cracked against the hard wood.

I could not breathe; the pain was like a knife stabbing through my side.

I screamed. I couldn't help it. The pain was so unbearable and sudden.

It was shrill and loud enough for the girls to hear. They came running up the stairs. "Are you ok Mummy, what happened?" I felt so saddened that this had happened.

The girls were both standing at the top of the stairs looking at me wide-eyed. I tried to disguise the pain I was in even though it was excruciating.

"It's ok, honey, Mummy just fell onto the drawers and hurt herself."

Smith left, leaving Bella with me.

I couldn't believe it. What the hell had just happened?

So many thoughts were running through my head, but I needed to get dressed and get Bella home. I knew I had really hurt myself. I couldn't breathe in. When I did it was like a stabbing pain. I looked at my ribs; they had gone a dark shade of purple already. I googled sharp pain to ribs after falling `[broken ribs]`.

For fuck's sake. I've got broken ribs.

He's fucking gone, that's it! Maybe I shouldn't have hidden the keys but it wasn't his car. I was justifying my own actions in my head.

`[Don't come back]` I texted him.

I was in so much pain, but I knew I had to get Bella home, so I drove her back to Smith's parents. Smith's mum answered the door.

"Hi, I'm just dropping Bella back. Can I talk to you for a minute?" Sofia and Bella ran through to the kitchen where all Bella's toys were kept. I walked half into the front room out of earshot of the children.

"I'm worried about Smith; he's acting really erratic. We had an argument. He was trying to take my dad's car. He can't keep using my dad's car. We should only use it occasionally if needed for the children, so I hid the keys and Smith got mad." I lifted my top and showed his mum the deep, now blackened bruise which had already developed on my ribs.

She looked away. "I still have maternal feelings for him, I can't." I was completely taken aback by her response. I could tell she wanted me to leave.

It was the oddest response to what I'd just said. She almost shooed me away.

"Gary will be back soon," she said, meaning Smith's dad, looking towards the front door. I did not stick around. Her response was enough. She did not want to hear it. It was her son. I got it, but if my son did that to his girlfriend, well he just wouldn't. I was pissed off.

It was strange; I expected her to be mad or show concern, or even talk to me. But she did not want to know.

I left with Sofia and went straight to the chemist to buy painkillers. I could not move as I was in excruciating pain. Cameron was still at his dad's and Moran was due to collect Sofia, so at least I could just relax and recover until the next day.

The next day my friend Melissa rang to say everyone was going out and talked me into it. As it was Christmas time, people were having drinks around their houses. I told her what had happened with Smith, and she told me to take photos of the bruise, so I did. I sent them to her, and she was adamant I should go out.

I took more pain relief and headed out to Melissa's. I wasn't myself; I was in so much pain. I thought if I drank alcohol that would dull the pain. I was trying to hide it, but my friends could tell something was up and one of the lads, my friend from school who I had grown up with, noticed.

"How did you hurt your ribs then, Zoe?"

"Ummm I just did."

"He did that to you, didn't he!" I wasn't sure why he even said that, but I was embarrassed, ashamed. I covered for Smith.

"Well, I'm not sure he meant to, we had a fight over some keys."

I did not think he meant to do it. I can be feisty. He wanted to leave and I was stopping him.

I justified everything to myself.

I should have just given him the keys.

It's just a car.

It was hard. When I was not with him, I missed him. I just wanted the old Smith back.

Looking back, I can see it clearly, the slow manipulation. The structure of our relationship had changed at this point. I felt like I would be lost without him. I'm not good on my own. Not that I would have ever admitted that to anyone else, but when I look at what I have dealt with throughout my life, this was definitely a reason I hung on.

It's this subconscious fear of abandonment that drives fierce independence on the outside and a difficulty in building a relationship based on actual love. It was a fantasy, one that I fed.

I did not answer the phone that evening, even though Smith kept calling. I went home after being out and felt worse. The pain in my side was unbearable. I didn't sleep at all that night, trying to dose up on painkillers.

Smith kept calling, then later that evening the pain got gradually worse. I was starting to worry now, as I could not actually manage to do anything. I could not even get out of bed. I was just lying in bed. I felt sad. Broken. In pain. I did not want the relationship with Smith at this point. Too many lines had been crossed but I also needed him. I was alone with no help.

Smith rang again. I answered.

"Hello."

"How are you babe? I can't believe you did that." Smith positioned it as my fault, an accident.

"Did what? I don't think I did it, Smith."

"How did you manage to do it then, babe?"

"You were pulling open all the drawers trying to find the keys, Smith! You can't just use my dad's car like it's yours, it's disrespectful."

"You fell Zoe, how are you?" he said, trying to divert my attention.

"In pain, excruciating pain, Smith."

"Baby! I want to help you, how are you managing with the kids?"

"They are at their dads', but they will be back in the morning and I can't move, it's a fucking joke."

"How about I come over and help you? I'm going to get some stuff for you from the chemist."

"Don't bother."

"Baby, I'll be there soon. I want to help you. I'll look after you."

He'll let himself in; he has a key. I could not really stop him and I needed help. I couldn't even sit up. I couldn't move. I was lying in bed helpless. I'd definitely cracked my ribs. I googled it again, and it said to use freeze spray.

I called Smith. "Can you get me some spray from the chemist then please?" I said, giving in.

"Of course, baby."

Smith let himself in and shouted up. "Babe!"

"Yes, I'm in bed of course, not able to fucking move, remember!"

Smith helped me sit up in bed. By now I was screeching in pain each time I moved.

"Let me spray this on." He lifted my pyjamas up to reveal the purple bruise.

"My baby, ok, let's get this on." He sprayed the Deep Freeze treatment on. I winced; it was freezing.

"Have you eaten?"

I was grateful he was there. At least I could eat something too as he made me food. I just wanted it to heal before the kids came home.

In the morning Wayne dropped Cameron home. I was up but still wincing with certain movements. Wayne usually comes in for a coffee so he noticed I was in pain.

"What have you done?" Wayne asked, concerned.

"I slipped on the decking," I said. Lame, so lame, and now I'm lying, but it was icy outside, so he believed it.

I felt so stupid lying; I felt disgusted in myself. But how could I say it was because I'd had an argument with Smith over taking my dad's car? That was too embarrassing.

All I wanted was to be happy. The relationship with Smith was the best thing that had ever happened to me. Smith made me feel amazing. So happy. So secure. I felt like I had finally met the one who I clicked with. He got me. He cared. Smith was my knight in shining armour.

But things had shifted so it was confusing. He was still my old Smith, but he was having these dark episodes and it felt like I was on a merry-go-round, bobbing up and down, one minute happy when Smith was having a good day then the next so low. Some days I felt as if I was going crazy.

My friends had started to notice things too. I found myself covering for him, putting on a brave face. In a matter of weeks I had changed from being happy, outgoing, the life and soul, to barely going out with my friends. Smith and I would sit apart in the kitchen.

I would be sat at the island with my laptop playing music. Smith sat on the sofa engrossed on his phone, not even present but in the room.

It felt really lonely. Again.

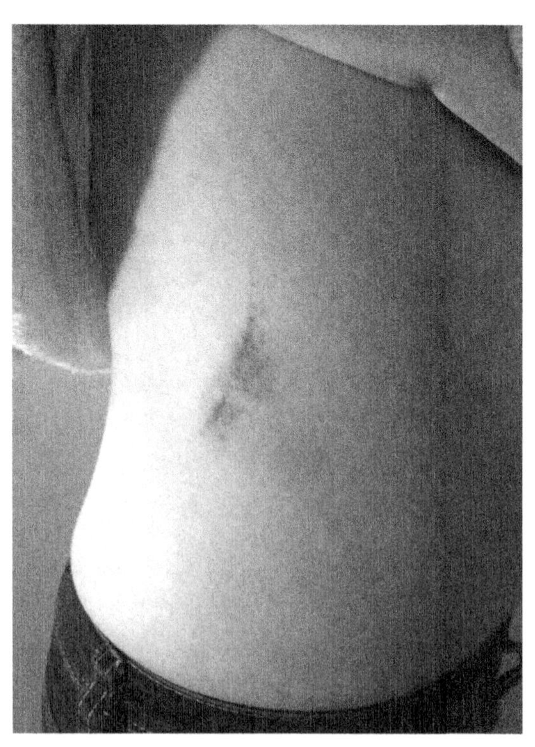

Zoe's broken ribs

RED FLAGS & REFLECTION

There was a theory developed in 1979 by Lenore E. Walker called 'The cycle of abuse', which explains the patterns of behaviour in an abusive relationship. The phrase is also used more generally to describe any set of conditions which perpetuate abusive and dysfunctional relationships.

These are the four stages:

Tension building > Incident > Reconciliation > Calm

There are many variations since Lenore's theory, and these helped me to understand the cycles I found myself in. Education is key to understanding and validation, so if you find yourself feeling confused or walking on eggshells in your relationship, read and research!

I found several books helpful throughout my recovery; I have included them in my resources section at the end of the book.

The tension had been building over several weeks until the incident with my ribs happened. It was all very confusing and out of nowhere. I did not know about red flags or abusive traits so I again justified Smith's behaviour as 'I must have fallen when Smith was going for the keys'. However, I now believe this was no accident. After speaking with professionals who profile abusers, it's clear to me that this incident put Smith in a position of power – the instigator of violence and my saviour – nursing me back to health.

This was manipulation.

It was to make me feel weak, vulnerable, and reliant on him.

Would you know what to do if you needed to break free from an abusive relationship?

CHAPTER 11:

The System

Often you can be a victim of something without even having the realisation you are a victim. This could be down to others minimising or gaslighting your situation or even your own denial or belief and sheer hope that things will get better.

I had felt pretty low for days. I knew what I needed to do but how would I do it? My relationship with Smith was becoming a drain and I could see a similar pattern emerging.

I was going through the motions of daily life. I seemed to be thinking about Mum a lot. I always did when I was low or felt sad. Somehow it highlighted what I had lost.

"I don't think I can do this anymore. I need some space." I managed to get Smith on a day when he was listening.

"I'm serious, I need time to think, can you go and stay with your parents? You need to sort yourself out. I can't deal with it, Smith. I've got too much going on. You are not happy. The drinking is too much. I have to think of the kids. We just can't go on like this, it's not fair, don't you think?" I asked him gently; this wasn't the time to fight. I wanted him to agree so this was partly his idea too.

I wanted him to go amicably. I wanted him to sort himself out. I still loved the old Smith. I still wanted him to return, of course I did. Who wouldn't? He had been amazing to me. Maybe if we had some time apart, he would get his shit together.

Smith agreed. "Ok, if that's what you want?"

I could not believe it. I was expecting a debate or at least resistance. I was pleased he was handling it like this. It gave me more respect for him. The length of time it took me to get rid of Moran was a joke and a complete waste of my life and time. I was so relieved.

"Do you want your key?" He looked upset.

"Well, yes please, there's no need for you to have it now. I really hope you sort yourself out, Smith."

Smith went back to his parents. We were still speaking daily; it was amicable. I wanted to create distance and space between us so I could think, decide how best to move forward, and give Smith a chance to realise his behaviour was not something I would tolerate.

It was sad that it had come to this, but this was the best thing for us. We needed distance. At least now I did not feel like he was using me. I could stop comparing the behaviour to Moran's and then maybe he would get his life back on track.

I felt like I was back in control of my emotions and my life. It gave me the chance to reconnect with friends. I went for lunch over at Jodi's and spent time with Melissa.

Over the next few days on my travels, out and about, I'd bump into people who knew Smith and knew me. It seemed like people were talking. It was quite odd. One day I was walking down the road and bumped into one of Melissa's friends who knew of Smith.

"Hi, how are you? Hey, you were going out with Smith, weren't you? Have you split up? I've heard some stuff about him."

"Hi. Oh right, what exactly?" I asked, curious at what she meant.

"He was apparently a right nightmare; he stalked my friend."

"Oh, right." I wasn't sure what I was supposed to say to that, but this wasn't the only thing. There were odd comments coming from all over. I was starting to get the feeling I did not know Smith at all.

I bumped into Sofia's auntie one day.

"Hey Zoe, how are you? Hey, are you not going out with Smith? He used to always come in the pub when I worked there. I never thought you would go out with someone like him."

"What do you mean?" I felt offended.

"Oh, you know."

"No, I don't actually, what is that supposed to mean? Someone like him?"

She didn't reply; she could tell I got defensive. What did she mean 'someone like him'?

I started thinking about the little things that had gone on over the time of being with Smith. Smith had told me about his ex, a girlfriend who was a police officer. She lived not far from me. "She was mad, Zoe, barking mad. She used to sit in the kids' Wendy house in the garden for hours waiting for me. She would not stop stalking me." I found this rather far-fetched. He said this quite early on in our relationship, so I had brushed it off.

Then there was that girl who messaged me saying Smith was messaging her mum on Facebook pretending to be the police. Now someone was saying he had stalked her friend.

Things just were not as they seemed. I wondered why all these people were saying this about Smith. This did not sound like the person I knew. I just could not get my head around it. My gut was telling me something was not right, and all these people could not be wrong. Smith never acted this way with me, so I was confused; he had been the best thing that had happened to me especially after Moran. I suppose I did not want to believe it. I had been groomed into thinking he was my knight in shining armour.

My first mistake was telling him everything about me on our first date. The abusive Moran. It allowed him to mould himself into the perfect man. Hindsight: I wish I had not been so open.

I was in mental turmoil. I did not *want* Smith to go, and I felt bad every day about it. He had helped me so much but the cracks were apparent now. I'd minimise them, shrug them off, and I threw myself into work. But Smith was still pushing for attention all the time. Constantly calling me.

Needing to know my every move.

I just wanted space but he could not leave me alone for a minute. It was as if he had totally unravelled. The contact was relentless.

"Baby, can I see you tonight?"

"Smith, I'm at work, can you stop calling me, I've got stuff to do. I'll talk to you after work."

"I just want to talk to you."

"Yes, I know but I'm at work." *Jesus, why can't he just stop!* I felt like turning off my phone but I knew I couldn't because of the kids.

I put my phone on silent.

I can see he's calling again.

I turn the phone over.

Head in my hands, I scream. *Why is he relentlessly ringing!* I did not want to talk to him at all. I needed him to just stop.

It was too much. Every day.

I felt so isolated at this point, more so than before because I did not want to tell my friends how I felt. I didn't want opinions. I was trying to deal with Smith by myself. What could anyone else do or say anyway? After hearing what other people had said about him, I also felt silly, embarrassed.

It was getting too much. Smith was not giving me the space he said he would. It was as if he'd upped the ante.

I wanted him to leave me alone. I needed time to think.

A text came through. "See you soon, I'm coming home."

What! Home! *Oh my god, what is he talking about now? This isn't his home.* I felt anxiety at every car that pulled up.

My phone rang again. I answered.

"I'm coming home tonight, babe." He was trying not to sound drunk.

"No! Smith! Do not come around here, it's a school night, the children are here, do not! You are drunk!"

What is he playing at now? His behaviour was so erratic, I never knew which Smith I was going to get.

This was exhausting. He never took no for an answer.

`[I'm outside]` he texted.

`[Why?! You can't come in, I've already told you.]` My heart was pounding. I was trying to stay calm, get the children off to bed. I turned my phone off.

There was a bang at the door. For fuck's sake, the children are in bed. I opened the side window.

There was a car at the side of my house. I could see his friend was driving. "You are not coming in, you are drunk and it's a school night. Go home, Smith."

"I don't care, LET ME IN!"

"Seriously, I'm calling the police if you don't leave. I've said no. Why have you come around? Why are you acting like this?" Did I just say that? To Smith? He's pushed me to the point of no return.

The fact that I threatened him with the police, I knew in my heart of hearts that was it. We were in new territory.

It is now OVER. And I had to make the call; Smith was not taking no for an answer.

I dialled 999. "Hi, police please."

"Police, how can we help you?"

"I have split up with my boyfriend and he keeps calling me all day over and over, then when I turned my phone off this evening, he turned up at my house drunk. My children are in bed."

"Is he still there now?"

"No, I just told him I was calling you and he has driven off."

"Was he driving?"

"No, looked like one of his friends."

"Ok, well he hasn't really done anything has he, so just give us a call if he comes back again." And that was that. They took no report, nothing.

I went to bed exhausted.

The next day, text after text after text.

[Baby I'm sorry]

[Baby I love you]

[Answer the phone baby]

[I'm coming home]

[See you tonight]

It was as if a switch had been flicked in him. It was unceasing.

A Facebook message, it looked like he had sent me an essay, it was pages long. I copied and pasted it into Google as the words looked familiar and I realised they were Boyz II Men lyrics! Is he for real?!

WhatsApp...

[I love you more than life Zoe, I can't live without you]

[Please answer the phone]

[Answer the fucking phone Zoe]

Texts...

[Baby, I'm coming home soon]

[Let's get married, we can be proper family]

[Wifey]

Voicemail...

"Baby my baby, I love you so much." His old self.

"Are you going to answer the phone Zoe? I'll keep calling." He sounds agitated.

"Zoe answer the fucking phone." Ok now he's mad.

"I'm going ... I'm going now baby, I love you..." He trails off, he's putting on a weak whispery voice, he's pretending to kill himself. He had threatened suicide before. Now he was pretending to do it.

"ZOE IF YOU DON'T ANSWER THE FUCKING DOOR, I'M COMING THROUGH IT."

That's it. I called the police again.

"Hi, I have called a couple of times but my ex still won't leave me alone. He keeps calling me and now he has left me so many messages, voicemails, WhatsApp."

"Can you turn off your social media?"

"No, you don't understand, he's not leaving me alone. I can't turn off my phone in the day, I have kids and when I turn my phone off, he threatens to turn up. He's threatening me that if I don't answer the door, he's coming through it. I'm here with my children."

"Ok, we will send some officers around."

"Ok thank you."

I waited for the police to arrive. A few hours go by and there's a knock at the door. I can see the high-vis jackets through the front door.

"Hi, come in." It's two young male police officers. "Come through." I walk through to the kitchen.

"So, you've called about your ex. Whoahh nice kitchen," officer number 1 remarks, looking around, giving the nod to his colleague.

"I'm sorry, what? Ok, umm thanks."

"Yes, gosh don't show my missus this kitchen, she'll want one."

"Umm ok," I said, confused at the fact they were not even paying attention to the situation I was dealing with, Smith's erratic behaviour.

"So you called about your ex calling you?"

"Yes relentlessly, he won't leave me alone, he keeps calling, leaving voicemails, listen here, I can play them..."

I play the different messages.

"He's pretending to kill himself on this one, listen..." I play it again.

They kind of snigger. "You need to find yourself a nice boyfriend, don't you?" He elbows his colleague, and they both laugh.

I'm sorry, WHAT?! My heart is in my chest playing the voicemails and they make jokes.

"Look he's sent this on Facebook , it's lyrics to a song. I just want him to leave me alone."

"Has he turned up tonight?"

"No."

"Well, he hasn't done anything then, has he?" They disregarded what I was reporting, which was quite terrible given I was not even aware of the amount of danger I was in.

"But he said if I don't answer the door, he'll come through it. What am I meant to do? My children are in bed."

"If he turns up, just give us a call," the officer states.

"Oh ok, thanks."

Every time I called the police, they said the same thing. "He hasn't done anything really, has he?" They were so condescending. "Until he does something we cannot act, unfortunately." No emotion. No care.

I was a sitting duck! This was a terrible failure in their duty. The police have a duty of care to the public; however, they did not even recognise or empathise with my situation. I just wanted it to stop. The police basically would not help until Smith had 'done something'.

There are laws they could have used. They did not. Instead, they made me feel like I was wasting their time.

Smith's behaviour and attitude was escalating, and he was scaring me with the threats about smashing the door. Although I never actually thought he would hurt me, I was fearful of the situation. I was embarrassed and ashamed and I did not want my children to hear or see Smith acting this way. I felt I was reporting something silly and irrelevant, something that I should just deal with myself. That's how the police made me feel.

His calling and texts were never-ending. Smith was contacting me day and night, disrupting my working day, and he would often be really drunk or sound weird, out of it somehow.

I was so frustrated but who the hell could help me?!

Yet the police brushed me off. It was just too much. I felt backed into a corner with this unrelenting contact and no-one to protect me or help. I felt vulnerable with the children at home and I could not burden Dad. He hates conflict anyway.

Things with Moran were no better, the usually shitty attitude and disruption. So not only was I navigating his bullshit still, I had this constant stress with Smith.

It was a living nightmare but I had to carry on ... regardless.

Since I worked from home, after dropping the children to school I started parking my car a few streets away from my house. I would walk through the adjoining alleyways and run into the house, hoping Smith was not nearby. That way he would not see the car and hopefully would think I was not home.

I moved my office desk into the loft, so I was no longer downstairs in the kitchen. I would keep my phone face down and periodically check it to make sure the school had not called. I would see hundreds of missed calls, text messages. All different numbers, but I knew it was Smith.

I had to manage everything around this stalking.

Even with my car a few streets away Smith was banging on my door anyway. There was no escape. I was completely drained.

One Saturday afternoon I had been out with Sofia. We'd had a lovely afternoon in town. Cameron was at his dad's. I walked through the front door and through the hall into the kitchen. My kitchen is open plan, large and airy with big bi-fold windowed doors at the end which open out onto my locked, enclosed garden.

Then I looked up and saw him. Smith was in the back garden! I jumped out of my skin. I had never expected him to be there. My heart was racing. What is he doing? How long has he been there? I ran out of the kitchen and said to Sofia, let's go upstairs. At that moment there was a hailstorm; it was the oddest thing. And then I heard him kicking at the side door.

Oh my god what is he doing, I was thinking. I was mad but had to try and stay calm for Sofia.

"Oooh look, Sofia, look at the big hailstorms out of the window." My mobile was in one hand and with the other I was pointing out the window to distract Sofia. I was in a complete panic.

I called Smith's dad first. "He's kicking my door in."

"Zoe, call the police!" his dad shouted down the phone.

"Erm ok." I put the phone down and called 999.

I could hear glass smashing, the thud of Smith constantly kicking on the door.

"I want to speak to you, Zoe!" Smith was shouting through the door.

"Please come quickly, my ex-boyfriend is kicking in my side door, he has smashed all the glass, I can hear him ... He's IN THE HOUSE, HURRY!" I heard the door open and his footsteps in the hall.

Then I could hear him coming up the stairs. "Smith is here, being silly," I said to Sofia and as he came through the bedroom door, I glared at him, looked at Sofia and just mouthed "Why?!"

Smith fell to his knees. "I'm sorry." He started crying. "Please, Zoe, talk to me." He looked so pathetic, I felt sorry for him.

"The police are on their way, I have no idea why you have done this ... none at all!" I was just shaking my head. I was angry, scared, upset, worried, embarrassed. Why was he behaving this way?

"You need to run," I said to him, shooing him with my hands towards the door.

"Really?" he said, looking behind him.

"Yes, the police are coming." He ran down the stairs and out of the front door. I watched out of the front window in Sofia's room as he ran up the road.

Even though he had smashed my door I was still not consciously scared of him. I never thought he would hurt me. I just felt so confused by his behaviour. I just thought he'd unravelled and needed help. It was really horrible to watch. I'm a strong person so watching his self-destructive behaviour was difficult. I cared for him, and I could not fathom why he was making life so hard. He was literally causing all of this himself.

Within a few minutes the police arrived. "He's run up the road, that way." I pointed which way he went. Both male police officers went running up the road, saying they would be back to take the statement later.

I could not believe what he had done. Smith had completely smashed in the side UPVC door, through the double glazing and through the door. I felt like I was in a bad dream, in a state of disbelief. *What is going on? What has happened to him? This is utter maniac behaviour.*

I had to get Sofia out of there; the kitchen was a complete mess. I needed to clean up and work out what to do next.

I had no other choice but to call Moran to collect Sofia early. I knew it was a mistake, but I had no-one else to help and she was going to her dad's anyway. I needed to get her away from the situation. I sat with Sofia, waiting for her dad to arrive. Moran walked in the kitchen. "You'd better tell him to go now, Zoe."

"What the hell do you think I've been trying to do? He won't leave me alone."

No-one was listening to me.

No-one was helping me get this man out of my life. I had no-one to turn to. Smith knew this too.

I was left in the house alone with a smashed open door. I did not even know what to do.

I called my insurance company and asked if they could send someone out to board up my door. I was mortified. *How on earth has my life come to this?* I sat in the kitchen with the smashed open door, freezing, waiting for the boarding company to turn up. It was a new low. They arrived and nailed a big piece of wood over the door opening.

I just sat and cried.

Later on, the police came to take a statement. I had already thought about what I was going to do. I was pressing charges.

I talked through the statement with the officer. "You don't have to press charges, you know." I was shocked that the officer even suggested I do nothing.

"Well, how will he learn if there are no consequences?! No, I am pressing charges plus I need to claim on my insurance, and I need a crime number. Why should I foot his bill? He smashed my door in, so he should feel the consequences. I don't go around behaving like that and if I did, I would expect something to happen to me!"

The police were trying to talk me out of this. Why? I wondered.

Not once did I feel I had the support of the police. Quite the opposite. I felt like a hindrance, like it was a nuisance to be calling them over for something they considered to be trivial. Everything I ever said to them was minimised. Every call I made, I had to repeat myself. Could they not read the reports against my address? It was obvious there were ongoing problems. He would not leave me alone.

They were useless. The system is useless.

I called Smith's parents. "Hi, Smith is at the police station, I don't know what is happening. He has completely smashed my door in."

"I'll sort your door Zoe; I've spoken to him."

Another odd interaction. His parents did not even seem to react. His father offered to fit a new door. He came round the next day to measure up and I met him and Smith's mum at the glazing company to choose the type of door I wanted. They never even really said anything about the fact that Smith had smashed my door to pieces. It was as if it was completely normal. His dad just said, "Smith is a twat."

At the window store Smith's dad turned to me and said, "If he turns up again, Zoe, you need to call the police straight away." I just agreed.

How had my life unravelled so much?

The smashed door

RED FLAGS AND REFLECTION

Hoovering is a manipulation technique; once an abuser thinks they are losing control of you, they will up the ante. Smith used this manipulation tactic a lot. He would send me messages making me feel guilty. He would apologise over and over, promising to change, declaring his undying love, and talking of marriage, our future, having children.

He would even get his friends to message me repeating all the above. All of this was an attempt to sway me into letting him back into my life. It was quite exhausting, and I suppose I wanted it to be true. He did not give me a minute's peace to gather my thoughts. Hence why I talk of creating distance from your abuser. You need clarity of thought.

At this time, I had resorted to contacting the police, a decision I did not take lightly. I thought if the police spoke to him, he would back off, however their response was terrible. They failed to protect me at this time and given they had back files and foresight it is extremely infuriating to me even now. They failed in their duty to keep me, a member of society, safe.

The advice they were giving me was incorrect and at times dangerous. You should not advise a victim to turn off their social media or phone if they are being harassed. All this does is create more of a reason for the abuser to turn up in person. The best thing you can do is get advice and create a safety plan.

The police did nothing about Smith and his incessant calling, texting, voicemails, and generally relentless contact. Instead, they told me to 'call back when he does something'. He had already done something.

He had broken harassment laws with the calls and texts, however Smith's behaviour had moved into stalking. The police did not recognise this, and I did not know that I was in a huge amount of danger.

If you find yourself in a situation similar to this with police not taking your reports seriously, do not think twice, escalate your report and speak with the domestic abuse or stalking lead in that force. If for some reason they also do not take your reports seriously, contact a specialist charity such as Paladin (the National Stalking Advocacy Service), Refuge or Women's Aid, any of whom will be able to advocate on your behalf with the police.

Police response to a victim's initial report is crucial. If a victim is dismissed, they may never call again. This could potentially result in the most serious harm, where a victim is seriously hurt or even murdered!

Police training is crucial; they should believe victim reports and investigate. That is their job. They should not minimise, victim blame or shame the person reporting.

Paladin National Stalking Advocacy Service's definition of stalking:

"A pattern of unwanted, fixated and obsessive behaviour which is intrusive and causes fear of violence or serious alarm or distress."

Would you know the difference between harassment and stalking behaviours or what to do if you found yourself in this situation?

CHAPTER 12:

The Monster

Smith had been arrested and given bail conditions for the damage to my door.

In the UK when you are arrested for a crime, depending on its severity, the police will decide if you can go home or must stay in police custody on remand until your court hearing. If you are allowed to go home and wait for the court appearance, they may put bail conditions in place which the offender must abide by.

After he was picked up by police, Smith would have then been taken to the police station to be processed then once the paperwork was completed, he would have been released. He was told he should have no contact with me or go anywhere near my house.

Now here is the problem. Police bail conditions rely on the person under these conditions being reasonable and adhering to the stipulations as set out in them. Often, and particularly in cases of domestic abuse and stalking, bail conditions can actually have the opposite effect and can aggravate the situation further, sometimes with fatal consequences.

The behaviour of domestic abusers and stalkers is well documented; it is about power and control and therefore bail conditions are hardly going to deter them given they are set out in a paper document. Do you think that is enough to deter a stalker hell-bent on contacting their victim? There is already a level of fixation and obsession so trying to reason with someone who is already unreasonable makes no sense.

Nothing changed. After being released on bail, Smith was not meant to contact me. But that did not stop him.

My phone rang. A number I didn't recognise. I knew it would be him. He had access to hundreds of phones and would always call me from different numbers.

"Hello."

"Hey baby, I'm out." Smith's voice was high, soft and caring. He expected me to be thrilled. His delusions were real. Did he really think that I was going to be pleased and ok with this? He was speaking so matter-of-factly, as if I should be thankful. It was quite strange. "I'm not allowed to speak to you, baby, but you'll speak to me, won't you? We'll get through this, I promise."

I felt sick in my gut, heavy, like a weight was on me, which would not lift off.

I was trapped, cornered like a mouse. *It's a cat and mouse game that I'm losing. When will this end? He does not even realise he has done anything wrong, which is the scary part. I'm hunted.*

Smith was delusional and this made me feel utterly helpless, as he was not going to take no for an answer. I needed to talk some bloody sense into him, make him realise.

He was talking to me like I should be feeling sorry for him. "I'm sorry baby, I messed up. You wouldn't talk to me baby, I just wanted to talk to you. I had to see you." This was the consequence of me not answering his calls; he turned up and waited. I was literally his prey.

"My door is boarded up, Smith, how could you?! Why the fuck didn't you turn up with a bunch of flowers, who the fuck smashes a door in and expects a happy ending. Sofia was in the house, you maniac!"

"Would that have helped?"

"What?"

"Bringing flowers?" Good god, he really does not get it.

"Not really, considering how you have been lately, but smashing my door, Smith, and Sofia was there! You are fucking crazy."

"I know, I learnt my lesson. I'll sort myself out, I'll get a job. I'll get myself straight. I know I've gone off the rails a bit. I love you. I'm sorry. My dad is going to sort the door, isn't he Zoe. We'll be ok baby, don't worry." He was begging for forgiveness, anything he could say that might potentially make me feel sorry for him. I was starting to feel like it was my fault, that I should have opened the door. Smith was now turning the lens onto me.

I continued to be angry at him, as he had caused me even more untold problems. "You know what Moran is like, you have given him the perfect excuse to give me more shit. How could you?!"

"Don't worry about him, baby." I could not quite work Smith out at this point; it was as if he did not understand why I was so mad. Moran would literally use this against me.

I felt alone and exhausted. I was embarrassed. Moran was furious and rather than supporting me in getting rid of Smith, he was attacking me too. I knew that this would fan his flames. I was getting it from all angles. I was trapped. Dad was still suffering too so I could not turn to him, not that he could help.

Over the next few days, it was the same, no let-up. Text after text. Calling me from different numbers. Smith knew how to hide from the police. There was nothing I could do. I could not prove that he was contacting me, and he knew it. Turning my phone off just made matters worse. I was so worn down at this point.

The last time I had cut him off, he kicked the door in, so I decided the only way to stop him was to meet him. Tell him face to face. I thought that when he saw what he'd been doing to me he would stop. I thought that if he could look me in the eye, then maybe he would realise. As long as he was sober and not on one, I thought he would see sense.

I felt like I had no other choice; what were my options? The police were already involved and did nothing. How could my friends monitor what he was doing? And I had no family close by who could help. It felt hopeless.

The children were at their fathers', so I decided to meet Smith. I answered his call. "Ok Smith I'll meet you, let's go for dinner. I'm not promising anything, but I want to talk to you."

"Really? Of course, baby, wherever you want. I can't wait."

I wanted him to see sense. He seemed vulnerable when he was being 'nice' Smith. I had invested a lot into our relationship. I wanted it to go back to the way it was in the beginning. Rose-tinted glasses, whatever you want to call it, but I felt sad he had lost himself.

My empathy and innate need to fix people were steering me to justify all of Smith's bad behaviour. I found myself minimising what he had done and trying to rationalise it. It was not ok, but I could not see this. Many victims go through this phase of self-blame, or belief that if they had done something differently the outcome would have been better.

The problem with this is that trying to regulate your behaviour to accommodate an abuser's actions is a dangerous combination. This is how they gain control, little by little conditioning you to behave a certain way so they can have that power over you.

I did not see this back then; only after educating myself did I realise a lot of my behaviours had a direct correlation with my relationship with Smith. I felt sorry for him, or he made me feel sorry for him. And more to the point, why did I feel sorry for him? He did not need saving.

Not just that, I missed the great connection we had at the beginning. Smith had met and cared for my children, we'd been on holidays, he'd picked up the pieces when my dad became suddenly ill. He had been good to me. I kept going over and over the things that we had done, so much in a short space of time really.

We had had everything, so I could not understand why he was destroying it.

I thought if I met him on mutual ground he would hear me, listen to me. I wanted to get into his head. I arranged to meet Smith at a local café bar near me. It's a place which is usually busy, and I normally bump into people I know so I felt comfortable in there.

We got a table. Smith was telling me how he had an interview set up with Jaguar for a sales position. He was sure that if he got himself a job, he could concentrate on that. I was happy and impressed that he had actually done that while we had not been together. I thought it was a good step. The job would give him responsibility, a reason to get up in the morning. *Maybe pressing charges was the right thing to do as he seems to be sorting himself out*, I thought to myself.

As it was approaching evening and it was a Saturday, the bar started to get busy. A few people I know came over and said hi, and I was having a few conversations with friends across the table.

Smith was not his normally chatty self with others, and he quietly pulled me to one side.

"Can we go back to yours and talk babe, I want to show you the emails from Jaguar. It's too busy in here, let's go back to yours. I want to keep talking."

"I don't think that's a good idea Smith, you're on bail conditions."

"I don't care about that; I want to talk in private. Ok, let me get you another wine." Smith went off to the bar to get drinks.

After another glass, Smith asked about going back to mine again. He had been lovely. I was in the company of friends. I wanted him to see I was supporting him, and I was trying to be the better person. In the end I agreed to go back to mine. After all, what harm would it do?

Smith said he would drive my car as I'd had another glass of wine. We arrived at my house. He immediately asked for the laptop and logged into his email. He wanted to show me the emails, which he did. I was so pleased for him.

While we were sat in my kitchen my friend Ceri called to check on me. We chatted on the phone. I did not tell her Smith was there. I knew she would worry or ask me why, so I just pretended I was home alone.

Ceri and I talked and talked, and I could see out of the corner of my eye that Smith was getting annoyed and agitated. He grabbed a piece of paper to write me a note: "Get off the phone Zoe."

I was telling Ceri "I'm not a battered wife, I'm fine". Smith should not have smashed my door, however I was talking about him and conscious he was in the room and he kept pointing at the paper to get me off the phone, but I also did not want Ceri to know he was there either.

I said my goodbyes to Ceri. I suppose I wanted Smith to see how my friends were rallying around. There had been plenty of people in the bar that I knew, and people were checking up on me. I wanted him to realise this.

The week before I had won a bottle of champagne at work so I said we could open it to celebrate his new job. Smith opened the bottle and carried on talking. I suppose I was being pretty matter of fact about everything, and my guard was down now I'd had some drinks. I was being very candid about everything; I'm not one to hold back and had no reason not to just be myself.

"Look, you can't make demands on me Smith, I won't have it. I'm a busy person too. Look at my door!" I pointed to the door which was boarded up, and looked at him with an upset expression. "How could you do that to me?"

I continued, "Why did you keep calling and calling and calling me? And threatening me. I won't be threatened. I need space. If I ask you to leave me alone, why would you keep calling me and drunk too?"

"I know babe, I'm sorry." Smith seemed to be listening. I felt like I was getting through to him. We were sat at opposite ends of the sofa. I smiled at him. He appeared withdrawn.

I felt happy that we had met up and I was happy that he had listened to how he was making me feel. I felt a sense of relief that his erratic behaviour was going to end. "Let's just move on, draw a line and see what happens." I felt like I'd finally talked sense into him.

"Look it's late, I'm going to bed. You can stay on the sofa or go. It's up to you. I don't think it's a good idea we jump back to how we were, Smith. You need to prove to me that you are working on yourself. I'm glad we had this talk and hopefully we can move forward now."

I know Smith had smashed my door, but he had never hurt me. I never had any fear of him, and certainly not sober or while we were trying to talk things through. This man had helped me at the most difficult time of my life, and yes, all his erratic behaviour had been impossible, but I felt I had got through to him. I felt comfortable that he was going to stop. I had reasoned with him.

I went up to bed.

Within what may have only been an hour or so I woke to find Smith standing over me asking me for money. It was still dark and, in my half-asleep state, I said, "No! I'm asleep, what the hell for?"

All of a sudden, I felt a searing thud and pain to the side of my face. Smith had booted me in the face and the force catapulted my whole body from one side of the bed to the other so that I fell off onto the floor on the other side.

It all happened so quickly.

I remember thud after thud raining down on me. Smith was stamping on my head. I could feel the hard sole of his shoe slamming my cheek and my face pressing into the carpet as I was trying to make sense of what was happening.

I felt like I was in a dream. It certainly was not a reality I recognised. It was like I was looking down over myself while Smith was attacking me.

"What are you doing that for?" I asked him in a normal voice as he rained down thuds on me. It was the most normal voice, as if it was a different person asking the question. An out-of-body experience.

My mother's photo was in its frame next to the bed. The old grainy black and white picture of her in a ball gown, looking demure. Was she watching over me as I was being brutally mauled by Smith?

I lost consciousness.

I must have lain there for some time because when I regained consciousness the room was filled with daylight.

I was slumped over the side of the bed near the bottom. I tried to lift my head. It was heavy. It felt huge. I could feel the swelling. I could see my white cotton sheets were covered in blood, all over the duvet cover. There was blood everywhere, like a horror scene.

I remember looking down through hazy vision and seeing my hands were red. I could taste metal in my mouth. It was surreal. I looked at the back of my left hand, and could see an open stab wound, flesh and blood everywhere. It was in a complete mess. I had been stabbed through the back of my hands. The police later said these were defence wounds where I had tried to cover my face.

My right arm felt floppy and was excruciatingly painful. It had been snapped in two, a complete break. Probably caused from him jumping on me.

I was trying to make sense of what was happening. I was so confused.

In the police reports it states that Smith had filled the bath with water and there was an eight-inch knife in bloody water.

He thought he had murdered me. He was cleaning the scene.

I came around. I was dizzy, disorientated. I felt sick.

What was happening? I could not make sense of it.

Was I alive?

Where was Smith?

I looked up. Smith was sitting on the other side of the bed, on the pillows at the top of the bed. Quite casually, with his feet up on the bed and holding a meat cleaver.

He was doing sawing and chopping movements, cutting his wrists.

"What are you doing? Stop doing that!" I couldn't bear to see what he was doing.

"We are going together, babe."

I felt a sudden whoosh of energy, for survival. I could not believe what was happening.

I'm going to die.

He is going to murder me.

"I'm not going anywhere. I have two children." I knew I had to get away; there was no way my children would be left with no mother.

"Smith, I need to get a drink." I started trying to get up, but I was unsteady.

"What are you doing?" Smith had the laptop open on the chaise longue at the end of the bed.

I knew I had to get away. What was going on? He had completely lost his mind.

"I'm going to get a glass of water." I made my way over to the loft stairs. Blood was being smeared everywhere I touched, spurting from the back of my left hand. The police photos showed how much blood was spread all over the house, in almost every room. There were hand marks and smears of blood all down the walls where I had made my way down to the kitchen.

I knew I needed to call the police, but I had to do this without Smith noticing. I had to get down two flights of stairs to the landline in the lounge. I did not have my mobile. Smith had taken that. I now know that while I was unconscious he had been sending Facebook and WhatsApp messages to my friends from my phone, pretending to be me. They did not even make sense.

One said `[I ok]`.

Another said `[What doing]`.

Did he think he'd murdered me when sending these? Or was he covering his tracks as I was still alive?

He was trying to change the timeline.

He was trying to get away with murder.

I was so woozy, only just managing to keep myself awake as I got myself to the ground floor. In the lounge I grabbed the landline phone off the cradle and pressed 999.

I felt a presence behind me and threw the phone onto the sofa.

It was Smith.

"What are you doing?!" He hadn't seen that I had grabbed the phone.

I thought at least if that call connected the police would come; they had been called so many times previously. The police reports confirm there was blood on the phone, but the call never connected.

"Oh, I'm getting water." I started walking into the kitchen but Smith turned me around to go back upstairs.

I was dying. I could feel the life draining away.

I started to feel weak. Ready to sleep. My fight was slowly slipping away.

Back in the loft, there was so much blood. I was weak. Woozy. Lifeless.

The only way I could get out alive was if he helped me. I had to plead for my life. For my babies' sakes.

The funny thing is, I'm not afraid of dying. I would be with Mum, but I could not leave my babies, not how she left me. No way.

"I'm dying Smith, please call me an ambulance." Smith was sat on the floor on his phone.

"Please call me an ambulance." I was pleading for my life. I remember wincing in pain. I couldn't take anymore.

"I'm dying."

Smith called the ambulance. He must have thought I was dead, but maybe as I had come round and was conscious, he thought he could try and get away with it.

Smith was on the phone to the ambulance operator for 13 minutes.

Here is part of that 999 call.

Operator:	Ambulance service. Is the patient breathing?
Caller:	… Er … love, we're both trying to breathe.
Operator:	Both of you? What's the address sir?
Caller:	… (inaudible)
Operator:	Sorry I can't hear you, 2… What was it?
Operator:	Alright don't worry, I'll get it from the … from the operator after. Just confirm your address sir.
Operator:	Whereabouts is that?
Female voice:	(background) Dying.
Female voice:	(background) (inaudible)
Operator:	Thank you. Now what's happened there, sir? There's two patients is there?
Caller:	Both of us.
Operator:	What's wrong?
Caller:	(sigh) We've had a fight (inaudible)
Operator:	And what have you done?
Caller:	I don't know what we've done, there's blood everywhere.
Operator:	Where … where have you cut each other?
Caller:	Everywhere.
Operator:	You've cut each other everywhere?
Operator:	Bear with me sir. Where are your injuries sir? Can you tell me anything about them?
Caller:	Neck, chest, arms
Operator:	Erm, erm … with a knife?

Caller:	(shallow breathing)
Operator:	I've let them know, we've got some help arranged ok, but I am gonna stop on the phone with you till we get there.
Caller:	Ok
Operator:	Ok? How is … how is Zoe doing there?
Caller:	(sigh) Zo?
Female voice:	Hmmm?
Caller:	You ok?
Female voice:	No, help me.
Operator:	Just explain to her that help's been arranged.
Operator:	Right, you're on a mobile phone, I want you to try and get and open the door. Just unlock the door for us.
	(Movement noise in the background)
Operator:	Have you managed to do it?
Caller:	It's open.
Operator:	Ok, how's Zoe? Can you have a look for me?
Caller:	Zo (inaudible)
Female voice:	(inaudible)
Operator:	Is that Zoe talking in the background still? (pause)
Female voice:	(shouting in background) Help me!
Caller:	Next to me
Operator:	She's next to you? She sounds quite far away. She turned the other way?
Caller:	Next to me

(ambulance control room noise in background)

Female voice: (noise in background) `Hello, help me.`

Operator: `Who's that shouting?`

Female voice: `Help me`

Operator: ... `who's with you?`

Caller: `It's the police`

Operator: `It's the police, they're with you? Ok, I'm gonna let you go. Thank you. Buh bye.`

When the ambulance and police arrived, we were both downstairs. I have no recollection of how we got there.

I remember them coming through the door, shouting "Zoe! Zoe!" I could feel myself going in and out of consciousness.

"Help me," I whimpered.

I was fighting.

Fighting for my life.

When the police and ambulance officers entered my house, we were in the kitchen. Smith was lying on the floor pretending to be out of it. His eyes were rolling in his head, although he had walked to unlock the door to let the paramedics and police officers into the property.

"I'm sorry," Smith said to the ambulance paramedic. This was documented in the police reports and the paramedic gave this evidence in court.

This was a calculated attack.

I was stretchered out of the house. According to the police reports I was naked from the waist down when the police arrived. I have no recollection why. It makes me sick to even think about this.

"What does the pain feel like Zoe, on a scale from one to ten, ten being bad?" I was in the back of the ambulance. They gave me huge doses of painkillers.

At the hospital unbelievably I could hear Smith nearby, in the next bay in Accident and Emergency. He was shouting "Is Zoe ok?!!"

Had they really put him near me?! It was frightening.

Coming around on the ward I was told by the nurses exactly what my injuries were. To say I was utterly shocked was an understatement. I was horrified Smith could do this to me.

I had a bleed on the brain, my right arm had been snapped, I had stab wounds to the back of my left hand; my tendons were severed, and they said I'd never use my hand again. The force of the blade had almost pierced the other side of my hand. My palm was bruised.

I had a stab wound to my neck 1mm from my jugular. Had he hit the vein I would have had four minutes to live. I had a cracked cheekbone, and my face was completely disfigured and swollen. I had slash wounds to my face, my torso and my arms. I also had a broken nose in several places. I had a bleed on the brain and had lost over two pints of blood.

I was lucky to be alive.

Why had he done this?! I still could not understand why the man that claimed to love me, who claimed he could never live without me, would do this. It was over.

Smith was remanded in custody after his trip to the hospital.

How could the police have got it so wrong? I had asked for help. Many times.

He was stalking me. The calls I made to the police highlighted many red flags that the police should have recognised, but instead I was classed as standard risk.

Domestic violence and stalking are complicated crimes. Stalking is often still depicted as a joke, and the police tend to minimise stalking behaviours as they seem unremarkable on their own. However, if you start to piece together the pattern then you see it's an escalation in behaviour and this is what is dangerous.

Police response is crucial in these scenarios and particularly the first call made to the police. If you get the brushed off, disbelieved, or have the abuse minimised this may be the one window of chance to save that victim from a life of hell or, worse still, death.

I have since campaigned alongside two fathers who have both lost their beautiful daughters, murdered by their ex-partners while on police bail conditions.

One of these is John Clough MBE, the father of Jane Clough, who was 26 years old and an A&E nurse at her local hospital. Jane was murdered by Jonathan Vass, who lay in wait in the car park of the hospital and stabbed her over 70 times with a 7.6cm blade. He then momentarily walked away but returned and slowly, deliberately and in cold blood slit her throat. Jane's colleagues did not even recognise it was her until she was taken inside the hospital.

Jane had predicted her own murder. She had kept a diary leading up to her death, detailing the rape while she was seven months pregnant and even six weeks after having her daughter; that didn't stop Vass and he raped her again in front of their baby daughter. Days later Jane found the strength to report Vass and go through lengthy interviews with the police. Vass was arrested and remanded in custody.

Unbelievably Vass's defence team applied for bail conditions and even though the Crown Prosecution Service had said there was a very high chance of the offender interfering with the witness, the judge granted bail.

Vass then went on to murder Jane. Vass got a life sentence and will be in prison until 2040. I have nothing but admiration for John and Penny, Jane's parents; they have set up a charity in her memory and have gone on to help hundreds of victims of domestic abuse and stalking.

Then there is Clive Ruggles, father of Alice Ruggles. Alice was murdered by her ex, soldier Trimaan Dhillon. She had met him through a mutual friend and they chatted on Facebook while he was still on tour. They eventually met up and started dating.

In this time Alice became withdrawn; the usually confident young lady had fallen out with friends, moved out of her flatshare with friends and moved in with a colleague. On a family holiday her parents noticed she had become withdrawn, and it came to light that Dhillon had been contacting another woman from a dating site.

Dhillon was becoming increasingly controlling of Alice, saying in one Facebook message that he was not used to being denied what belonged to him, a very ownership statement. Alice began ignoring his messages, but the psychological effect was profound. She tried to continue to be nice to him as this was in her sweet nature, however he would not take no for an answer, so Alice contacted the police who issued him with a Police Information Notice.

A PIN can be issued when there are allegations of harassment. It's quite similar to bail conditions. Alice was reassured by this, however Dhillon did not stop, so Alice called the police again seven days later. This time they did nothing. She felt completely helpless.

Five days later, Alice was dead. Dhillon drove 120 miles to Alice's flat and broke in. He stabbed her and slit her throat. Alice's flatmate found her dead in the bathroom. Dhillon was given 22 years in prison.

The most chilling thing about Alice's story is her 999 call to police which has since been released and can be found on the internet. Alice is very sweet in the call, explaining that even after Dhillon had been given a PIN he was still contacting her and even left flowers on her downstairs bedroom window. Now this may seem innocuous on its own, however this is the problem. Police were not collecting the evidence, the pattern and escalation of Dhillon's behaviour; it was taken as a one-off event. This should have been taken more seriously. It cost Alice her life.

Since then the College of Policing advice and the HMIC/HMCPSI recommendation from the 'Living in fear' report of July 2017 has stated "Chief constables should stop the use of Police Information Notices (PINs) and their equivalents immediately". This has yet to be seen in all police forces. The PIN in this case escalated circumstances.

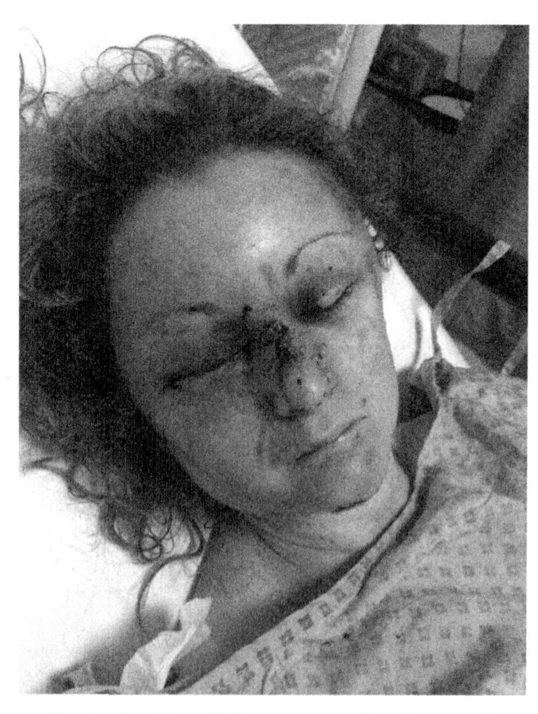

Zoe in Accident & Emergency after the attack

RED FLAGS & REFLECTION

The hoovering had increased over this period. I was worn down, exhausted and so alone. Smith had upped the ante AGAIN. His apologies and contact were stronger than ever. I was backed into a corner. Informing the police felt like a useless thing to do as (a) they would not do anything, like before and (b) Smith was calling me using many different mobile numbers not linked to him. I was trapped, cornered, hunted.

With hindsight, looking back and knowing what I know about Smith, I was in a huge amount of danger meeting him. But how was I to know that?! Do I now think the attack was premeditated? Yes.

His behaviour was often odd; he was obsessed with *NCIS*, an American crime show, and with being able to break the system, circumvent the rules. He was always looking at the 'West Midlands Most Wanted' list online. One day he even got arrested with a fake firearm, something he laughed off as a joke. I was not sure why a grown man would find that funny. Like I say odd behaviour, like he was testing what he could get away with.

Psychopaths are cool and calm under pressure; this is why an abuser can look like a well-balanced person when police turn up to a domestic incident. However, if they do not get their way, they are prone to emotional outbursts and fits of rage, usually perpetrated behind closed doors.

Smith charmed and sweet-talked me away from the bar on the evening of the attack. We had alcohol. My guard was down. He lured me back to my house. He was angry. He had lost his power and I did not know my honesty in telling him this was my demise.

I no longer had any intention of getting back with him and I made this clear that evening. This was likely the trigger for his rage. The loss of power and control over me had resurrected the monster.

If a perpetrator thinks they have lost power and control over you, this is when their behaviour will change dramatically. Our relationship had gone through various cycles of abuse but until this night it was very much in stealth. I was not even consciously aware I was in an abusive relationship. Since researching EVERYTHING about domestic abuse, I now know I absolutely was. When I told Smith it was over, alone in my house, I did not know then how much danger I was in.

In the UK two women a week are killed by an ex or intimate partner. More than half the women killed by men who were an intimate partner in 2018 were murdered after attempting to leave the relationship (Guardian: https://www.theguardian.com/uk-news/2020/feb/20/over-half-of-uk-women-killed-by-men-die-hands-current-ex-partner).

It is absolutely crucial that if you are looking to leave an abusive partner, you do this as safely as possible. Specialist charities can support with this planning and provide you with advice on how to leave with caution.

It is very important that the abuser does not know that you intend to leave.

Would you know what to do if you wanted to end a relationship you fear is with someone abusive?

CHAPTER 13:

The Recovery or Is It?

Alone in the hospital ward and sitting blankly in my hospital bed, I had not looked in the mirror yet. I could feel my disfigurement, but I had no idea of the extent of the damage. I could not look. I did not want to look.

No-one assured me it was ok, so I knew it was not. Broken and empty, I was void of any emotion and in complete shock.

Smith tried to kill me.

I had to say it again to myself.

Smith tried to kill me.

The man who claimed to love me.

What did I do to deserve this?

Why did he do this to me, his 'princess'?

The first few days were a blur. I was on morphine, which pretty much turns you into a zombie. I was in and out of sleep, the nurses looking after me, topping me up with pain relief. I had an operation on my left hand where my tendons had been completely severed. As my right arm was completely broken, both arms and hands were bandaged from my elbow down to the tips of my fingers.

I had stitch tape on my face, my neck, my shoulder. I felt mummified, broken and disfigured. I was under various different consultants and departments in the hospital due to the various injuries: the neurology department for my bleed on the brain, orthopaedics for my broken arm, maxillofacial for my cracked cheek bone, psychiatry for the trauma. It was a lot.

The time ticked by slowly. I had nothing to do. I had no smartphone or TV. My phones had been taken as evidence. My auntie had brought me some magazines but they were full of normal things in life, and I felt completed disjointed from normality. The magazines just highlighted that the world was still turning yet mine stood still.

I just sat there with my thoughts. I could hear nurses pushing the trollies up and down the corridor giving out the pain relief and doing the food rounds. I was empty and felt soulless without my children. I felt so ashamed of what Smith had done to me and so horrified that he was capable of this.

I was jumpy, on edge with every bang or noise. In a state of constant anxiety. If I heard a man's voice in the hospital corridor it would make my stomach turn over, thinking it was him. My body would tense in fear. It was not a conscious fear; it was a physical fear. My body would react involuntarily; I would get breathless and start shaking.

My dad and my friend Melissa came to see me, but I wasn't very coherent. Wayne called me. "Shall I bring Cameron up today, Zoe? He is wondering what is going on. Cameron is not daft, he knows something is up. Although I won't bring him up if you don't want me to. Are you ok?" He was concerned. He always wanted to do the right thing by Cameron and me.

"Wayne, I have no idea what I look like, but I know my face is bad and I don't want to scare him. We probably need to wait for my face to heal. I'll speak to him and tell him I'm ok. I'd love to see him, Wayne, but it's probably too soon. Just tell him I fell down the stairs and say the doctor said in a few days. Tell him that I have some bruising to my face, so prepare him for that." Wayne was a worrier and I hated to lie to Cameron, but I obviously could not tell the children the truth. Not yet anyway.

I did my best to reassure Wayne. I knew he would be hating this situation. He does not like bad things happening and I can only imagine what his reaction was when he received the phone call from the police to say that Smith had attacked me. He would have been in so much shock and felt helpless, however I knew he would help with Cameron and keep him for a while so I could get better.

I later found out that when Wayne went to collect some of Cameron's things from my house for school, it was like a murder scene with blue and white police tape around the doors and police in forensic suits going in and out.

Wayne walked over to speak to the police officer who was positioned outside. Realising he was upset, she asked him if he wanted to sit in her car a minute before going into my house. She was bracing him for the scenes, the aftermath of my attempted murder.

Wayne sat in the car with the female officer and broke down, visibly upset and crying. No good parent wants to see any harm to the other parent of their child or have to break awful news to them. Even though our relationship had ended around five years before, we still remained good friends, and stayed close for Cameron. We always kept a united front. I respect Wayne so much for this. We work together as parents.

Wayne told the officer the story about my broken ribs. "Zoe told me she slipped on the decking; do you think he did that?"

"She probably never told anyone what was going on as she was most likely scared." The officer was explaining that I must have been in an abusive relationship for a while. "She has probably been hiding it from everyone and it's likely to have been going on over time and she was too scared to say anything."

When Wayne told me this afterwards I was so annoyed. How dare she judge me like that? It was a damaging assumption. She did not know me. I still find it frustrating how people judge and assume things based on their own perspective on life. Maybe she thought she had seen this situation before, but every single situation is unique. Prior to these two occasions, Smith had not been physically abusive towards me or the children, quite the opposite. Now this is not me defending him, however I know that when people make assumptions where children are involved this can be extremely detrimental. The system is set up to blame the victim of the abuse and even more so if they are a parent. Unfair? Yes.

I never recognised Smith's relentless contact as abuse. And I was not scared of Smith, and neither were the children. I was just beyond annoyed with the stalking and blamed him for his own unravelling. If anything, I thought HE needed help. He played on the 'poor me' syndrome (https://www.laurarichards.co.uk/top-10-poor-me-syndrome-tactics-i-mean-signs-and-symptoms/). Someone making you feel guilty for their behaviour is not ok.

I felt sorry for Smith. I'm a strong-willed person, so when I said it was over and to leave me alone, I meant it. I just wanted him to understand but Smith would not accept it, so I felt the need to explain this to him and had therefore unknowingly put myself in danger.

Domestic abuse is complex. Friends wonder why you don't 'just leave' but it's really not that simple and I did not recognise his subtle and insidious manipulations as abuse. It was not until afterwards, looking back over the relationship, that I realised he was pushing the boundaries from day one. This was all part of the grooming process.

I had my gut feeling something was not right with Smith but I chose to ignore my own intuition. Instead, I tried to help him as he unravelled over the last few months of our relationship, which eventually ended in him trying to kill me.

However, Smith's behaviours prior to the attack were also a far cry from what I had put up with from Moran. The relationship with Moran was very obviously not good although abusive was not a word I would have used at the time; nevertheless he had done many things I knew made him a bad person for me to be around. He would scream in my face, called me every name under the sun, cunt, slag, whore; he threatened me, attacked my dad, disrespected me in front of friends, stole my car, removed me from a business, lived in my house without paying his way. So in comparison my relationship with Smith was amazing, until the unravelling, the drinking, the lying, the manipulation. I did not recognise the grooming and I was also not aware of his past. So I went out of the frying pan, into the fire.

I had become desensitised to abuse, thinking this is how men act in relationships. I was also not the only one dealing with an arsehole either. It was standard to hear my mates moaning about how their boyfriend was treating them. Is this what women have succumbed to?

So when Smith was harassing me I was not scared of him, I was angry.

When I made the decision to go back to mine with Smith, I was also not scared. He wanted to show me the emails. He was sorry. He wanted to make amends. I fell for it, of course I did. I cared about this man. This was not just any man. He was the man I slept with every night before the relationship broke down. The man who saved me when Dad went into hospital. The man who built my confidence back up after it being trodden into the ground by Moran. The man who collected my children from school. Made the dinner when I came in from work. Took me out at the weekends. Treated me. He was not the monster that turned up, not in my eyes.

He had made me feel special over the short time we had been together, and I so needed it after the toxic relationship with Moran. Smith and I had good times. He did everything right in the beginning, so I did not see the subtle red flags, the crossing boundaries, the financial control, the control around my time, who I spent time with, how long I took getting ready. I just thought he loved me.

It was only when he started to lie that this was unacceptable to me and I pulled him up on this behaviour that I would not accept. Then he showed himself to be a psychopath, capable of murder! I had no idea.

That's why I was numb. The whole thing was a lie. My entire relationship. I was in shock but there was no doubt in my mind that it was over. I never wanted to set eyes on him again.

A few days into my hospital stay, the nurse entered my room. I had just finished breakfast. "There is a social worker here to see you Zoe, do you feel up to it?" The nurses were so great. I cannot thank them enough for making me feel so safe and the care I got was beyond amazing, although I wondered what they thought of me. I wondered if they judged me.

"Yes, it's fine, thank you for letting me know." I gave a grimace. I don't think I had smiled since I came around from the attack. I was just blank. The pain relief medicine kept me numb, painless and empty.

"Hello Zoe, I have to come and see you due to the nature of what happened to you. I'm from Coventry Social Care. We have to ask you some questions, is that ok?" he asked, explaining. He was a nice guy, probably mid-forties.

"Yes, I understand. I ran a child protection agency for five years. I understand all too well why you are here," I replied.

This is social worker protocol. It was a 'domestic', and they needed to understand if I was likely to go back into the relationship with Smith as he would clearly be deemed a danger to my children. Social services' job is to protect any children in a family where there may be violence. If I gave any indication that I would be staying in the relationship with Smith, then that would have been a safeguarding issue. Of course, there was no way I wanted to be near that monster ever again. He could have killed me or worse; what if the children had been there? There was no way I wanted him anywhere near any of us ever again.

I told him what had happened and then he asked, "Zoe, will you see Smith again?" He was looking at his pad and paper, poised to write notes.

"Rest assured I will not be seeing him again and he is remanded in prison with no chance of getting out. I am going to court so he will not be getting away with this. He tried to kill me!" My brave face cracked and I got tearful. "I can't believe he did this to me."

"I'm sorry, we have to ask." He seemed like a kind man.

The nurse came into the room and noticed I was upset. "Zoe, I think that's enough, are you ok?"

I looked at the social worker. "I never thought he would do this to me but there is absolutely no way I want that man near me or my children again. He is in prison, and he will be staying there for a long time. He tried to kill me," I repeated, as I was still in shock.

After the social worker had left, I lay there pining for the children. I felt helpless.

The mobile phone I had in the hospital was terrible. Since my iPhone and work BlackBerry were being kept by the police as evidence, I had been given an old Nokia to use, so at least I had contact with the outside world. But the buttons were hard to press given my hands were bandaged and I had to stand by the window to get any signal, which was tiring.

I had spoken to Wayne and Cameron on the phone, so I knew Cameron was ok. I was wondering how Sofia was as I had not seen or heard from her at all. Moran and I had exchanged texts, although his were curt, with no empathy, no care, not even for Sofia wondering where her mummy was. I did not expect anything more from him, to be honest. I knew he would be revelling in this.

I had to agree that he didn't bring Sofia to the hospital. At only four years old at the time, she did not want to see her mummy all bruised. It hurt me inside not to see her but it was the right decision until my face healed. Moran was so mean to me it took all my strength away to deal with him, so it was better to avoid it. Sofia was safe, that was all that mattered. I just needed to get well and back home.

The nurse came into my room again. "Sorry Zoe, the police are here now, they need to take a statement from you, are you ok with that? I can tell them to go if you've had enough for one day." She looked at me, concerned.

"No, it's fine." I thought maybe the police could tell me more. Maybe they had spoken to Smith. Smith could not deny what he did, so what was he saying?

Two detective constables from the Criminal Investigation Department (CID) department at West Midlands Police came to the hospital. The CID department deal with the investigation of serious crimes. DC Davies, the officer in charge of the case, was a small lady, like a typical cop from the TV. You know the detective types who always look inquisitive, straight faced, to the point and factual. DC James had a softer look, however both came across very professional and seemed to have empathy.

"Hi Zoe, we have met you before. You might not remember. We took a statement when you were in Accident and Emergency, but they needed to look after you. You were in a bad way, so we want to go over what happened again if that's ok?" I had no recollection of giving this statement. They had given me ketamine due to my injuries, so I had been fairly sedated at the time.

I had to go back over the attack and what I remembered, which was not much, and when talking about it I got tearful. It was the shock and saying it out loud; it made it all the more real. Maybe they could piece together what the hell had happened because I had no clue why he hurt me.

I asked both the DCs, "Why did he do this to me? Have you spoken to him?" I started to cry. It did not feel real. It was like I was talking about someone else.

"We have, Zoe. I interviewed Smith in the station after we arrested him at the scene," DC Davies explained.

"I can't believe he did this to me. What did he say? What did he say happened?" I wanted to try and understand what he was thinking. Did he do this on purpose? Why? If DC Davies spoke to Smith straight afterwards then I wanted to know what he was thinking. Was he mad at me? Did he say he wanted me dead? I wanted to know.

"He says he cannot remember. He asked how you are, and he started crying when we showed him a picture of your face. We took it in the hospital when you arrived. I can't really tell you anymore, Zoe. We are building a case."

"I don't understand what happened, I'd called the police previously. He smashed my door. I was still mad at him for that, and I told him that, but we met to discuss things as he would not stop relentlessly contacting me. I wanted him to give me some space, I was trying to talk sense into him."

I was so dazed and confused. He loved me yet he tried to kill me. I was still extremely weak at this point, both physically and emotionally. I would sometimes daydream about the good times; my mind was playing tricks on me.

I knew what Smith had done was wrong, however it did not stop me reminiscing. This is where victims can become confused and convince themselves that maybe their abuser did not mean it, or they would never do it again. I had to constantly tell myself the reality. You could not really get away from it but your mind plays tricks; I was emotionally connected. Smith tried to kill me. What other explanation could there be? Knives, meat cleaver, texting my friends, cleaning the weapons. There was no other explanation. I had to keep reminding myself of this. He was not a good person.

About a week into my stay in hospital, they allowed me to have more visitors. Melissa came in every day and my dad, Jodi and Ceri came one evening. Jodi told me she looked through the doorway of my room and almost walked past. She thought I was an old woman. My face was so disfigured she did not even recognise me and when she came into the room, I could tell by her face that I looked terrible. Jodi could not hide what she thought. It was all over her face.

"Oh Zo." Her hands were over her mouth in shock. It was horrible. I felt like I was in a goldfish bowl. I was embarrassed. Embarrassed I had allowed this to happen to me.

Everyone was trying to keep the conversation upbeat; it was odd. Small talk. What do you actually talk about when your friend has just been nearly murdered by her boyfriend? I noticed I kept repeating myself. Jodi and Ceri looked at each other and I recognised why. I was so frightened.

"I've just said that, haven't I? Why am I repeating things?" My brain was all jumbled. This scared me so much; I did not want to have brain damage. I needed to get better.

"It's ok Zoe, it's fine. Maybe you should get some rest." They were concerned. I could see them looking at each other with worried faces.

Then Moran walked into my hospital room with a bunch of flowers.

What is he doing here? After all the blunt texts and not letting me speak to Sofia, why had he come in to the hospital?

He walked over to the bed, leaned over and pretended to kiss my head. Then he whispered in my ear, "You've done it now; you'll never see Sofia again."

I could not quite grasp what he had said to me. *I'll never see Sofia again. What does he mean?* I started to feel triggered, on edge.

Moran then started with his self-righteous speech out loud. "What were you playing at, Zoe? Anything could have happened." I was so angry. What was he doing in my hospital room and how was this my fault? At that moment the nurse walked past the room and heard me say, "Who let him in?" I was agitated and getting flustered. He had come here to abuse me by the hospital bed, and the nurses fell for it and let him in because he had a bunch of flowers.

"Right, you need to leave." The nurse ushered him out of the ward but before he left, he placed an envelope on the end of my bed.

That's weird. "What is that?" I said to Jodi as she passed me the envelope. I opened it and I could not breathe. My throat closed. Total and utter devastation came crashing over me. They were court papers for custody of Sofia!

Moran had been to family court in the days between the attack and visiting me in hospital. He had got an ex-parte family court hearing. Ex-parte means that it's an emergency court sitting, and the respondent (me) does not have to be present. So, the case goes ahead without you being able to respond or defend your position.

The bastard! This was not the act of a caring father. It was to punish me.

"He's taking her. He's taking her from me." Everyone around the bed looked at me, shocked.

"I cannot believe it. How can he do this to you? And now?"

"Wow, this is pure evil, when you are so ill in hospital, that he would come up and do this to you. He has waited for you to be at your lowest. What a coward. Poor Sofia!" My friends were in shock and my dad, well, he could not understand this at all.

"Get my laptop!" I was almost shouting and sat bolt upright in the bed. "I need my laptop, I need to write to the judge, this is all lies, and he will be saying anything to keep her. He is doing this to punish me and nothing else. Why would he hurt Sofia and Cameron like this if it was not for his own gain?" I read through his statement. He had put that I drink too much, and go out with abusive men. Well yes, Moran was one of them!

Everyone left shocked and Dad spoke to my auntie who brought my laptop to the hospital the next day. I did not sleep that night. The nurse gave me extra pain relief; I was distraught.

I knew Moran would not care one hoot about her brother Cameron and separating the children. This was about winning for him. I had to get my practical head on and fight back. I should have been recovering but Moran had involved my children and I knew the devastation involved with family courts all too well after running my childcare business.

This is not a system you should ever choose to enter. I thought I could write to the judge and they would do background checks on Moran and see he was not a law-abiding citizen and had numerous convictions. This would prove he was a liar.

This was the lowest of the low. How could anyone separate a mother and their child, especially the father? It was evil and more, and the system had allowed this.

The judge on the paperwork was female. I wondered if she had children, if she had given any thought to what this would do not only to me but both of my children. The impact of Moran being handed this power was detrimental to us all.

The judge had taken his application, full of lies and the limited information about my violent assault, and decided that I deserved to also have my child removed into the hands of her father, who would use this perceived power over me to berate, ridicule, embarrass and be so unbelievably cruel. This decision was made in an emergency hearing and without any representation for me present.

This practice is barbaric. This is probably the worst thing that can ever happen to a good mother other than losing a child to death. I felt broken.

It also made zero sense. They were not suggesting removing both children. The courts would not be looking at Cameron and neither did Wayne question my ability as a mother. He knew my children had amazing lives and he certainly would not hurt his own child by hurting his mother. How had the courts decided this was the right thing to do, especially given the circumstances? My mothering of Cameron was never in question. Now the judge had split up the siblings, as the order was just about Sofia. Had she even considered this? Clearly not.

Moran was an opportunist, and he seized this moment when I was weak to deliver the evillest act against a parent.

I have often said that I would rather have been attacked again than feel the pain of having my four-year-old daughter taken from me for no other reason than I was a victim of someone else's violence.

How could anyone justify this decision? How could the court act without facts? How could they allow a convicted criminal to apply into court for residency of a child without any background checks whatsoever?

I was sick to my stomach. Disbelief echoed through my head. All sorts of thoughts were running through my mind. I knew how ruthless family court is. I thought, this is it. He will destroy us all and he will do it with a smile on his face and with the law on his side, all because I was attacked by Smith as the court will hold me responsible for Smith's violence.

The cruel brutality of this was inhumane. I was so scared of what Moran was saying to Sofia. Given half a chance I knew he would just erase me from her life. Moran's own father had done this to him as a child and removed the four children away from their mother for a period while they were school age. I knew he was capable of this, as this was his 'normal'. Maybe Moran was damaged by this. He had turned into an extremely selfish man, with no shame or conscience and would not think twice about the hurt he would cause as this was his revenge. He felt entitled to it.

I wrote a statement to the judge outlining all my concerns. That Moran grew up in a dysfunctional home. He would not think twice about erasing me and I asked the judge to consider the timing of this. This was not the act of a loving father but the act of a man looking for revenge and the opportunity presented itself in the form of Smith's attack.

In my hospital bed, unable to sleep for the fear and worry of losing my daughter, I was typing and typing. The nurse came in. "Zoe, you should really be resting. I understand this is important, but you need rest."

I remember crying, getting angry and asking the nurses what they thought. I was utterly mortified I was in this situation. My life was slowly being destroyed by two men: Moran and Smith.

My auntie posted the statement I had written to the court. It took me a couple of days to write it, but at least once it was sent, I could concentrate on my recovery. I was still struggling with my memory. My long-term and instant memory was intact but my short-term memory was damaged.

This was scary. I needed my memory.

My arms were still bandaged tightly. My right hand was free, but the left hand was completely covered, and it was wrapped like a claw. After several days, the consultant wanted to take off the bandage on my left hand to have a look at how it was healing. I never gave it a thought; I just thought my hand would work.

"Zoe, we are just going to have a look how you are healing under here. It was a tricky operation as the tendons on the back of your hand were completely severed, so we had to stitch them back together. It is possible you will not be able to use this hand again." The consultant said this in a matter-of-fact sort of way.

I was horrified.

"Pardon me, I will not be able to use my hand? But I need my hand." I started to cry. He took the bandage off and I tried to move my hand, but nothing. No matter how hard I tried to create a fist, my hand would not respond. It was so strange, sickening.

"I NEED my hand! I need to type." The consultant gave me some exercises to do daily and left the room. I sat there looking at my stupid hand.

WORK! I was looking at my hand. *Work, you stupid hand.* I squeezed and squeezed. I could not accept this. I thought the bandages had restricted the movement, but it was actually my hand; it no longer had any power. I worked on my hand every day, determined that I was not going to allow this to be the case. I could not have permanent damage.

While I was recovering my auntie and uncle had gone to my house to clean up. They were met with the sight of my once immaculate bedroom now completely covered in blood. It was everywhere: on the bedding, splattered up the walls, on all my clothes, in my shoes, in the bath where Smith attempted to clean his weapons, in the toilet downstairs, smeared down the walls where I had managed to get downstairs, and on the bannisters. They had dragged the sodden mattress out of the house and put it in the garage, stored out of my way so I did not see it when I got home. I had no idea everyone was having to sort all of this, while I was in hospital.

It was hard for my friends and family to have to go through this too. Their tough friend, now in hospital being basically ambushed by not just one but two men. It was truly surreal. On one of her visits Jodi told me she had spoken to her cousin who was a Police Community Support Officer (PCSO), which is a kind of police officer. She knew one of Smith's ex-girlfriends who was a police constable. Apparently, she had been in a relationship with Smith, and he was abusive in their relationship and had been to prison for harassment of her.

I was shocked. Was this the Carmen he had told me about? I only found this out while I was in the hospital and was appalled. He had done this before. Smith told me he had a crazy ex-girlfriend. He told me stories about Carmen that I believed. They were not true. All the things he had accused Carmen of, he had done himself. He made up stories about how Carmen would hide in her children's Wendy house in the garden waiting for him. I now know this was him talking about himself and why would she hide in her own garden anyway? It was outrageous. More about Carmen later.

Pay close attention if a man tells you their ex-partner(s) are crazy. This is often leakage and them disclosing what their behaviour was like in their previous relationships.

I'd been in hospital a week. It was the weekend and I decided I needed to look at my face. I had avoided this until now because I could feel the swelling and that was enough.

I went into the bathroom and looked up into the mirror. I was horrified at what was looking back. My face and head were swollen, and I had grazes to my face which looked like carpet print on one side and shoe print on the other. My face was a mixture of red, blue, green and purple. My right eye was yellow and bloodshot. I could not really see as I did not have my contact lenses in, which was probably a good thing.

I called Wayne. I told him my face was not great so he would need to prepare Cameron. I asked him to bring him to the hospital that evening at visiting time. Wayne, Dawn (Wayne's wife) and Cameron arrived that evening. Cameron hid behind his dad when he saw me. He looked so scared at seeing my face. I felt terrible. "Oh darling, Mummy is ok." I was so happy Wayne had brought Cameron to see me though. Thankfully he had no idea what had happened, and I did not want him to know. The full horror would clearly come out later but for now all he knew was Mummy fell down the stairs. I just hugged him. "When can we go home, Mummy?" Broken, I replied, "Soon my darling."

After they left a rage inside me took over. *What fucking animal does this and who deals with all the shit I'm going through right now?!* My heart was broken, my babies separated and clueless. My superpower, my strength in the face of adversity, was underneath itching to get out. I was not going down without a fight.

I vowed I was going to fight tooth and nail to get my family back together. I could not stop thinking about Sofia after the visit with Cameron. I wondered what she was doing.

The court hearing date rolled around. I had been in hospital for two weeks, so I told them I was going to attend. The hospital advised me not to leave as I was still not well, but I needed my family back together. I got dressed and left hospital to attend court.

I was not ready for what was going to happen next.

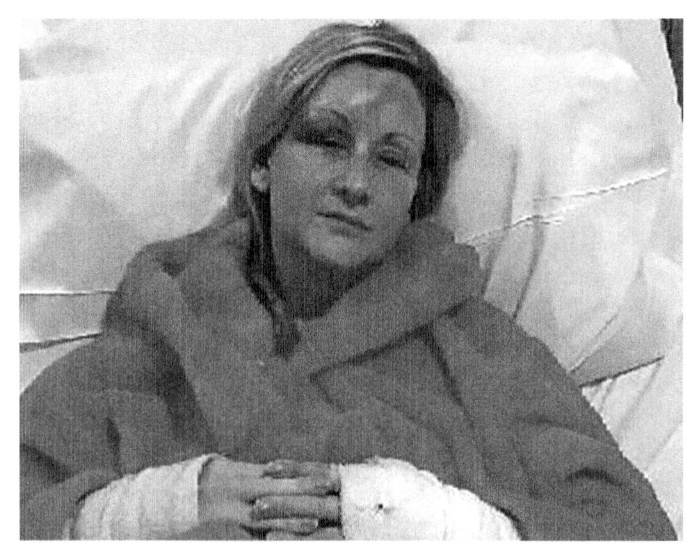

Zoe in hospital, still recovering before having to discharge herself to represent herself in family court

RED FLAGS & REFLECTION

In society we often make the victim feel like the abuse they received was avoidable. This perpetuates self-blame. This self-blame can lead to Post Traumatic Stress Disorder (PTSD) and victims can often have chronic feelings of anxiety, guilt and shame.

I was battered within an inch of my life. I was weak physically and I was emotionally very vulnerable after the attack. I kept going over and over what happened that night to try and make sense of it, to try and understand why Smith would try to kill me, why he would destroy his own life, never mind my own, by acting this way. Did he really want to die and want me dead too?

None of it made sense but of course it wouldn't, would it. I'm not a psychopath so I can't think like a psychopath.

I knew I had to keep my mind strong. Trying to understand your abuser's behaviour will get you nowhere; you will end up in a cycle of self-blame and trying to rewrite what happened in your head. It will send you mad, so don't do it!

Abusers will get into your head even when they are not physically present. This is all part of the grooming process. The love-bombing and overt affection is to create an emotional bond. This is what you need to undo and you may want help in doing this.

If you have had an abusive partner, do you find yourself wondering about them? Trying to work out why they did what they did?

CHAPTER 14:

All Rise Kangaroo Court

Sometimes you must reach your lowest level to muster the strength to fight, as the only way has to be up from that point. I had gone through the most horrific ordeal in terms of violence but in my eyes the worst was yet to come.

Family court in the UK is not a place for women who are victims of domestic abuse. There is a culture of victim blaming and often mothers are blamed for being victims of the abuse they receive and are blamed for their abuser's behaviour.

There are many examples of mothers losing their children to their abuser, as victims of domestic abuse often don't present well in court. This can be for several reasons: maybe they don't have the financial means for representation, or maybe they are so traumatised by the abuse they have received that they look broken in the court and of course this process is also retraumatising. All of this perpetuates the narrative that victims of abuse are not good parents. However, it's the abuse that put them there, so wouldn't it be better to support these mothers?

I discharged myself from hospital to go directly to the family court hearing, my face still bruised, and wearing clothes that were not appropriate for court. They had been brought to me at the hospital by a family member.

I should be in a suit, I'm thinking, looking down at my dreadful outfit.

I was in a fluffy jumper and trousers. I knew this was not a good look, however I tried to remain positive. *The judge will have read my statement I sent into the court, and she will remove that stupid order.*

I shuddered as I arrived at the court building. One of my other aunties was with me. She was in her seventies and had made the trip from London to Coventry to support me, so I did not go alone. It was raining. We walked up to the large glass-fronted building, cold and soulless. As we walked in you could hear the odd shout echoing through the high ceilings but other than that, silence. It felt like the building held a lot of misery, pain and sorrow.

Looking around at others hanging around, clearly waiting for their own court hearings, no-one looked happy. You could feel the tension. I walked up to the front desk.

"I'm here for a hearing, what do I need to do?" The lady explained I needed to go through security. I walk through the metal detector, like the ones at the airport when you go on holiday, however this was not that feeling. Far from it. I had a sick feeling in my stomach and an empty ache. I had not seen Sofia or heard her voice for over two weeks. I missed her terribly.

I kept thinking, *I shouldn't be here.* In a court. I am the victim, yet I felt like I was being punished.

Smith was in prison; it made no sense. I could understand if he was out, and I had gone back into a relationship with him, but that was never going happen. Moran knew this too because that's why our relationship ended.

He was punishing me for that.

But how had Moran, a convicted criminal, who had been convicted of various crimes and been in prison for an accumulation of driving offences and one conviction of GBH Section 18, managed to convince a court to listen to his lies? The lies he submitted on a court form that he had handwritten and had scribbles and crossings out on it. Just statements like: Zoe drinks too much. Zoe drinks three bottles of wine. The whole application was an attack at me. None of it read like a concerned father. He never even talked about Sofia in the application or raised any concerns about her wellbeing or health, so it was clear to anyone with a trained eye that this was an application of punishment.

The guard directed us upstairs to a waiting area. "You need to wait up there until your name is called," he said blankly, pointing in that direction.

My auntie and I waited at the top of the stairs on some wooden benches.

"Are you ok?" Auntie asked. I had gone ashen. I felt distraught. I was still so poorly. I should have still been in a hospital bed, recovering.

"I can't believe this," I said, looking at Auntie and shaking my head. "Hopefully the judge has read my statement." My stomach churned and my heart was in my mouth.

"I know love, he's a bastard. How could anyone do this to you, especially now. It's obvious what he's doing. Why has he chosen to do this now? Because he would never get away with it. Just try and stay positive." I just looked at the floor.

I'm a good mother. I am the sole provider, the breadwinner, the children live in a wonderful loving home, so surely the judge will see sense. I kept reiterating this to myself repeatedly.

I'd written to the judge. She would have checked Moran out and realised he was not the man he was portraying himself to be. *He is a criminal who's using the physical attack against me to take Sofia away. It will be fine.*

At that moment I felt Moran's presence walking up the stairs. He reached the top and smiled. He smiled at me!

"What the fuck are you smiling at?" I mouthed at Moran.

"Oh if you are going to be like that, then that's it", and there it was. The real ugly Moran. The punisher. Because I wasn't begging for his forgiveness or grovelling to him, he wanted revenge.

What did he expect? Did he think I would beg him; did he think I would be friendly? WHAT exactly did he expect my reaction would be?!

He walked away and sat further up the corridor. Urgh, he made me sick. He was dressed in a smart suit, coat, trousers and shoes. Not his usual attire. *Oh yeah he looks the part,* I thought to myself. This was his stage; he was so goddamn smug.

The smiling. The threats. The lack of any empathy. He was not thinking about Sofia. He wanted to win. He was enjoying the power. It was excruciating. I wanted to wipe that smile off his face.

How dare he drag me to court in this situation, having to discharge myself from hospital, for a hearing, for what?!

I'm not a bad parent because I was battered by a maniac. I had written this in my statement to the judge `[If I was hit by a bus and had to cross a road again, would I be told I couldn't be trusted to cross the road again?]`. This was a stupid situation. No-one knowingly puts themselves in a situation where they will be brutally attacked, so how could I be blamed for it? I was being blamed and punished for Smith's attack on me.

Our names were called. My stomach hit the floor.

That animal Smith had not only nearly killed me, but he had given Moran the ability to do this. I felt so vilified, so attacked, so judged. Everyone against me but I had done nothing wrong. I was the victim.

The usher showed us where to stand. I was shaking. I was bruised and sore. I just wanted to go home. We took our places.

"All rise," the usher called out.

It seemed so ridiculous. I wasn't on trial.

I'm not a criminal. I haven't committed a crime. I haven't done anything wrong other than be in a relationship with a man who underneath his Prince Charming façade was a monster. My relationship with Smith was being used against me, as if I was to blame for his actions.

The female judge entered. She was an older, pompous looking woman. She made no attempt to look either of us in the eye. She addressed us both by outlining the case and highlighted that we were both litigants in person. This meant that both Moran and I did not have legal representation. So it was just us, the judge and the court usher in the room. The judge looked positively annoyed by this.

Moran got up to speak and demanded full custody. He told the judge I was a bad mother, I drank every day, three bottles of wine at a time, which I found remarkable given my job was to drive up and down the country. I could not believe the bullshit that was coming out of his mouth and the judge was just listening to it.

I felt so weak. I was listening to lie after lie coming out of Moran's mouth. It was unbelievable. All the things he described were his behaviours. Imagine how this feels, just standing there being branded all of this by the man who has treated you so badly. It was disgusting. I knew Moran had some criminal convictions that could prove he lied too. He had told me previously he had been convicted of drink driving but here he was telling the judge he did not drink and was teetotal. It was astounding, the bullshit he was coming out with.

I was so ill, and this process was making me worse. I just stood there, flabbergasted that the judge was even allowing this. I hoped she would have done checks on Moran and on the information I had written to her.

The judge looked at me. "And Mother?"

"None of that is true. Yes, I have been attacked but I am a good mother to both of my children." I had no idea how to conduct myself. I was so not prepared for this. I just thought that they would check and realise with Moran's criminal history that this was just him trying his luck. It was crazy; I was being blamed for something I could not control.

The court did not check any of the information. I have since found out that family courts do not carry out background checks on an applicant's criminal history on applying to the court, so pretty much any Tom, Dick or Harry criminal can put an application into court and be granted a hearing. How can that even be right? They may request them further down the line however it was too late in this instance. What if Moran had been a child predator; he would have sole custody of a child. That is not right.

The judge was visibly annoyed by the whole thing. She took one look at me, looking down the bridge of her nose at me, bruised and standing there in my fluffy jumper.

She turned to Moran. "Daughter stays with Father. Mother can have access overnight on a Tuesday to be collected from school and dropped into school the next day and Saturday day for four hours."

My world just ended.

I could not breathe. My throat closed. My eyes welled up.

Why is she punishing me?!

What about Sofia; she has not seen or spoken to her mummy for weeks?

Flashbacks of losing my mum went through my mind. Crushing emptiness. A feeling of a total loss of control.

The judge made an assumption! She clearly never read my statement or checked Moran's background. She had taken his lies and perjury to the court as the truth. Sofia was my daughter too and I had done NOTHING wrong.

"No!" I shouted out. "She'll be missing me, that's not long enough." The judge got up and walked out. She completely ignored my plea.

This was an absolutely violation of my human rights.

Moran had Sofia half the week already before all of this. Why was that not enough? Why did he want more power?

He wanted full power and control. He wanted to erase me.

He wanted to put the final nail in the coffin and rip my daughter away in the cruellest way.

What kind of person can do this?

That was it.

My daughter had been thrown to the wolf and he did it all to punish me. No care for Sofia or Cameron or anyone else. I could not even fathom why the court made that decision.

Cameron was allowed home. If I was a bad mother, why was my son allowed home? I found out afterwards that Moran had contacted Wayne to try and get him to side with him in the case. Wayne said no and asked him not to do this to me while I was still recovering.

Wayne is a decent man and that would be the response of any normal human. Why choose to kick someone when they are down? Because he knew that was his only opportunity.

I had no idea how I was going to break this to Cameron. He was eight years old at the time and he worshipped his sister. They were so close.

I was destroyed. I could feel Moran smirking, gloating that he had won. Was this the act of a loving parent? No.

He got what he wanted. He tapped his papers and walked out.

I waited for the door to close behind him before I got ready to leave.

How was I supposed to accept that decision? The courts had made a huge mistake and if this could happen to me, it could happen to anyone.

I walked out to Auntie. I shook my head and just cried in her arms.

I was in a complete daze. I could barely stand up. I couldn't see, I couldn't breathe. Utter disbelief at what just happened. We got a taxi back to my other auntie's house and I just sat on the sofa staring into space.

As the news sank in, I got slowly more and more angry with the injustice of it all. How could a convicted criminal walk into a court and get custody of a child without any checks? Yet he couldn't get a job in a school or hospital, but he walked away with a piece of paper, a court order saying he had all the rights! After standing there and lying through his teeth. I knew only too well this was an injustice; my whole career had been working in child protection and criminal screening.

The courts had failed. I wanted this known. I needed to highlight what was going on there. I was utterly horrified.

All through my life whenever I was at a low point or something bad was happening, I would think of Mum. She gave me my superpower, my survival instinct.

At this time, I felt so disconnected from the entire world. Having a child taken from you when they are alive is like grieving but the child is still alive; this is worse than death. And to top it off the person taking her away was her own father.

As I had discharged myself from hospital, I had several follow-on hospital visits booked in with various departments. One of them was a psychological meeting with the IAPT (Improving Access to Psychological Therapy) team.

They wanted to check my mental health. They did an initial screening call, following me completing a questionnaire assessment. All I kept writing was "I just need to get my daughter back". Do you have any suicidal thoughts? No, I want my daughter back.

Do you struggle to sleep? Yes, because I need my daughter home.

We went through the sheet on the phone and after telling them the entire story about Smith attacking me and now the father of my daughter, Moran, using this attack to remove my child from me through family court, they immediately discharged me.

"Sounds like you need to get through all of this legal stuff Zoe, then maybe you can refer yourself after everything has calmed down."

I did not need treatment; I needed a good solicitor! The way I felt was situational. Had none of this happened to me, I would be fine. I was down due to the attack; I was broken because my daughter was being taken from me when I needed my family most.

I was getting angry, which was a good sign. I channelled this anger and got laser focused on getting my daughter back. The injustice was incomprehensible to me.

Wayne brought Cameron straight home as soon as I got back; it was amazing just to give him a cuddle. He walked into the house, his big brown innocent eyes looking up at me.

"Are you ok Mummy?"

I hugged him. "I'm fine matey, you know me. I'm tough, naughty silly stairs." He did not need to know the truth. Not yet.

I was broken inside, however on the outside I had to keep a strong stance for the sake of Cameron. It was hard but I did not want him to worry. I told Cameron that Sofia was staying with her daddy until Mummy got better. It was heartbreaking as he missed her so much. He had not seen his sister for weeks either and this would be his life if Moran got his way permanently.

The following day we were able to pick Sofia up from school. I arrived early and went and spoke with the headteacher first. I explained what was happening and how I was now in court fighting for Sofia.

When I collected Sofia, her little face was so angelic. She had grown.

"Hello darling." She looked at me with sadness in her eyes. She looked confused. Where had her mummy been all this time?

I got her in the car. "Darling, Mummy had an accident on the stairs, so I had to go into hospital but I'm ok now."

"No!" Sofia snapped back. She seemed so confused. It took her a while to settle, and I worried that Moran was filling her mind with rubbish.

"Are you having a nice time with Daddy?"

"Daddy says I have got a new mummy now."

I was floored. I was not expecting that comment. What was he playing at, telling her that?

I was outraged.

"I am your mummy sweetheart; your daddy is being silly." I was furious underneath. What the hell did he think he was doing messing with her little head.

I tried not to focus on the separation to Sofia; instead whenever Cameron and I had her for contact we made sure we had the best time. The three of us. We went to Cadbury World, Legoland, out for food; I bought toys and we had so much fun. They were precious times.

The family court had a lot to answer for. Yes, Moran was the bastard who put the application in, however how on earth was this allowed? Such a flawed system. The word 'family' should be removed for a start as it totally smashes families apart. It antagonises an already tempestuous situation.

There is nothing in that process that supports families who are in conflict; there is nothing remotely 'family' about it. It is an adversarial system that pitches one side against the other. Which is wrong. Families who find themselves in the system invariably need support, not more conflict. It is counterproductive. It is no place for a family that already has animosity. All the system does is perpetuate the problem.

What continued from that day forward would never have happened without the court granting Moran that court order! He then had a false sense of power and control. He would consistently threaten me with court whenever he wanted anything at all, even silly things. It was exhausting.

"You'd better be on time Zoe, or you'll go back to court." I was never late collecting my daughter, but he would say these things to wind me up, to get a reaction. "If you are late dropping her off, I'll tell the court!" He was like a relentless petulant child. The fictitious power given to him by the court allowed him to act like the school bully. Any opportunity to kick more mud in my face with a smirk on his, he would.

Moran used the court as a threat and weaponised Sofia. Good father?

This was a living nightmare, with my children at the centre of the destruction being emotionally ruined in the process. It was excruciating to watch, with one hand tied behind my back. Moran would taunt me often. "Well that proves you're a shit mum." "Why do you think the courts gave her to me?" This should never ever have been allowed to take place.

I needed to get focused and start building my case. It's no longer innocent until proven guilty, like it is in criminal court. No. It's guilty until proven innocent and even then, you are still tarred with a guilt brush.

It was like being in Elizabethan times when they test to see if you are a witch. Women were tied to a ducking stool and dunked under the water in a pond or a river. If the woman floated, she was a witch. If she did not, she was innocent. However, that did not really help the innocent, did it? They were drowned anyway.

This is how it felt in family court as a victim of domestic violence. It's a no-win situation. You are to blame.

Between the times having Sofia and when Cameron was at school, I was doing as much research as possible. I spoke with a law firm who arranged a meeting. I asked my uncle Roger to go with me. He did not want to come in with me, so he waited in the car.

I walked into the solicitor's building. There was a young lady sat typing away at a front reception desk. She did not look up immediately, although she must have sensed I was there.

Too important, I think to myself, rolling my eyes. I sigh.

"Yes?" said the receptionist, not even looking up from her computer. "Hi, I am Zoe Dronfield. I have an appointment, I called yesterday about urgent legal support needed to get my daughter back from her father who is threatening me. He is saying I will never see her again. I was the victim of an attack that is being used against me."

"Oh yes, take a seat." I looked around. Considering this was meant to be a family solicitor's office it felt far from family orientated. I had not been in many so did not really have a preconceived idea, but I felt like I had no connection with this place at all. The grey walls and dull carpet. No colour or life in the place. Then a lady came out and asked me to follow her to the office. She was one of the solicitors of the firm.

We both sat down at a small round table and I gave an explanation of what was happening. "Sounds awful," she said coldly. There was little emotion coming from her, in fact her tone was rather flat and uninterested. I felt judged and humiliated.

"So we need to find you a good barrister," she said, and I nodded. I had no idea; I was being guided by her. She did not seem very caring, rather very matter-of-fact in the way she was talking. Could she not see the emotional turmoil I was in?

In the UK the solicitor is the person who prepares the court files and gets the case files ready to be produced in court. A barrister is legally trained to defend a case in court so they do the speaking in the court rooms. The solicitor tends not to talk but does all the paperwork outside of court.

"So, I need a solicitor and a barrister?" I looked at her, trying to understand.

"Yes, you need a good barrister too for a case like this." A case like this? What does she mean?

She started pulling laminated A4 sheets out on the table with photos and bios of barristers in their full court attire. Court wigs and gowns. She lined them up on the desk for me to make a choice.

I'm so confused.

"So we have this one, they are £500 a day, this one she's good she is £1000 a day or we have this one £2000 a day, very very good." She looked up at me.

"Pardon me. Are you being serious?!" I just glared at her.

"Oh, and they are the costs for the barrister, our fees are here." She pulled out another piece of paper with a list of charges from £10 a phone call to £50 a letter. I was dizzy.

Is this some kind of joke?

What the fuck is going on? I look at the photos. I'm meant to decide whether to use the expensive shit barrister at £500 a day, to an extortionately expensive barrister who is 'very very good' but wait for it ... she added:

"However, we cannot guarantee the result you want. So you may not get your daughter back." She looked at me, her head tilted to the side, offering some sort of false empathy.

I felt sick and now I was frightened. What the hell was happening to my life?

"I'm a good mother, with a good job, money in the bank and a couple of properties, how can this even be possible? I've never even been in trouble with the police, yet I'm here building a case to defend myself. I don't understand why I'm even in this situation. I was attacked. I am the victim," I snapped back at her, and she did not even flinch. I was sickened by the process. It was cold and heartless.

"So, I can be bankrupt with or without my daughter!" I raised my voice.

She just looked at me with the most patronising face. I was so angry.

I am a professional woman and never in my life had I felt so humiliated and judged through no fault of my own. I was furious. The power that one person has in family court is truly staggering and unjust, especially given the impact. Did the judge have any understanding of the trauma and abuse she had caused by handing Moran this court order? He was literally legally abusing all of us: me, Sofia, Cameron, my dad, Wayne, all of us. The dynamic had changed, and he was the puppetmaster. I was wrong. I got up and left.

I went home and started researching as much as I could about family law. The rights I have, the laws I can use, what other parents have been through. I found the Women's Aid forum and sat for hours and hours reading every single post about family court, what's involved, the thousands of women in my position who had lost their children to an abusive father.

I was in shock. I was sure I was going to lose her. Everything I was reading was so biased against mothers who were victims of domestic abuse.

There were reams of women who had posted. Topics included Life after abuse, Getting out, Family court being used as a legal weapon, Rollercoaster, I'm getting out, I have not seen my daughter for 3 years, My children won't talk to me, I'm having a bad day, When will this end... The list went on and on and on. All women experiencing domestic abuse and if they were mothers most were being dragged through family court.

Until this time I had some basic knowledge and understanding of domestic abuse; my stepmother had experienced it, some celebrities had come out in the media as having been through it, I had experience supporting families when I ran my company, and there was even a music video I would often play as I liked the song called 'Time' by Chase and Status that depicted domestic abuse. I used to play that with Smith all the time and I'd even tell him how the video made me so mad.

Even Moran told me a story about how his stepmother committed suicide and his dad had threatened to hang his mum at the end of the garden, however I never really knew or understood the true trauma and insidious behaviour of domestic abuse.

You think it happens to other people. That it would never happen to you. You would not put up with it. However, the truth of it is, you do not know you are even in it until it's too late. Leaving an abuser is the most dangerous time and post-separation abuse is rife, especially in family court. Perpetrators of abuse up the ante; they do not like losing control and everything is about their ego so their manipulation will escalate to any means available to them, including the courts.

I just kept reading everything I could find about domestic abuse and family law and I could resonate with many of the women's experiences. It was like abusers all have this blueprint. The pattern of abusive behaviour is always very similar and so is the response to these women too. Like myself they had been let down, disbelieved, or had their abuse minimised. They had been blamed and shamed for the abuse THEY suffered. There is a stigma attached to women who have been abused; they must have deserved it or at least done something to cause it.

I was in a state of shock, disbelief, and realisation for days. I would get up, take Cameron to school and just sit in the corner of my sofa in the kitchen with the laptop open. I would be there for hours on end, reading, researching. I bought book after book and trawled the internet. I provide a list of the books I read and some other good books I've read since in the resources section at the end of the book.

The fact that I was not alone was the biggest validation for me and there was some comfort in realising this was happening to others, because it gave me hope that maybe this could be changed. All these women could not be liars. This was a collective of the truth.

It helped as otherwise I would have questioned myself, 'Maybe if I had acted in different way, then the abuse would not have happened'. This was not true. Both Smith and Moran were abusive in different ways. This was to do with them, not me.

Since my ordeal, whenever I speak with a victim of domestic abuse my first piece of advice is to not even try to fathom why the abuser is this way or question your own behaviour. You are not responsible and it will send you literally insane thinking this way. The reason you cannot understand them is because you are a healthy, normal, non-abusive person and if you had changed your behaviour, the abuse would likely be worse. Abusers want to condition their victim. This is why leaving can be so dangerous.

As a victim it's important you understand that you are not to blame for the abuse, nor should you feel ashamed. The shame lies solely with the abuser.

RED FLAGS & REFLECTION

Appearances and education are so important, particularly in family court. It is a place where you are looked at, judged on information that is often not even fact checked, so you at least need to present well. It's a pantomime. I walked into that court room expecting the court to have done their due diligence and for the judge to have read my statement and realised that Moran was a criminal opportunist. That did not happen.

The judge will not look at anything unless it's in the legal bundle. That was my first mistake. There was me thinking that this process was set up to ensure abusers cannot abuse and good parents keep their children. It's often quite the opposite. I found the family court process to be harsh and lacking in empathy.

You really need to be on your A game when going through family court proceedings. Things you have done or said can be presented to the court to paint you in a bad light, so be ready with answers. I made a few slip-ups and sent Moran a couple of emails swearing and telling him to basically fuck off and leave me alone. He presented these in court. In hindsight, it was a reactive thing to do, and I played into his games. He had also done the same but in hindsight we just looked like argumentative children. It's much better to use the Grey Rock Method.

The 'Grey Rock Method' is often advised by psychologists when co-parenting with a narcissist, or someone with no empathy. Keep any communication to a minimum; keep it brief and factual. Do not get baited into an argument. The theory is the narcissist will get bored and move on, with a bit of luck. Just try and remove any emotion as this is what they feed off; they want reaction.

Moran tried his very best to upset me in any way he could, and it was so hard not to react, especially knowing that Moran spent the time he had with Sofia trying to brainwash her into thinking she had a new mummy. He also knew that by getting her residency switched this changed the status quo; it was perceived by the court as Sofia's normal. It was not. I was the main carer. I clothed her, fed her, paid for everything. Moran dipped in and out when he felt like it or when it suited him.

I had to stay very strong through this process. It could have very nearly killed me. I couldn't sleep. Couldn't eat. It was so worrying. I was worried sick about Sofia and Cameron as well, as he was really suffering. Also, no good parent wants to be branded a bad one, so that was literally soul destroying. It was truly horrific. However, I could not reveal this to Moran or the court. You have to become an emotionless robot.

Do you think there is enough information provided to you by the judiciary about the process when/if you find yourself in the court process?

CHAPTER 15:

Victim Blaming, Education and Self-Care

Backed into a corner, I knew the only way out was to get myself organised and educated, and start building my own case for family court. Knowledge is power. If Moran was the great dad he was trying to portray, then he needed to answer some questions as to why he had chosen this time to go after Sofia.

Why had he never built a case before?

I had never done anything wrong to him, or to my children, quite the opposite, so this hatred he had towards me was purely because I had ended our relationship. It was revenge for his loss of power. So, he was now using Sofia to exert this over me again. If the courts had bothered to ask certain questions, they would have seen for their own eyes Moran was an opportunist, and this was because Moran was an abuser himself.

Abuse comes in all forms, and you may not even recognise certain behaviours as abuse. We can become blind to bad behaviour because it is normalised, or we have become desensitised to it over time.

Moran had chipped away at my self-esteem. When you think of domestic abuse, you think of the battered women with the bloodied face, like the attack I received from Smith. That is something you cannot argue with; it is there in front of your eyes. However often domestic abuse is hidden and it's this abuse that often creates more lasting emotional damage. Before I met Moran, I was happy-go-lucky, a strong businesswoman, however he gradually wore me down. I lost my business and almost my home and now he was trying to take my daughter. He wanted to destroy me.

His abuse led me directly into the arms of further abuse. I was an open book for Smith, an easy target, and when Dad became ill, that was Smith's 'in'. The emotional abuse I endured from Moran had broken down my sense of self, so I welcomed flattery, any flattery. Smith knew this because I told him on the very first date. This made me vulnerable.

If someone systematically crosses your boundaries when you ask them not to, they are being abusive. It's that simple. We all have the right to say no and expect to be treated in a certain way. If someone is not meeting your needs, then you need to question why.

Domestic abuse is complex, and abusers don't turn up with three heads and start knocking you about on day one. The relationship will start out great, more than great. They will make you feel like the most important person in the world – this is the love-bombing stage, the idealisation. You will be sucked in by this, especially if your head is filled with bloody fairytales like mine was, and I had previously been consistently put down by Moran. I walked headlong into another abusive relationship and furnished him with all the tools he needed to manipulate me.

The next phase, once they have you sucked in, is where tension builds or you get discarded. This is to create uncertainty and catches you off guard. Gradually your perfect world will start to unravel, however by then you are invested in the relationship. You don't immediately jump ship the second the sea gets rough; you think you can change the abuser, or you try to change yourself to please them or for the abuse to stop.

Domestic abuse is a drip, drip, drip effect. It does not happen all at once so when you finally realise you are in a relationship that is abusive it can be extremely difficult to break free. The abuser has created it this way. Professionals need to understand this dynamic. Social workers would often make remarks to me when I ran my business about women living with abusers like "Why doesn't she just leave?" or "It's her own fault, she keeps going back". This is an uneducated and ignorant response. It's not that simple.

I often use the analogy of the frog. If you drop a frog in boiling water, it will jump out immediately, however if you put the frog in cold water and slowly turn up the heat the frog will boil to death.

This is like domestic abuse. It's a pattern which escalates over time, so you are often not conscious the abuse is happening. Hence why some victims do not even realise they are being abused until they come away from the relationship and look back. This is also why time and distance are key to keeping a victim safe. The victim needs to recognise the abuse and she will only do this with the space and time to do so.

I continued to research domestic abuse and the effects it has on families and how it is used in the family court arena. I found that most victims of domestic abuse were women, and those who are mothers often have their children removed because of this fact. I found this remarkable and barbaric. I also found that children were being removed and put into the care system at an alarming rate after the Baby Peter Connolly case that I mentioned in chapter 6. There was definitely a culture shift and you can see this in the care proceedings data.

Baby Peter Connolly died in the care of his mother, her boyfriend, and their lodger. He was extremely badly abused, and the injuries he received were the cause of his death. This created a huge focus on child abuse and social workers were removing children with much more haste than before. Of course, this is the right thing to do if there are safeguarding issues, however from what

I was reading this was happening for very questionable reasons and good families were being ripped apart rather than supported, because of their misunderstanding of domestic abuse and fear that there would be another Baby Peter Connolly case. Something had shifted. They were using the term 'failure to protect' by the mother. So, if a mother was a victim of domestic abuse, she was now also held responsible for that abuse.

There are videos online posted by frantic parents having their child/ren forcibly removed by social workers and police. Social workers were turning up supported by uniformed police to rip children from the arms of their families. This would often be late at night, probably to catch the family off guard, and they would take the children into care. Imagine the trauma that child goes through. The children screaming, crying, being prised from their family. The social worker forcibly uncurling the child's fingers clutching at their mother. I know many families who have been through this ordeal and, even worse, mothers who have had their children removed from them through force, only to then be placed with their abuser. How can anyone in their right mind think this is remotely ok or humane? The trauma for that child being made to live with an abuser is lifelong and as a parent you have to sit and watch from the sidelines while your child is legally abused. It's abhorrent.

There was one case when I had my childcare business where a mother had all three children removed and put into care because she was a victim of domestic abuse. I challenged the social worker on this, and her attitude was "Well why doesn't she leave him?" At the time, I did not know what I know now and that sounded like a very simple solution. However, the reality is trying to end a relationship with an abuser is extremely difficult and given the response from professionals, from the police to social care, if you blame the victim then what chance does anyone have? Why is the focus not on the abuser?

When I was running my business my carers supported children on the protection register and supervised family contact visits for those going through court proceedings. I sat with many families and my heart bled for them. There was little or no understanding about domestic abuse from social workers. There was also limited training around domestic abuse and it rarely included real life case studies. I was appalled by some of the decisions being made by social workers. It was as if common sense had completely gone out of the window because some of the decisions being made by professionals did not even make sense.

Outdated laws have affected professional practice and have driven a culture of victim blaming and there is a presumption that a child should have contact with both parents at 'any cost'. Something that I challenge, strongly. On one hand a mother would be vilified for not leaving an abuser. If something occurred the mother would be charged with a 'failure to protect' for staying in the relationship, however if she did manage to get away then she would be made to facilitate the contact between the abuser and the child. Common sense, anyone? This is so dangerous and another campaign I have worked on is to stop this culture of contact 'at any cost'. Surely an abuser should lose parental rights?

There were so many double standards. For example, the mother who had her children removed because she smelt of alcohol on one contact, however the father was a full-blown alcoholic and had custody of his kids but that was ok. Why? Why was the mum different? This difference in standards between one end of the city to the other was stark. My business ran across Coventry and Warwickshire. Often it was down to the social worker's judgement on the case, never mind the social worker had only just stepped out of university, had no children of their own and limited life experience.

I was consuming so much information at this time, reading everything I could get my hands on and piecing it all together, that it became very clear to me the system was completely and utterly flawed, social care, family court, police, victim support, the justice system. None of these services were joined up. Not one of them put the victim at the centre, only when they were blaming them. It was not victim-centric at all.

There are fundamental things wrong with how the family court system operates. As I've already mentioned, the accuracy of claims is not checked in the family court. Applications are accepted based on hearsay, and the judge will then decide and make an order based on a balance of probability. A dangerous decision-making process given facts are not checked or verified. It kind of makes a mockery of the law, in my opinion.

I also found there was little recourse for families unless you spent hundreds of thousands of pounds on the appeals process or attempted a judicial review. A judicial review is a type of court hearing that reviews the lawfulness of a decision or action by a public body.

I tried both the appeal and judicial review.

I wrote to the court demanding that they look at the judgement that the judge had made, and the court wrote back to me saying that I could appeal or if I had a complaint about the judge's conduct then I could write to the court. But get this, if I did send in a complaint my complaint would go to the judge I was complaining about.

Do you think that judge would hold up their hands and say "Sorry, I got it wrong"? Of course not. That's like asking a child to mark their own homework.

So, with the system set up the way it is, the most vulnerable people suffer and more often than not it is the victim of abuse who is vilified by the courts under the guise of 'failure to protect'.

This is the term used when usually a mother who is victim of abuse 'allows' domestic abuse to take place in the home. No-one ever asks why the abuser abuses. I found an amazing book written by Lundy Bancroft called *Why Does He Do That?* which was my saving grace going through family court with an abuser. It is falling apart now; the pages are folded, there are sticky notes marking pages and I have underlined and highlighted throughout the entire book.

That book validated the extreme situation I was in, and my feeling that this process I was in was unjust and incorrect.

However, I consider myself to be very lucky. I have amazing friends. So, although I was going through the worst ordeal of my life, they all rallied around as much as possible. One of my close friends, Maxine, put me in touch with a close family friend who is a solicitor and she introduced me to another solicitor who spent years in criminal law and was now a partner in family solicitors, Mr Hawley from Brindley Twist Tafft & James in Coventry. He was appalled when he heard what had happened and arranged to meet me the very next day. "No time to waste, Zoe, can you come to the office tomorrow with all the paperwork?" I was so amazed at his urgency.

Walking through the double glass doors into the reception area, it was fresh and there was a friendly receptionist who smiled at me as I walked through the door. "You must be Zoe," she said and I felt at ease immediately. I looked around and there were magazines for adults, some children's books and in the corner some toys. *This feels right*, I thought as I sat down to wait.

Within a minute Mr Hawley walked out to greet me and shook my hand. "Zoe, right, let's get started." He walked with authority and with an air of urgency he directed us to a quiet room. I told him about what had happened, being attacked by Smith and being served court papers in my hospital bed by Moran.

I also explained that I had been to another firm and left in tears as it was all about the money with no guarantee of a positive outcome. This was not about money but clearly I had to consider this. I could not end up broke, as how would I provide for my children then? I just wanted my daughter home where she belonged with her brother. It was heartbreaking to think about all the stages of her development I was missing.

While we were sitting at the big boardroom desk, Mr Hawley's PA popped her head around the door and asked if we wanted coffees. Mr Hawley was reading through the papers and making the odd voice note on his dictaphone. We sat quietly for a few minutes while he read. I drank my coffee. I was shaking. I had become used to this feeling which I can only describe as being cold, when you are shivering. I think it must have been a trauma response, a trigger. I was holding it together on the outside but on the inside, I was triggered. I was hyper-alert and it was as if I could feel the blood running through my veins.

My Hawley took a deep breath and let out a huge sigh as he looked up from his papers. My heart was pounding out of my chest.

"He's a bastard, well both are, Zoe. Smith obviously doing that to you but what is this Moran playing at?" Mr Hawley looked at me, horrified and concerned. He was a good man, a father of five children. It turns out Wayne's new wife Dawn had worked with him many years before. What a small world.

"What a bully, Zoe." He looked across the desk at me.

"He wants Sofia all to himself; he had shared care of her with me. There was no need for this. It is purely for revenge because I ended the relationship. He hates me because I stopped putting up with his shit."

"I will help you, Zoe." He seemed to be physically annoyed by the whole thing, shifting in his seat and sighing.

"David, I will pay you the money, I have a house, I have a good job. I need legal representation. I cannot do this alone. My dad is really poorly, and I don't have a mother. Women are losing their children left right and centre being victims of domestic violence. This just cannot happen to me! It will destroy my children's lives. Moran will erase me from Sofia's life. I know what he is like. He has already lied; he is a compulsive liar. He will tell Sofia all sorts to get her to hate me. His own father did this to him as a child. He is one of four, and he has told me how they used to run away from his mother outside school. His dad took them away from their mum as kids. He is trying to do the same to me. It's history repeating itself because it's his normal. It's sick. Cameron will be emotionally scarred his entire life, he is so sensitive. I can't let this happen."

"Don't worry Zoe. We are going to get this bastard," David said. I let out a huge breath of air. Finally I could breathe. I instantly felt at ease. He was on my side and emotionally involved. This was the right solicitor for me!

I knew this was only the start, however by his body language I could tell Mr Hawley was incensed. He was going to help me and that meant the world to me.

"Right, we need to find you the right barrister for this case, a mother, someone who can relate to you and then I want you to meet them. It's called a conference. I want you to meet them face to face and tell them what has happened, exactly what you have told me."

I could have kissed him.

The relief that someone was going to fight with me. David knew exactly how to handle people like Moran; he had seen them his entire career in law. A bully who is an opportunist. Smith, well he's a psycho, but what Moran was doing was premeditated, cruel and not justified at all.

My strength was building. The resilience to keep going. My superpower was rising.

David told me to keep a log of everything Moran said to me from that day on. Any texts, emails, every conversation; if he was being abusive, document it. Document everything. He asked me to find anything I could find on Moran too: criminal convictions, background, anything at the school, anything he had done in the past that we could use to show the courts the truth and what his real character was. Then he said to get character statements from everyone I know, my friends, colleagues, doctors, schools, everyone! This was going to prove who I was as a person. I literally asked everyone I knew to write me a statement. I am so grateful to every single person who did this for me too. They will never understand the importance and the impact this had. I had to prove Moran was a liar.

I was building my case. Moran had no idea and I was not about to tell him either. I did not want him to know that I was now instructing a legal team. It felt good to finally have someone on my side who did not treat me like a victim but stood shoulder to shoulder with me, bolstered my strength and validated my argument.

It's hard for victims of domestic abuse to get access to legal help and I know I was very lucky. I felt guilty for this every day; some women are just too broken to even fight through the system. I was not entitled to legal aid, which is a form of financial support from the government. My case did not meet the threshold as Moran was my 'previous' partner so I could not claim. The rules have changed since my case, as I along with others campaigned to have the burden of proof of domestic abuse reduced so victims could access financial legal support and the timeline was extended so that it included ex-partners. I cannot do anything retrospectively about this for myself, however I am glad to have paved the way for others. You should absolutely seek legal advice if you find yourself in similar circumstances and make sure you speak to as many legal professionals you can, to ensure you work with the right one.

Of course, Moran carried on messing me and Sofia around on contact days, however now I felt that at least I could build a picture to show the judge so him messing me about did not feel so abusive, in fact it gave me more ammunition. I also started to implement the Grey Rock Method when communicating with Moran. If Moran tried to bait me, I would just ignore. I have to say this was hard, especially given the circumstances, and look I'm not perfect. I did have my off days when I sent a text like `[Oh fuck off you idiot]` and Mr Hawley would tell me off. "Zoe, keep it together."

It pissed me off; he would goad me constantly. This was all a power and control game to him. He didn't care about Sofia and how all of this total upheaval was upsetting her life and he made damn sure he was being as disruptive as he could.

He changed her doctor, her dentist, got her hair cut. He went on overdrive trying to present himself as this perfect parent. This is the man who would bring random people back to the house in the early hours when my children were in bed. He was a bloody hypocrite.

Then he did something that any mother would dread.

I heard from his sister he was thinking about moving to Dubai and was going to try and take Sofia with him. I did not think for one minute he would go through with it. I was wrong.

Moran had put an application in to the family court for full residency and not only that, but he also wanted to remove Sofia completely out of the jurisdiction altogether by taking her to live permanently with him in Dubai.

This made me panic. I had heard about children being removed from the jurisdiction so this was something that the court would consider, and my instant thought was *He is going to kidnap her!*

When that letter landed on my doorstep, I rang Mr Hawley in a blind panic. "I've had another court order for her passport now! And he wants her to live in Dubai. He's moving to Dubai, God knows how. He doesn't even have a salaried job, no stable income. His brother-in-law has got him a commission-only job selling real estate. Sofia will never come back from there, Mr Hawley." I was in a blind panic.

So many questions ran through my mind. The courts would not allow this, surely? Would the court allow him to just take Sofia to a foreign country? Do they realise you need money to live there? It's private healthcare, private education. Moran did not even have a regular paying job.

Moran was emailing me schools he was thinking of enrolling Sofia into. I was sickened by his brazen disregard for Sofia's wellbeing. How did he think removing Sofia completely from her mother's life at the age of four years to a completely foreign country with a totally different culture, where he had no support network, was a good idea?

He was serious. This was serious.

"Ok Zoe, where is the passport?" Mr Hawley asked me, rushed.

"In my house," I said, slightly panicked by his tone.

"Get it out of the house, give it to a friend, anyone who can keep it safe and you trust. Do not tell anyone else where it is. He is not getting the passport, Zoe. We will deal with this at the next hearing."

After this I did some research around child abduction. This was harrowing, but I found out that whoever applies for the passport as the parent is the owner of that document. I went abroad every year, so I had applied and paid for Sofia's passport, thank goodness. So the advice on the site was to contact border control at your local airport, explain you are going through court proceedings and under no circumstances should your child be taken out of the country without your prior consent or the court's.

Border control were helpful. They explained that a caveat would be put on her passport and should someone try to go through border control with her passport this would be flagged. They would not be allowed to cross the border unless consent was presented. This put my mind at ease temporarily, but that was not a conversation I thought I would ever be having in my lifetime.

Thank goodness for Mr Hawley. He kept me strong, he kept me sane, and he made me think rationally and gave me solutions. Without that representation I would have fallen apart at this stage. I told him about the caveat. "Well done, Zoe." I was still so vulnerable. I did not realise it at the time but when I look back now, he was my saving grace.

This also highlights how many good parents lose their children as they cannot afford representation. Without Mr Hawley's support I have no idea how I would have dealt with all of these things being fired at me. Due to the threshold for access to legal aid being dramatically reduced there were so many litigants in person in the court and often it is the abuser who is financially secure, meaning it is the victim, the most vulnerable (again) who has no legal support.

It is very easy in this situation for the abuser's legal team to present the mother as unfit, and with the mother left to represent herself her argument would not come across as strongly. I consider myself to be a tough person but after what I had been through, at that time the family court process nearly broke me.

I would 100% advise anyone in this situation to 'get educated' and seek as much advice as possible until you find your Mr Hawley.

The family court is a truly horrible place. I did not want to say the things I did but I had no choice but to bring Moran down with the truth because he was trying to do this to me with lies.

Who wins in that situation, with each side slinging mud? The court gets paid, the legal teams get paid, the abuser wins; they enjoy the conflict. It is the victim that loses.

Parents need support, not war. Instead, they are bled dry financially or thrown to the wolves. It is the most archaic institution still functioning today. They believe that any father applying to family court must be 'good enough' even if he has beaten and terrorised his wife/partner and/or been convicted of violent offences. It makes no sense. There are changes being pushed in UK Parliament, however changing laws is a lengthy process and can take years.

Mr Hawley wanted me to meet with the barrister, so we went to her chambers in Birmingham. She was a smallish woman who came across as quite strict and tough. She was straight to the point. I liked her. I just hoped she liked me and wanted to fight my corner. I went through everything, but she was extremely honest. "Zoe, there are no guarantees, but I will do my very best. It is disgusting what you have been through. This is not the act of a good man to try and completely destroy you when you are at your weakest and lowest." That was good enough for me. I believed her. She was also a mother, and I was hoping that now she had met me she could put herself in my shoes.

I had my up days and down days. Some days it was enough to just get Cameron to school and then I'd spend the whole day crying uncontrollably, or just sit numb after reading about all the women having children removed. My friends rallied round as much as they could, but I was completely broken some days. This is normal. Let yourself be sad, let that emotion go. Sometimes you need to release these emotions to build yourself back up. Just try not to stay there.

By this point my story had broken in the news. My local newspaper in Coventry had run a story about my attack and this went viral on the internet. This was then picked up by the *Daily Mail* national newspaper and then the rest followed. The *Daily Mail* article was shared nearly 8000 times and then I was being tagged into posts around the world. Japan, Hong Kong, New Zealand,

Australia. It was crazy. So many women and men were getting in touch with their well wishes and support. They didn't know the half of it. This was just the reaction to my attack and the injury picture that went into the paper.

I was being contacted daily by other people going through or who had been through a similar situation. On social media people were sending messages of support and disbelief. Old friends from school, old work colleagues, strangers. It was so nice to have such support and even from those I did not know. It all helped with my recovery. It helped me find my strength. It gave me the drive to keep on going and it also made me angry that so many other people had been in similar situations. This anger was to be the force that started my campaigning.

And it was at this time that some additional and sinister information started to come out into the open about Smith. Many of Smith's exes contacted me, saying they too had been in a relationship with Smith and he ended up being abusive. They too had struggled to end the relationship and that was when Smith upped the ante by harassing them, turning up at their houses uninvited, even letting himself in. Many had also been on fast response with the police, so the police knew his behaviours were a pattern.

One told me a story of him telling her to stay home and checking the engine on her car was cold so he knew if she had left the house. Another talked of stalking behaviours and abuse towards her son. The pattern was the same: each of them had been in a relationship with him for around a year before he unravelled, and most of them were professional single mothers. In total over the weeks of my story being in the press, 13 women came forward. It was unbelievable to me that he had been allowed to get away with it each and every time. There is no way all of these women were making it up and they did not know each other. It was truly crazy.

I knew by this point I had a long, hard battle on my hands and I needed to be as strong as possible. I had to beat these manipulators with my mind; it was all I had. I started looking into how to get over trauma or abuse. I knew I did not want counselling – I did not want to go over the past – but I needed some sort of support to help me get through the court cases I had looming.

I enlisted the help of a therapist. I wanted to build on the motivation other survivors had given me. I felt compelled to do something, but I was nowhere near there yet, although I knew with some support I'd get there.

What I needed was confidence, clarity and validation. I needed a vision to succeed. A clear path to success and to laser focus on it.

I found cognitive behavioural therapist Mr Kilmurry at DK Hypnotherapy who specialised in behavioural change management, regression, and growth mindset. This was exactly what I needed.

At our first meeting we discussed the therapy I was looking for and the outcome I wanted to achieve. Firstly, I needed to understand what had happened the night of the attack. I still could not comprehend why Smith had done that to me, in terms of the memory of what happened. My wounds were defence wounds – stab wounds to the back of my hands – but I did not remember covering my face or anything really about the physical attack and I wanted to remember more about what happened that night. What was I saying/doing when he was physically attacking me? This was important to me to know but not crucial, as my priority was Sofia.

"I want to know what happened; he stamped on me but why did he start stabbing me? What did I do, say? Where was I positioned? What was I doing? I just want to know."

Mr Kilmurry looked shocked. "Most people want to forget, however it's good that you want to try and address it head on so you can move on. This is a personal choice," he said. He offered me something called 'regression' therapy where you attempt to go back to the incident of the trauma.

I know some people will ask why I needed to try and get into this part of my brain to understand, however I needed answers. The blank was worse for me, although your brain is an incredibly clever muscle and it had probably deleted parts of the information to keep me safe. The parts that I do remember are harrowing; even so I still felt the need to go back. This was not because I wanted to try and understand Smith, but for my own knowledge of what happened!

I arrived for my first session at the DK practice. He had a big wooden desk with various items on it: a skull with the areas of the brain mapped out, spiders in glass cases for phobia work, and it was a fluffy environment, with cushions and blankets on the comfy chairs. He worked with all sorts of people with a variety of issues: phobias, eating disorders, fear of flying, you name it, but he specialised in 'change your mind', a solution-focused approach. This was perfect for me. This is what I do as a day job for others in IT. He was a professional of the mind.

I sat back in the chair. "So let's go back to the night." Mr Kilmurry was trying to take me back but it was no good, I could not regress. I was so frustrated. "I knew this wouldn't work on me," I said to him.

"Ahh Zoe that's probably why, if you don't believe and relax then maybe it will not, however it could be that you were actually unconscious for that time after the first blow," he said.

It is not always possible to regress; it depends on the brain trauma. I also think I am too front of mind. I can't let go and I was dealing with so much at this time. I decided we should move on from the regression.

Still, the session had helped in many ways, as it gave me clarity around the information I already knew. Nothing had changed in the information I had already given to police about the attack.

Over the next few months, I saw Mr Kilmurry two to three times a week to work on confidence, clarity, fitness and just general wellbeing to get me into the right frame of mind for court. I needed to be strong, stronger than ever. I needed support; I could not rely on friends. You soon realise that you are becoming a burden, or at least that's how I felt, and friends of course get back into their normal daily routines.

My life stood still, while the world kept turning.

My dad was also still recuperating and I did not want to worry him with the extent of what was happening. He was going through his own recovery and it was the same with other family members: they were busy conducting their own lives.

Mr Kilmurry was there when I needed support; he would only be a text away if something happened and that was often daily at this point. There was always something, a text from Moran that would trigger me, another newspaper article, another victim looking for support. Another victim of Smith! Mr Kilmurry was my support network throughout all of this. An absolute rock.

One of the sessions was one Mr Kilmurry called a flooding session. Warning: they are probably not for everyone; I believe that your recovery is personal to you. My personality is not to dwell on the past, but face it head on and with the future in mind. So, the flooding sessions were taking me back to the trauma situation and reliving that scene but with control. It was exciting and empowering.

I arrived at the flooding session with Mr Kilmurry. The class was nothing to do with my session with Mr Kilmurry; we had just gone along to incorporate it into my therapy. It was held in a local school sports hall. There were around 20 men present at the Krav Maga session, which is a form of Russian combat. The session was with knives, pretend bendy rubber knives, but they looked very real. Mr Kilmurry had spoken with the guys before the session and told them my story. They all lined up to build a tunnel using gym mats they were holding, and using my shoulder I had to smash through the middle. I barged and bashed through them all, until I emerged at the other end.

It was liberating. My strength of mind was growing daily with all these confidence sessions. It was a crucial part in my recovery.

Mr Kilmurry also took me capoeira sessions, which were amazing. It's an Afro-Brazilian form of martial art combining dance and acrobatics. We also did parkrun, went to the gym, went for walks. Mr Kilmurry would literally pull me out of a hole if I was falling into one. All of his work was practical, forward thinking and strength focused.

There is benefit to counselling, don't get me wrong. You need to get that shit out of your head, however I had spent a lot of time with friends and family going over and over the story, getting it out, talking about it, plus all the reading. It was practical, forward-thinking, focussed therapy I needed to bring Sofia home.

Everything was about building me up to be strong, confident and ready to take on the court process. I was not only preparing for family court but I also had the criminal court case pending.

I had given written statements and video statements, and whenever anything else cropped up I would keep DC Davies in the loop. I often found out bits of information that I thought might be helpful in my case. For instance, I was cleaning out my bathroom one afternoon. I had one of those organiser storage things that hang on the back of your door; it's where I keep my extra toothpaste or shower gel. I emptied it all out and found a business card. I never put it there but I could guess who did, Smith. It was a female's card. I wondered if that was his next target and thought about contacting her. I did not, although I gave the information to the DC.

Contact was becoming strained with Sofia too. Moran was being his usual disruptive self and there was another no-show for my contact with Sofia. He texted:

`[she's poorly she's not well enough to come this week]`

Any excuse to keep creating distance between me and my baby girl.

This time I called the police. There was a court order in place and he was breaching it. I decided I needed to report the constant abuse and threats from Moran and now he had breached the contact order. It needed to be documented and recorded for court. How was it ok for him to threaten me with court, when he was the one in breach!

However, the police response was disgusting, more judgement, more minimising the impact of this abuse.

I called 101 which is the non-urgent number for the police. Two male officers attended my home to take a statement. I explained everything. The attack, the ongoing abuse and threats. "She is my four-year-old little girl," I pleaded. It was useless. They had zero empathy.

Male officer 1: It's tit for tat.

Male officer 2: Can't you just get on?

Male officer 1: We cannot do anything, why can't he have his daughter?

Male officer 2: It's a civil matter.

I knew I had to keep reporting and documenting everything because there was no way I could allow Moran to take her to Dubai.

I would never see my daughter again.

Zoe and David Kilmurry after finishing a half-marathon which she arranged to raise money for the local domestic abuse charity, Coventry Haven

Zoe doing her half-marathon with supporters

Zoe at parkrun

Zoe during the flooding session with the Krav Maga group doing pad work

Zoe during the flooding session with the Krav Maga group

Zoe sitting in a boxing ring at one of her confidence classes with David Kilmurry

Zoe speaking at the Leeway Domestic Abuse Conference

Zoe with David Kilmurry at DK Hypnotherapy Practice

RED FLAGS & REFLECTION

Document everything, times, dates, and also include the impact on how this made you feel; read everything, get professional advice, build allies where you can, and take care of yourself both physically and mentally.

To come through the other side of domestic abuse takes an awful amount of work but it's worth it and you can do it!

See my list of books and charities where you can access support and advice and also how I can support you.

Education and knowledge is power.

Power yourself up!

What recovery methods would/did/do you use to get over abuse? How could you help someone going through abuse?

CHAPTER 16:

Witness Intimidation

It was a few months after the attack. Smith was still on remand in prison and we were awaiting the trial date. It was a Saturday morning; the sun was beaming through my window. Spring was here. Not much to be happy about but the sun at least gave me a reason to get up and fight another day. Cameron was with his dad, and I was home alone.

I had just made a coffee and was standing in the kitchen, looking out the window and contemplating what on earth was happening to my life, when the phone rang.

"Hey babe, it's me." I was almost sick.

It.

Was.

Smith.

He was calling me from prison. *Is that even allowed?!* I'm thinking to myself. *How can he be allowed to contact me?* It was a withheld number, so I could not tell if it was from a prison phone.

"What? Why are you calling me?" I said. My voice was quiet. My heart jumped into my chest, my throat went dry, and I felt goosebumps all over me.

I went silent. I wanted to hear what he had to say. I mean where is this going? Why was he ringing me? The fucking audacity!

"Baby you fell down the stairs, I was trying to help you," he said. Seemingly this is what he had convinced even himself, going by the tone of his voice.

"Are you fucking kidding me, you tried to kill me Smith!" I couldn't contain my anger. I was furious. Furious he had ruined my life in one evening, furious I was now fighting for my daughter, furious that he even thought I would believe his story.

Was he actually going to try and convince me I was stupid? Or had lost my goddamn mind?

Why had I attracted this shit? It made me realise very quickly that I have no boundaries, and if someone crossed them I would enable and excuse this behaviour rather than challenge it. I was far too forgiving in relationships and put up with way more shit than I should have, now to the point that Smith could literally think he could convince me it was only a fall – with all of those injuries. I was horrified. I was codependent and a fixer which are vulnerable traits when bumping into a sociopath and narcissist; they can smell an empath/codependent a mile away. They seek them out. I felt hunted, again.

Smith switched attitude the second he realised I wasn't going to play ball and I was never going to believe that bullshit, that 'I fell'.

"If I wanted you dead, you'd be dead Zoe." *Wow! There he is, there is the real ugly Smith.*

The evil core reared his head. I'd never seen or heard him until the attack. I got the Prince Charming mask but here he was in all his glory; the mask was off. The man-child not getting his way so he resorted to threats and violence and fear.

My entire relationship with that fucker was bullshit but I had the wake-up call of my life. Did he even realise or care what devastation that attack had caused? My daughter was being controlled not loved, my son was in counselling at school because the separation was seriously affecting him, and Smith had the audacity to ring me and pretend it was an accident!

Cameron had struggled over the last couple of months not having his sister around, so I had arranged for him to have someone to talk to at school. I wanted him to have an outlet. When I was a child, after Mum dying, I could not speak to my dad for fear of upsetting him so I know all too well children need a third party to offload to. To also make them feel special and deserving of support.

So, this was my life in a nutshell. I was back at home alone with my eight-year-old son and could not work due to my injuries. I was now receiving threats from prison from my attacker and receiving a constant ream of threats via text and email from Sofia's dad, who had interim custody of her anyway.

"Are you going to court Zoe? I'm looking at 10 years. I need to know what you are doing."

I listened to his pleading in shock.

He was swinging between trying to be nice, through gritted teeth – I could tell – and when he realised he wasn't getting anywhere with the nice act, he switched again.

"If you go to court Zoe, I know people in here now and they will pay you a visit." And here came the threats.

Smith must have thought he could sweet-talk me around. He was wrong. Once my feelings are switched off, they are gone forever. This is a skill I have learnt since childhood.

As soon as I put the phone down, I called the DC in charge of my case. She was really grounding and calm. Very professional and it seemed like she had seen it all. She said she would need to come around to take a statement.

"Don't answer the phone to numbers you don't know, Zoe," I was told. Bad advice. I think that the police sometimes say things in the moment without really thinking about the consequences of their words. To tell me not to answer the phone when I was clearly being intimidated from prison was not the answer. The police should have been acting to make sure that (a) it did not happen again; I am a victim and a witness in a serious case and (b) they needed to gather evidence to charge Smith as the stalking was continuing even from behind bars.

"So how are you going to catch him for witness intimidation if I don't answer the calls?" I challenged them. I am not going to sit in my house alone and be scared. I'm just not. The police have a duty to keep me and my family safe, all of society for that matter, however it felt to me they just kept failing. Another institution with a serious lack of understanding around the complexity of domestic abuse and stalking. I was in a constant state of disbelief, something I have become accustomed to while dealing with the system.

None of it makes sense to a victim going through it, especially if they have no understanding of how institutions 'should' be run. I do, which is where my frustration stems from. We all think that somehow the police, health, victim support, even different departments in the police such as frontline officers who attend calls and CID (the Crime Investigation Department) talk to each other. Also the criminal and family court. They do not. It's disjointed. There is not one process to follow. No-one seems to know what they are doing, and nothing is joined up.

When I called the police to update them on anything, I had to tell my story repeatedly, which is retraumatising for victims. You'd think they would be able to look at some summary notes and reduce the impact on victims of serious crime. I talk more about the disjointed system in the next chapter.

The DC continued to advise me, "Ok well next time Smith calls, you'll need to make another statement and call the prison to get them to check his cell. He must be using a smuggled mobile phone as he couldn't call you from the prison phone."

The DC by now knew my personality and that I was not going to let him get away with this. Fight, flight or freeze are all trauma responses. I am a fighter.

I was not going to be bullied and especially not from behind bars and if he thought I was, he had completely misjudged who I am. I was furious at the audacity. I was also numb. I was getting it from all angles, so it was a case of 'bring it on'. I knew he could not get to me physically and why would someone else that he had just met in prison do something to me? Unless he paid them, and I knew he had no money, so he was clutching at straws.

"That's fine, I will do that. Then at least you can have this put on his record." I was so annoyed with their previous response that I should not answer my phone. Why yet again should I be isolated and how would they get the evidence to convict him if I just didn't answer the phone? He would just get away with it. This policing infuriated me.

Smith did call again, of course he did. He is a stalker.

There were many calls over the next few weeks and often it was a silent call, or I'd hear men in the background saying things like "Are you going to court?" and laughing and then saying "Your house will get burnt down".

I reported it to the prison each and every time. They were useless.

"Oh he's probably on the landing, by the time we get there it'll probably be gone; they'll hide the phone."

I wonder if they'd be so blasé had it been one of their family members being threatened.

I made two statements to the police about the calls where Smith and I spoke, and I made numerous calls to the prison and kept a diary of every single missed call I had from an unknown number. I had to collect my own evidence, and this is key. If you are being stalked, harassed and abused the police need this information in order to build their case. They cannot do it on your word alone, so if you are going through something like this, document everything. Times, dates, where you were, what was said.

Then one Saturday he called again but this time he forgot to withhold the number.

I called the DC immediately after the call. "I have the number! I have the mobile number he called off; he forgot to withhold." I was shaking. I had the time, the place and the number.

The DC explained to me they could do a check against the number to see which mast the call pinged off and if it was near to the prison then that would be evidence of the call.

It was. And stupidly Smith had also called his family members from the same phone, so the story he made up when he was interviewed at the prison did not add up. He said that I had arranged for someone to drive near to the prison to make the call as I was 'stitching him up', but fortunately for me because he had also called one of his family members from the same phone he was bang to rights.

Since you only need to provide an element of doubt in court for something to be dismissed, he had revealed his own lies by making this mistake. We had him for witness intimidation!

It was at this time that I encountered a charity called Paladin National Stalking Advocacy Service and I met Laura Richards, its founder. Laura Richards is a criminal behavioural analyst, formerly of New Scotland Yard, and an international expert on domestic violence, stalking, sexual violence, homicide and risk assessment. Laura founded Paladin in 2013, and it's the world's first national stalking advocacy service, having successfully campaigned to change the law on stalking. It has since changed laws around this type of abuse worldwide. Laura has spent her career tracking offenders like Smith and by now I realised that I was dealing with someone who was not going to give up, since he was continuing to offend even from behind bars so I knew I needed support from an organisation that could advocate on my behalf with the police, because their response to most things was quite frankly terrible.

I had a brief conversation with Laura on the phone and then we arranged to meet up.

Laura is a force to be reckoned with, a trailblazer, and when it comes to domestic abusers and stalkers, she knows her stuff. She has spent her entire career profiling these types of offenders and can dissect any case to understand it. She speaks with authority, having spent her career profiling perpetrators, analysing hundreds of domestic homicides and she also wrote the Oxford University Press book *Policing Domestic Violence*. I was honoured to be speaking with her. Laura and I discussed everything. She asked me to explain how my relationship started with Smith, how he was in the beginning. Well he came on quite strong to begin with, and crossed my boundaries after date one; if you recall he turned up outside my house the very next day. I had brushed this off as keen and was flattered. Then she asked me questions around other scenarios, for example the incident with my ribs. She also asked me how Smith had managed to get the knives into the bedroom.

I explained that a few months before Smith had picked up the children from school and when I got back from work he told me my back door handle had been damaged; the lock was prised away from the door. It looked like someone had tried to break in. Smith had also been through my kitchen cupboards and found a set of cooking knives I had bought a few years before that were just hidden at the back of the cupboard.

Smith said that we should keep a couple of knives under the bed as protection. He said, "If anyone gets in the house when we are in bed Zoe, then we need to defend ourselves. There's no way out of the loft." I never thought anything of it and thought it was reasonable.

It was Laura who made me look at this differently. "Do you think he broke the door on purpose, Zoe?" It had not even crossed my mind. However now we knew that Smith had been abusive before to ex-girlfriends there was every chance that he orchestrated the knives in the bedroom. So, was my attack premeditated?

I explained to Laura the response of the police telling me "he hasn't done anything" so they could not act. This was wrong! They were wrong. They had failed to even categorise what was happening to me as harassment; they had not even checked his historic offending to understand the risk he posed to me at the time of me calling 999.

There were many red flags that Laura recognised just from our initial conversation. I was infuriated that the police had failed me and continued to fail me repeatedly. I did not come across as a weak victim, or a broken person; was this why they dealt with me differently?

It was as if they did not see the red flags due to my strong attitude towards my situation when reporting it, but they still failed to pick up on the risks, the red flags that were present in every situation I had been in with Smith when the police were called.

The fact that Smith was a serial offender, the making of threats. One in two stalkers who have had an intimate relationship with the victim, when they make a threat will act on it. This is an alarming stat. It's from Australian research by Rachel MacKenzie and Troy McEwan (https://www.stalkingriskprofile.com/about/rachel-mack, https://www.stalkingriskprofile.com/about/troy-mce). Threatening to kill himself was a huge red flag and a risk marker. If he was prepared to kill himself, then this posed the question that he would not think twice about killing someone else and was a prerequisite to homicide. The police should have recognised this, however I was classed as standard risk. They failed to take evidence of the voicemails where Smith was pretending to kill himself, all the text messages, Facebook and WhatsApp messages.

What I now know is that on the risk assessment they carried out they said I was not scared. This meant they marked the risk level lower. This was another huge mistake. Just because I said I was not scared, even though clearly there was reason enough for me to call 999. I was not necessarily fearful as my first response when being asked that question would be that I was angry, however I was scared enough to call the police, to want his behaviour to stop. He was behaving this way in front of my children; I did feel apprehensive about him turning up to my house drunk, and the threats about coming through the door. His behaviour was forcing me to change my life and my routines to accommodate his abuse.

His behaviour was that of a stalker and Laura validated that for me. He was fixated and his obsession was obvious to anyone trained in this type of behaviour. Laura profiled him perfectly.

How had the police missed so many fundamental things? I felt failed by them, violated by their lack of response. Their attitude was to minimise my experience in an attempt to give a false, reduced view of the risk of harm I was in. Had they checked Smith's historic file they would have joined the dots and acted accordingly.

They failed to investigate my reports properly and I was nearly murdered! They had it on file he was dangerous; he had done this before to one of their own officers along with the other victims who came forward. They know he was and still is a serial offender.

I was yet to find out the extent of what he did to Carmen, however I knew Smith had been to prison for three months for harassment and that was enough for Laura.

Laura made me look at the situations I was in with Smith previously through a very different lens, and it became so apparent to me that Smith was in fact a dangerous abuser who had done this before and had been allowed to 'get away with it', so his offending went under the radar. This gave him his sense of entitlement over the women he was in a relationship with and he became a master manipulator. There were many victims before me so by the time Smith started the relationship with me, he had honed his techniques.

I knew I had to speak out; I knew I had to raise awareness around these system failings but first I had to get the trial out of the way. However, I was doing the ground work to highlight these failures and atrocities.

Many other victims are living in immediate fear. They cannot publicly speak out or call out the professional failures they endure. Often victims suffer in silence. If you are going through something, and a response from those privileged enough to serve does not feel right, get more advice. As I explained previously with the solicitors I went to after my first appearance in the family court, you may not always find the right one immediately but please don't give up. Please do not think that every response from professionals will be the same. Call back, speak to someone else. Move your requirement for advocacy to another service; ask for another officer on your case. Expect more.

While going through my ordeal I had support from various agencies for various different reasons. There was local domestic abuse charity Coventry Haven, who helped me have my house all secured with reinforced locks and alarms on the windows and doors. I was working with Refuge, the domestic abuse charity, who supported me with the family court process. I had an advocate that would attend the hearings with me. That was invaluable; the family court process was the worst because Moran was not the attacker so my case was classed as private proceedings. However the fear of losing Sofia was real due to the fact that I was now having to defend myself as a parent, against a father that was deemed to be a good man, saving the day from Smith. Little did they know the reason I was with Smith in the first place was due to Moran's abuse.

I was also using the Women's Aid forum which I've already mentioned, just for research to help me understand what other women were going through. I had been in touch with the Centre for Women's Justice for support around family law. I was also in touch with an abduction charity who helped me to get the caveat on Sofia's passport and now I was being supported by Paladin, the National Stalking Advocacy Service, and was working directly with Laura Richards. For my mental health I continued to work with DK Hypnotherapy, and I was going to the gym to keep myself physically fit.

So, after giving my statements to the police about the witness intimidation by Smith, I had also sent two text messages to Smith's dad and one to his sister on Facebook. One Friday evening around 9pm Cameron was in bed, and I was just turning off. My phone rang, and I answered it hesitantly as it was a withheld number, however the police by this point had spoken to Smith so I thought it would not be him.

"Hi is that Zoe, it's West Midlands Police," said an officer on the end of the phone.

"Oh hi," I said, wondering what the hell had happened now.

"We have had a report that you have sent messages to the Smith family and we need you to come for a voluntary interview at the police station on Sunday."

"I beg your pardon!" I was furious immediately. Were they actually being serious?

I was being asked to go to the police station for MY harassment of the Smith family, however it was Smith who was threatening ME from prison and I was the victim of near murder. How was the police response to them so different to when I was reporting Smith's harassment and stalking behaviours towards me? They said there was nothing they could do but here they were threatening me with a harassment charge!

I was livid.

"I'm sorry, you do realise I'm a victim of domestic abuse don't you?" I said, utterly pissed off at the officer. It was late on a Friday night, and given what I had been through I did not think it was appropriate to be calling at that time, especially given the information too.

The officer let out a smug laugh. "Oh, you are not going to pull that one are you!" I was disgusted at his response and even more mad now. How the hell can he justify talking to me like that?!

"Pardon me! What is your collar number?" I asked abruptly.

Following that conversation, I was furious not only at the Smith family's audacity, which clearly proved to me that this was where Smith got his entitlement from, but at a police officer speaking to me like I was somehow less of a person or was using domestic abuse as an excuse.

I called Laura Richards. I explained what had happened and she was as incensed as I was. I told her I was going to the police station alone as they wanted me to go on Sunday and I would just tell the truth.

Laura warned me not to do this. "Do not go without legal representation, Zoe." She arranged for a solicitor to do a hundred-mile round trip to meet me at the station on the Sunday. This experience was a joke. How could they justify the response to my three messages, in comparison to what I had endured?

The solicitor met me at the police station on the Sunday. I walked through into a barred cell and they read me my rights.

"You do not have to say anything but it may harm your defence if you do not mention when questioned something you later rely on in court. Anything you do say may be given in evidence." It was utterly ridiculous and off the recording the officer who was interviewing me said he was sorry and he made it clear he felt it was wrong. I was outraged and angry. The Crown Prosecution

Service (CPS), who make the decision whether to take a case forward to court, threw it out. It was not in the public interest, but still I was furious. How dare they treat me like that but yet Smith 'got away with it' every time he offended.

I just do not understand how these so-called professionals can make these decisions without any thought to the repercussions. I made an official complaint about the officer on the phone and was told the threshold for harassment is three contacts. The police agreed that their response to my three messages was disproportionate, and they apologised, but really, was that enough? Not really in my view, which is why I campaign to change our system.

The inspector and boss of the police officer came to see me about what I wanted done about his attitude.

"Look, I don't want him to get the sack, however does he realise that making comments like that about domestic abuse is extremely damaging? He needs training. He needs to understand that the public look up to the police and look to them for guidance. To disregard me, saying I was pulling something by saying I was a domestic abuse victim, was wrong. Had he looked at the file before making the call then maybe he would not have been so flippant, given I was almost murdered!" I snapped at him furiously.

"How would you feel if it was your daughter?" I raised my eyebrows at him. I was so angry. I was not going to let anything go.

The police officer was sent for additional training. Throughout this process I have challenged the system when I have found it not to be fair. It really does feel like everything is stacked against the victim.

Shouldn't it be the other way around?

Zoe with Laura Richards on the terrace at the Houses of Parliament

RED FLAGS & REFLECTION

More failings by those who should know better. It will never cease to amaze me, the incompetence of those who are meant to protect and understand. I was just horrified at most stages of my journey at the sheer lack of understanding of domestic abuse and the intricacies of how this abuse plays out and how abusers manipulate the system.

One thing about me is I do not like injustice, and I will not tolerate it either. Every organisation, whether it be the police or a private company, must have a complaints procedure - use it!

The incident when I was called on a Friday evening by the police advising ME I might charged with harassment for sending three text messages when the text messages were sent trying to stop my intimidation incensed me. I was furious at the utter incompetence and complete lack of authority anyone has in the system to stand up and make a stance for victims. In the grand scheme of things, what were three text messages?

It's just not ok to treat a victim of almost murder with such contempt, when they did nothing about Smith harassing and stalking me before almost murdering me. Keep your anger and channel it, that's my advice. I made sure the complaint was seen through. Yes, I was also dealing with a shitload of other stuff, but for me making sure these errors are highlighted at least means that someone else will be spared the stupidity.

Once you formalise a complaint,

a. it must be dealt with professionally and within protocol

b. it must be documented so it can be called on as evidence should you need it

c. and most importantly it can be used by them to improve.

Professionals do not always get things right and we must call this out.

Don't be afraid to use your voice.

Have you ever been treated unfairly by professionals there to serve the community? How did you deal with it?

CHAPTER 17: Final Hearing?

Four months after the attack, it was the 'final hearing' in family court. This was when the decision would be made where Sofia was to reside moving forward and this would be ordered by the court. It is a position I never ever thought I would be in; it felt terrible but here I was. Unbelievable. This could be the day that Moran could take Sofia forever, to live in a foreign country.

The fear of losing my daughter and going through the family court process in my mind was worse than the attack by Smith. I would rather have been attacked violently and it be over with, than to be branded a bad mother, lied about, my reputation completely pulled apart. This prolonged agony, the bitterness, the vilest insults that flew around, it was truly soul destroying. Moran wasn't doing this for shared care; he already had shared care of Sofia. I never ever stopped my daughter seeing her father. He had done this out of spite, control and to teach me a lesson. He made that very clear the day he left the flowers by my hospital bed, along with the court papers to take Sofia away.

The separation felt like a lifetime from Sofia, my baby. None of our contact time felt like quality time. Moran made sure of that: cutting contacts short, turning up late, picking up early, texting me abuse, all to interrupt my time, even verbally abusing me in front of her knowing I would not want that so I would have to leave her quickly to avoid a confrontation. That hurt so much, seeing Sofia's innocent little face looking back at me wondering why Mummy was in such a hurry to get away. The cruelty that Moran was raining down on me was vicious.

Cameron was still having counselling at school. He was really struggling some days because he was such a sensitive young boy, and he loved his sister dearly and only knew life with her in it. He would often ask, "Why is Sofia not at home, Mummy? Why does Moran take her away from us?" Cameron did not understand what was happening with the family court, but he had the intuition to understand that it was Moran keeping her. Also, my dad was struggling. Although he was out of hospital, we had all sorts of problems with his social care housing. The extra worry around Sofia was just not needed or warranted.

My dad would often get really annoyed about Moran serving me with family court papers while in hospital. "What's wrong with the man, Zoe?" he would say to me, looking desperately upset and helpless. "He wouldn't do that if I was up and about." It hurt me to see it hurt my dad.

I had no choice but to fight on. Moran was hurting my entire family including his own daughter, just to punish me for ending the relationship years before. All of us punished because his weak sense of self and ego were damaged. By this point in the proceedings, I had spent over £14,000 on legal fees. But I had to tell my truth; I had to expose his lies.

By now because my story had gone in the paper, I was doing a lot of work online raising awareness around domestic abuse, the process, how it is geared up for the perpetrator. I was documenting my journey on social media and the support I received kept me strong.

One of my friends Claire posted `[Head up, shoulders back]` in response to my court selfie I took the day I was heading into our family justice system to hear our fate. That saying stuck with me throughout the entire journey. Every time I was in a judgemental situation, that's what I'd think: *Head up, shoulders back.*

Claire was also a victim of domestic abuse and the family court process. I never really knew Claire before this although she is from the same city. It's funny how life events can draw people to you. We had mutual friends, however we had never met. When she heard about what I was going through via social media, she reached out to me. I've had this a lot and I must thank every single person who has stood by me through this truly horrific time.

Claire had also been in a seriously violent relationship. Her ex had poured petrol over her, threatened to set her on fire, beaten her, thrown her into the street naked, just awful disgusting immoral things. She had to run to the neighbours with no clothes on. He was a violent man known to the police and even while he was spending time behind bars for armed robbery, he dragged Claire through the family court. Unbelievably the system allowed him to submit an application for custody of his son from prison!

How can convicted criminals and prisoners in Her Majesty's Prison be allowed to do this? He was granted days out of prison to continue to harass Claire. I have heard this a lot. The problem is the criminal court and the family court work in very different ways and do not share information, so they often work against each other, putting the victim of abuse right in the middle of this broken and flawed process.

I remember Claire telling me the story of her ex turning up at court in the prison van, f-ing and blinding at the judge, causing mayhem in the court. He had applied for residency (custody) of his children. How can any sane person think this is remotely ok? And believe it or not, he was awarded custody of his son. Claire was allowed to keep her daughter, so they separated the children like puppies in a litter and her son was given to the dad although he was in prison at the time, so the son had to live with his then girlfriend until his release. That is utter nonsense. Welcome to the topsy turvy world of family court where anything can happen.

Claire is now alienated from her son. She doesn't blame him, of course not. He is her little boy, but as a teenager now he has been told all sorts by his dad over the years and has become completely estranged from her. The system is truly unjust. There is no recourse either. You are expected to go down a lengthy, expensive appeals process if you don't like the judgement.

I have met many women who have been through this awful system, all with similar stories to tell. It was like we were all in a secret club, victims of abuse, blamed for the abuse and bonded by grief. An understanding of something we never wanted to be a part of.

Often when I talk to my 'normal' friends who have no knowledge of family court, they cannot believe their ears and just look on in disbelief. It is difficult to even portray the extreme helplessness you feel. I say 'normal' as most people do not go through a family court to organise their children's lives after a separation. It is like you are in a game where your children are placed in the middle as pawns and the system enables further abuse by proxy.

My friends would often ask, "Why would the court not protect the abused mother?" I would have to explain the culture of victim blaming, the no-win situation, damned if you do and damned if you don't.

After working with Mr Kilmurry of DK Hypnotherapy, he encouraged me to start a Facebook group to support other victims and this had grown over time. I set up a page called 'I want my mummy' plus a personal public profile and I was getting daily messages from victims looking for guidance or support. I was posting anything I thought could help someone else going through the same ordeal, and the page soon became a one-stop shop of information to support victims of domestic abuse going through family court.

It included any relevant laws, guidance on the court process, petitions for change. We were a club of abused parents wanting answers and justice. A club of women and some men, who had been victims of a system that does not play fair.

The family court process allows an infinite number of applications to pursue any vexatious claims. As I mentioned earlier, applications are not checked or verified in any way. It's absurd really. In my case they had switched residency to Moran in a hearing where I was not even present. How is that justice? And what if he had been a paedophile? The court would have been responsible for putting Sofia directly into harm's way. Moran is not by the way, thankfully, but you get my point! And this does happen, more than you think.

Moran submitted application after application, and he hadn't even cared enough to write them himself – they had been written by his fiancée. I knew it was not his handwriting.

Goodness knows the lies he told her to get her to side with him. It made me sad that she was so influenced by him. I put this down to her being young at the time, and not having children herself she probably never really understood the enormity of what she had done.

How awful to attack another woman you don't know, without a shred of evidence, just the word of a bully. I felt sorry for her. This happens a lot too, abusers hoodwinking their new partners into thinking their ex-girlfriends are mad. This is how Smith and his family had presented his ex-girlfriends. This is a huge red flag. I would recommend anyone with any concerns whatsoever with a new partner to carry out what is called a 'Claire's Law'. I will mention more about this in my reflection at the end of this chapter.

So, this was the 'final hearing'. Today I would find out who would be awarded residency of Sofia and whether the judge agreed that Moran should have residency and take her to live in Dubai, away from everything she knew.

Judge C had all the information and wanted to hear from us in person. My legal team had presented bundles of information. My professional background, the fact that the children have always lived together and with me, having regular contact with their respective fathers, they both go to an outstanding school, they have a strong friend network, I live in a good area, I own my house, I am a businesswoman, I own a rental property which houses victims of domestic abuse, I am a law-abiding citizen with a good job, I have a strong network of friends and family rallying around, with many providing character statements to court, friends, parents of children from the school, work colleagues, my bosses, professionals. And most importantly, the simple fact, I am a good mother. I was just an unfortunate victim. We had reams and reams of positive counterevidence against Moran's unverified lies.

All that being said, I was never given any indication I would just walk out of the court room with residency of Sofia, quite the opposite. The odds were against me. Moran had switched the status quo by getting an interim residency order while I was in hospital; he had constantly submitted more and more applications giving the impression he was the doting loving father and he was using his fiancée to show some sort of stability. By now he had even got her pregnant but was still leaving for Dubai.

I met my solicitor Mr Hawley at his office. He was driving us to the court. "Why didn't you wear your glasses?"

"I don't like them, I normally wear contacts, why?"

"You look more staid, Zoe." I rolled my eyes. Honestly, I thought. What a pantomime. Everything is positioning, not fact.

If I turned up in a clown suit would that make me a bad parent? Probably.

I shuddered as I went back to that unwelcoming place. It has a sober, stale atmosphere, and I could feel the tension in the air. The ceilings are high so everything echoes, and you can hear family names being called over the loudspeaker as people are summoned into the court rooms. Back to the reception desk, through the metal detector. I hated that place.

Mr Hawley and I made our way through security. "Let's go and get a coffee, we have a bit of a wait." He pointed to the café sign. It was a tiny café room, old and tired looking. We got coffees in horrible paper cups and Mr Hawley's legal secretary arrived.

"Barbara will meet us upstairs. You ok?" Mr Hawley asked. I felt ashen.

"Huh." I rolled my eyes, pursed my lips and took a sip of my coffee, shrugging. At least I was dressed for the occasion this time, in a smart black suit and crisp white shirt. Although of course I was not ok. This was pure hell. I wanted to scream from the rooftops, HOW DARE YOU SAY I'M NOT A GOOD MOTHER, YOU DON'T KNOW ME! But that would play into all of their hands, now wouldn't it. I had to stay calm, play to the pantomime.

My heart was racing now as I was watching the door open and close. Looking around at the other people waiting, everyone looked so sad, broken, depressed. Nothing good was happening in that building. You could feel the misery in the stagnant air.

My Hawley noticed my fear. "Just be yourself, Zoe, and try not to get angry. Don't speak unless you're spoken to." He knew how passionate I got about the injustices in the family court. I just looked at him, tipped my head to the side and smiled.

"Moran is likely to be able to cross-examine you today, Zoe. He is a litigant in person so he may be asked by the judge to ask you questions," Mr Hawley informed me. I was shocked.

"HE can cross examine ME! How is that even allowed?! Is this a kangaroo court? He is a criminal and not a barrister or legally trained. How can he address the judge and cross-examine me?! It would be laughable if it was not so serious. A convicted criminal, bully and opportunist now has the floor of the court. I thought I'd heard everything, clearly not!"

"Case call for Dronfield."

It was time.

My hands were clammy. My heart was pounding. We walked into the court room.

We were ushered in and told where to sit by one of the court staff.

My barrister was already there in the court room. Mr Hawley sat next to her. His legal secretary and I sat behind.

I was legally strong but I did not feel it at the time. I felt weak. I felt emotionally broken.

Moran was sitting on the other side of the court room. He was there on his own. He looked pathetic. He was no longer legally represented. He only had a solicitor for the first couple of hearings and they do not speak in the court room; you must instruct a barrister if you want someone to talk on your behalf so it's likely he did not want to spend any more money. And he probably felt he did not need to as his game of destruction was already working through him submitting constant applications to court.

To submit an application was just over hundred pounds, a small price to pay for a man who could control what everyone was doing with that small fee. I just hoped the courts would see sense seeing as he had submitted so many and often for ridiculous reasons: to have Sofia's passport removed from me, to amend contact times to suit his life, to place enforcement on me if I breached, to threaten me with prison or have assets ceased. He had even tried to arrange for my contact time with Sofia to be supervised. This was sickening, as if he wanted to portray me as a danger.

I hated Moran for doing this to us and I hated the court for allowing it without a single piece of evidence.

Moran and I sat on either side of the court facing the judge's empty chair waiting for the judge to appear, with the usher sat facing us at the front. The room was furnished with dark brown wooden benches and there was a court logo almost the height of the wall behind the judge's chair. Moran had a large ring-binder folder in front of him. I wanted to laugh, it was so utterly pathetic. This was the man I wrote the business plan for and took to retail conferences to show him how to buy stock for the clothes shop we had. I helped him figure out the shop till when he was shaking with fear at the thought of customers coming in. His normal attire is street wear, to fit his drum and bass pirate radio DJ persona. Yet here he was dressed smartly in a suit.

He was revelling in his opportunity to attack me, an educated woman who comes from a good background.

Time stood still. My mouth was dry. I could feel his presence. He just kept looking down at his papers. Was he enjoying this?

My barrister looked annoyed, slightly irritated. She acknowledged me by turning, nodding and mouthing "Ok". I gave a half smile. She started preparing herself, looking through her papers. As Barbara was the only barrister on the case, she was the only person who could address the judge, unless of course the judge asked someone else to answer a question and because of this Barbara would have to direct the case. I found this infuriating as she had to help Moran at times, to ensure the trial was fair, but clearly it was I who was paying for her time.

"All rise."

We stood up as Judge C entered the room and sat down, then we followed suit.

He went over the applications and highlighted the asks of the applicant, which was Moran. "So, you are looking to gain full residency of your daughter? The reason given is Miss Dronfield was the victim of a ferocious physical attack by her ex-partner Smith who I understand is in prison. You believe Mother will get back with Smith and she always has relationships with violent men." He looked down his nose towards Moran. He nodded.

"Yes, that is correct Your Honour," Barbara confirms.

I try not to react. My chest is tight with anger. YES, HE IS ONE OF THEM (violent men)! I want to scream.

"And you are looking to remove Sofia from the jurisdiction completely to live in Dubai with you. You have a job lined up in real estate, is that correct?"

"Yes, Your Honour," Moran responds. He thinks the judge is on his side, I can tell.

My eyes go wide, and my eyebrows rise. I look at Mr Hawley who just gives me a look to stay calm. I'm screaming inside. *It's not a proper job; it's his friend who is giving him a job out there and I give him three months and he'll be home. He can't sell a house, he struggled to sell a t-shirt!*

The job was also commission only. I wondered if the judge had considered this. He would need money for schooling, for healthcare. I had proven that Moran even claimed my tax credits (benefits you get from the government if you're on a low income) while living in the UK. I wasn't entitled to them, so Moran claimed them instead. It's so frustrating not being able to talk. I was wondering if the judge had read all of this information. How would he raise a child there? Would he ask?

The judge was doing all of the talking for Moran at this stage, outlining his ask to the court. "Ok so I think let's hear from you both, Miss Dronfield could you please take the stand?"

This is it. I'm shaking inside but holding it together on the outside.

I walked over to the stand. It felt surreal. This was something that happened in films. The judge addressed Moran: "So you can ask Miss Dronfield any questions you feel will help the court please?"

Moran looked startled. He would not have been aware he would have to question me. I was shocked that the judge expected Moran to ask me questions. *He can't speak publicly*, I thought to myself, half amused by what would happen next. What was he going to do or say?

I had to look at him. I had not locked eyes with him since the first meeting in the court after discharging myself from hospital. A bit of vomit went into my mouth. I raised my eyebrows as if to say, "Go on then".

Moran starts, "So I put it to you..."

Oh my god, Moran thinks he's a lawyer! He had clearly watched too many movies. Did he actually say that to me?! The judge looked fondly at him. *Oh my god, as if he got brownie points for saying it,*

I thought to myself. I literally could not believe my ears or eyes. Was this happening? Like really? It felt surreal but the judge was taking this seriously, embarrassingly so.

Moran cleared his throat. I could tell he was nervous, but he was trying to look like he knew what he was doing. "Um what will you do if this happens again?" He looked uncomfortable but revelling in the experience all the same. The perceived power the court had given him with the order plus allowing him to cross-examine me, had him fluffed up like a peacock.

It was hard for me to stay calm. I wanted to scream, "SHUT UP YOU FUCKING IDIOT, do you want to tell the judge all the things YOU have done to me over the years, why does it feel like I am on trial?!"

"I'm sorry, I don't quite understand the question," I said, shaking my head at him. I was trying to highlight that the question was rather stupid, given I did not know I was going to be attacked in the first place. I had not chosen to be in that situation.

"Just answer the question Miss Dronfield," the judge jumped in, seemingly annoyed with me for not answering.

I was shocked but I pushed back to further highlight the stupidity.

"I don't understand the question because do you mean physically? If it happened again, would I fight back?" I was being sarcastic, trying to let the judge see how stupid the goddamn question was.

I was on trial for being a victim. I had to explain how I would deal with an attack again. It was absolutely preposterous.

The judge made Moran move on. I think I made my point.

"Do you drink three bottles of wine a night?" Oh seriously, here we go.

"No, I don't think I could, do you? Does anyone? It's quite a lot." More stupid questions and accusations. It was an embarrassment to our justice system giving Moran the floor of the court. What a stupid process.

Moran was clutching at straws because he had nothing, just lies. Which you would also think was perjury in a court of law. Apparently not in the family justice arena.

"No more questions," he said and sheepishly sat down. *Well, that was pathetic*, I thought. After having gone through this, I gave it a lot of thought, the fact that Moran was allowed to cross-examine me. It really beggared belief. I asked other victims if this had ever happened to them and it seemed to be a common practice. I was horrified that a victim could be potentially cross-examined by their rapist or attacker.

I have campaigned since against this outdated practice and this has now been abolished under the Domestic Abuse Act which was given Royal Assent in May 2021.

"Ok, you can step down Miss Dronfield. Please take the stand," the judge signalled to Moran. It was his turn to be cross-examined.

As I had a barrister, she would be the one to cross-examine him. Barbara stood. Moran looked so uncomfortable in the dock. Barbara looked at him with an inquisitive face then folded her arms in front of her. Holding her papers in one hand, she took the odd glance at them and began pacing the floor.

I looked at Moran; I could tell he had not thought this through. He looked so petrified. He knew what was coming. His past was about to be exposed. His lies questioned. Let's see how he holds up under this pressure of a legal barrister.

"So, do you think Miss Dronfield is a bad mother?" my barrister asked as she stopped pacing and looked straight at Moran.

"Yes," Moran said smugly.

Barbara looked down at her papers. "So, all the years Sofia has been alive, would you say she has thrived? Would you say she is a happy child?" She paused to look up at Moran and raised her eyebrows.

"Doing well at her nursery?" she quizzed quickly. She gave him a smile.

"Yes, very happy." Moran started to relax a bit, smiling as if proud.

"And in that time, while at nursery and you say she is happy, Sofia was living with Miss Dronfield and you both had time with Sofia. Is that right?" Another pause.

"Urm yes," Moran answered.

"So, would you say Miss Dronfield has done a good job raising Sofia?" she asked, raising her eyebrows.

"No, she drinks wine," he said stupidly.

"So, if you thought Miss Dronfield was a bad mother as you suggest in your applications, why have you only brought this to the court now?" She tapped the tips of her fingers together.

He started to stutter from this moment on. He had been rumbled. He had nothing on me now and nothing historic. He was shifting his feet. He looked over at me. I looked back blankly, but inside I was screaming, *You have NOTHING!* He looked at the floor.

"So, you say Miss Dronfield drinks. I'm partial to a glass of wine. Do you drink?" she continued.

"No, I don't drink," he said. "What a liar!" I wanted to shout but I stared ahead as blankly as I could though I couldn't help the small huff that came out.

"So how do you explain your criminal record for drinking and driving then?" Again tapping her fingers and looking down at her paperwork.

He shifted.

Barbara continued. "Have you been to prison?" she asked, eyebrows up and looking directly at him. *This is great*, I was thinking. I did not show any emotion though. You cannot predict.

"Erm yes but that was ages ago." He was stuttering again.

"Yes, but have you been to prison?" Barbara raised her head as if to wait for a yes or no answer.

"Yes."

"So, you say Miss Dronfield is a bad mother, yet you have been to prison and I am looking at a list of criminal convictions here. You have all of these criminal offences, but you want the court to believe you don't drink yourself and Miss Dronfield who has no criminal history is a bad mother? It seems to me you flout the law at every opportunity. You have many offences."

"Your Honour, may I list what we have found?" The judge nodded. "Drink driving, leaving the scene of an accident, driving while disqualified, possession of drugs Class A, GBH Section 18." The judge looked over at Moran, aghast.

Moran looked at the floor. I felt sorry for him, stupid I know, but I have empathy. Why had he brought us to this place? This was his fault.

I never wanted nor needed to be here. I know family court is brutal, but he insisted on dragging me there. Did he think he could keep his skeletons in the closet? Did he really think I was going to let his past slip by while he told lies about me to take Sofia away? Of course not, I was going to dredge up every bit of true and awful information I could find about him and provide proof. He had nothing on me other than I was the victim of a violent attack. That did not make me a bad person or mother.

The judge started to look quite annoyed at Moran following Barbara's questioning. She had highlighted that Moran was in fact a liar, hell-bent on revenge. He turned to Moran and asked him a question.

"Do you think that a four-year-old little girl should be taken from her loving mother and never see her again? She has not seen her mother for some time to date." He looked straight at Moran. Was he testing his empathy or reasoning? I was glad he asked that question because Moran's answer would reveal a lot.

"She can Skype," Moran said weakly.

The judge raised his eyebrows. He looked appalled. "Do you think that's acceptable for a four-year-old little girl? I'm not sure she would even grasp the concept."

I'd done my homework on this judge. He was known for his harsh decision making. This did not faze me; in fact, I was glad. I wanted someone who was going to follow the letter of the law and not take any of Moran's BS. This proved to be right. Thank goodness. At least he could see through him. I found out that Judge C had written a book about adopting a young boy from Romania. *He must have a good heart*, I thought.

I was holding out all hope. I had been back and forth to court so many times that I was hoping this was it. A final decision. The right one. It felt like we were in the court room for a lifetime.

The judge addressed us both. "I think I have heard enough. Let's reconvene after lunch, then I will come to my decision." Judge C got up and walked out of the room.

"Court adjourned for the judge's decision."

I waited for Moran to walk out of the court room first. He had to pass us and I could not bring myself to look at him. I keep my gaze on Mr Hawley then followed him and his legal secretary out. Barbara had already left the room.

Just outside the court room there were old-fashioned benches and across the corridor was the ladies. I nipped in there before we were all going to head to the on-site café to grab some lunch. Barbara was in the ladies washing her hands.

"What do you think?" I asked her.

"I really can't say Zoe, he was playing with me in there a bit when I was talking about the laws on removal from the jurisdiction."

"Who, the judge? I couldn't read it either. Oh I feel sick. I really don't know what I will do if he allows Sofia to be taken to Dubai. Does he realise that I will never see her again? Moran will sever all ties without a second thought. He told Sofia, a four-year-old, she has a new mummy. This is not someone who should be allowed full control of a child's life."

"I know, Zoe. Let's get some lunch." Barbara really could not tell which way this was going to go. She looked at me, hopeful, and maintained her professional demeanour.

I followed Barbara to the café but I couldn't eat. This had become my normal response to this trauma I was going through, not eating. I felt sick. I had lost so much weight over the last four months. I was about seven and a half stone and very pale.

As we sat and ate lunch Barbara was telling me about her daughters, who were in uni. She seemed like a lovely woman with a great family. I envied her. I never asked for this horrific situation I was in but here I was. This was the hand I was dealt.

I thought about how it must be so hard doing the job of a family barrister. You would have to emotionally detach from every case. I would find it extremely difficult. Especially if the judge ruled against you and a child's life was exposed to danger. I thought about the family court process and how it is just one person's decision on the outcome of a family dynamic. It did not seem right. That person has never met the family and is making their judgement based on information presented in that case. There seemed to be far too much room for injustice especially given the information is often hearsay or not fact checked.

"Case for Dronfield" came over the speaker.

We were being called back in. My throat was dry.

I watched Moran walk into the court room first. He had been sitting on the benches in the waiting area. Barbara looked at me and nodded.

We made our way back to our places in the court. It felt surreal. This was it.

This was where my daughter's life and that of everyone around us could be ruined and changed forever.

"All rise." The judge walked into the room. I was trying to read the expression on his face but it was impossible.

I was holding my breath and bracing myself for the worst. I was praying the judge had seen sense and through Moran's utter nonsense.

My legal team were so professional, no-one showed an ounce of emotion. We all just stood facing forward waiting for the judge to sit, so we could. Mr Hawley looked at me and gave a nod.

I gave a half smile from the corner of my mouth. I could not even look in the direction of Moran.

The judge addressed us both. "You have both given me your sides of the story. I have made my decision."

He paused.

The judge turned to Moran. "You are leaving the country to live in Dubai. I believe it right that Sofia will reside with her mother in the UK and continue her education in this country."

I had a huge intake of breath. *Does this mean she can come home today?* I looked at Barbara, I looked at Mr Hawley. Barbara kept looking at the judge and Mr Hawley gave me a wink.

The relief was palpable.

The judge continued to address Moran. "You are to have Skype contact with Sofia from Dubai. Miss Dronfield you must arrange for a non-molestation order against Smith and have no contact with him whatsoever." I nodded.

Of course! I thought. I wouldn't be here if it wasn't for that nutter.

The judge turned to Barbara: "Can I ask you to draw up the relevant order?"

"Yes, Your Honour," she replied.

Moran did not even react. He started to gather up his papers.

Mr Hawley turned to me again, and I smiled a huge smile at him. Tears welled up in my eyes.

I whispered to Barbara, "Can I collect Sofia from school today and take her home?"

Barbara immediately addressed the Judge. "Your Honour, Miss Dronfield will collect Sofia from her school today and thank you."

The judge nodded, got up, it was announced "Court dismissed" and he walked out.

The sense of relief was overwhelming. I could breathe again. *My baby is coming home!* I was so excited to tell Cameron. My mind was racing and my heart was pounding.

I was so happy, but I knew my journey was not over, however at least I had got over a major hurdle and pulled my family back together. This was something I should never have gone through at this time. Moran was a wicked and cruel man; he did not deserve Sofia.

I turned to David. "Thank you so much. Thank you, thank you, thank you." The right decision had been made. Well done to Judge C; common sense and evidence prevailed. The facts were considered properly.

No-one is perfect in this imperfect world, however he did his job right that day. He looked at the facts, the evidence I had collated, and did not assume. I would love to know why Judge W made her decision to remove a four-year-old little girl from her mummy, punishing me and her brother Cameron for my attack.

She made an assumption and that was not her job. Judge C did say something that I found totally unrealistic in his summing up. He said that he hoped one day Moran and I could have a coffee together and forget this ever happened. I'm sorry, Judge C, but that will never happen. I will never talk to that man again for as long as I live. From that moment I would only communicate via email. I blocked all contact in any other way; that way I could keep every communication as evidence.

After settling Sofia back in her own room at home I booked a holiday for just the three of us and we flew out to Egypt for a week. It was magical. The kids remember that holiday to this day. It was just the three of us; it was euphoria!

It was over.

Or was it?

Cameron and Sofia on holiday in Egypt after four months of separation, following Zoe regaining residency of Sofia

RED FLAGS & REFLECTION

Each time I spoke out, whether on my social media platforms or if I was featured on the news or in the newspaper, it triggered a flurry of contact from people, some who were also victims, and they would offer words of support and well wishes. This really helped me get through some difficult days. The validation from talking to others who understand your journey is so valuable to your wellbeing. You need to be believed. You need to feel heard. I got great strength and determination from this.

It gave me the drive to continue my fight and made it compelling for me to help others, to change the system and to stop the injustices victims face daily when navigating our justice system. I wanted to close gaps in the process that seemed glaringly obvious to me.

Earlier in this chapter I mentioned Claire's Law. This is a disclosure scheme which allows the police to share historic information about previous domestic abuse offences that a new partner may have. However there is no duty for them to do this or to identify if someone is a serial offender. Also if they say there is no history, it does not mean there isn't one. Therefore the system is flawed.

The law was named after Claire Wood. Claire was 36 years old when she was murdered by her known domestic abuser ex-boyfriend in 2009. He strangled her and set her home on fire in Salford in the UK. An offender's criminal history was previously confidential. Claire's father campaigned along with others to make this change.

Something I find difficult with this scheme is that it puts the onus on the potential victim to make the request. I know I would never have done this, given I did not even recognise I was a victim. However, as we become more informed around domestic abuse, I would hope that anyone reading this in the UK who has doubts about a new partner uses this service. You apply at your local police force.

It could save your life!

Are you aware of the various orders available to you in family court? And do you know which one to use should you need to access this service?

CHAPTER 18:
Two Courts Same Day

It was 10 months since the attack when the DC informed me of the date of the trial in the Crown Court. I was spending my days on self-care, making sure I was prepared for the two-week-long trial. I had got up to start my daily routine while the kids were still in bed and as I walked down the stairs, I could see the silhouette of the postman walking back up the path away from my house. He had posted a large envelope through the letterbox. I wondered what it could be as it looked important. My stomach churned. *What now!* I thought to myself, trying to stay in a positive frame of mind but I was again triggered and could feel the blood running through my veins.

I go to the kitchen and just stare at the envelope while putting on the kettle.

I open it and start reading. It's another court date but it's not for the trial for Smith, it's another hearing in family court for more changes around Sofia. Since the 'final' hearing there had been more. There is no such thing as a 'final' hearing as applicants can just keep on submitting exponential applications.

I feel sick. *When will this end?!* How was I supposed to prepare myself for Crown Court, an attempted murder trial, when Moran was constantly trying to pull me down too and disrupt every inch of my life? And as the family court do not vet this process, he could continue to put in never-ending vexatious applications, which was a complete joke.

I read on through the papers. Moran had now applied for an enforcement order. He wanted an order to be enforced on me with penalties. I could not believe it; the audacity of this man was astounding. I wouldn't mind but he had made the decision to leave and live in Dubai and now he had returned to the UK because that decision failed (go figure!) and the second he landed he reverted to his demands, using the family court as a tool of abuse. It was tiring having to deal with his petulant child behaviour. I found it truly unbelievable that he could not communicate in a normal manner. He had to schedule a court hearing for everything. It was a total waste of everyone's time. Sofia was having contact with her dad. He needed to win and was still just hell-bent on punishing me. Family court is the perfect playground for someone who wants constant attention and conflict.

I looked at the date on the letter. That date seemed familiar. I read my message from the DC confirming the Crown Court date. *It's the same date!*

My heart started racing. How the hell had he managed this? I was furious but frightened at the same time. Moran was back and now he had managed to disrupt the court process by getting a hearing date for the same date as the Crown Court case I had to attend as the main witness and victim. How could I do this? I stared at the page in disbelief. *He's done this on purpose*, I think to myself. I feel sick. They were not even scheduled at the same court.

So, on the same day I was supposed to be putting a potential murderer behind bars at Warwick Crown Court, I was meant to attend a family court hearing for custody arrangements of my daughter in Coventry Family Court and the order threatened me with consequences as what Moran had asked for was an enforcement order. What a dilemma and disgusting position to be put in. I was meant to decide to convict a maniac or keep custody of my daughter. I had no idea what happened at an enforcement hearing, but I had heard many horror stories of residency being switched, and this was always a fear.

I read through the application documents. He had simply written a paragraph of utter lies. Something along the lines that he had minimal contact – he had not had any contact he chose, so this was a lie or due to his own doing. He also wanted Sofia to attend his wedding. I already knew this as Sofia had told me and I had no problem with her attending, and actually I thought it would be lovely as she was to be bridesmaid. However, he was positioning it to the court that I had said no, another lie! I found it utterly disturbing that he could waste so many people's time for such a ridiculous request. He wanted it ordered by the court Sofia could attend the wedding. I found this bizarre.

The handwritten application, which clearly was written by him and not his fiancée this time, had big crossings out on it where Moran had scribbled the application.

I was utterly confused by how the system allowed this much power to a convicted criminal over another person, who was law abiding. The printed summons from the court read that this was an enforcement application, saying I had breached a previous order and not allowed contact. This was again utter rubbish. I went through the dates and started building my evidence of where in fact Moran was the one in breach. By now I had learnt to document EVERYTHING.

However, reading the document further, the threat was very much aimed at me. It read:

[To Zoe Dronfield: You must obey the instructions contained in this order. If you do not, you will be guilty of contempt of court and you may be sent to prison, fined or your assets may be seized.]

Another application picked up by Judge W, the delightful female judge who made the initial judgement to remove Sofia from my care. What was this woman thinking? Does she do her job as a judge, or does she just believe any poppycock that passes her nose?

Obviously, this was now a huge worry. My fury at this judge's ignorance was pounding through my chest. This woman had met me once, as I stood bruised in court having discharged myself from hospital, a victim of a ferocious attack and not once but twice this judge had made hugely detrimental decisions which would impact my and my children's lives forever. How had she come to the conclusions she had?

I spoke with my solicitor. "You could ask for a sick note from the doctor." This felt wrong. I wasn't sick. I was sick and tired, but I was not sick. Why didn't the courts understand there was a bigger picture here? It was not just about what Moran wanted. Judge W seemed completely biased and against me for some reason. I'd love to meet her one day and for her to look me in the eyes and tell me why she did what she did. She constantly believed any old hearsay rubbish submitted to her in applications, handwritten, illiterate and abusive, without a shred of evidence. This was not law. This was a failure in her duty as a judge.

I wanted to understand why the family court were not aware of the Crown Court proceedings. At the time I did not know that they function in complete isolation from one another. Clearly, both cases were hugely important so why did they arrange a family hearing on the same day? I obviously could not attend both. One was being held at Coventry Family Court, the other in Warwick Crown Court around 30 minutes' drive (assuming no traffic) away. And the most obvious point, how could I be in two places at once?! Another glaring failure of the court process, which made me feel like I was not important in this whole process, however I was the victim in an extremely important and expensive case held by the Crown. You would think things would be joined up. The cost of me not attending Crown Court would have been substantial; Smith would have walked free and Sofia would probably have been removed from my care due to failure to protect or some other made-up guise. The consequences of missing either case were huge, costly and dangerous.

How could anyone endure such nonsense without losing your mind? And I often felt I was, or actually that the whole system was completely bonkers. I was quite furious and frightened. I needed to have a record of this; I needed to highlight this extreme failure. I wrote to my MP Jim Cunningham; more on this later.

So, as advised by my solicitor Mr Hawley, I arranged a doctor's appointment. I gave it some thought, and this would be a way I could get this ridiculous situation documented. However even this was not straightforward. I arranged a consultation with my GP and explained what was going on: the attack and the offender who was on remand. Now the father of my daughter was dragging me through family court with a constant stream of lies. I was struggling to sleep, and clearly very stressed.

As I was talking, I started to cry. It sounded a lot; it sounded unbelievable. I shocked myself while I was reeling this all off to the GP. I felt so disgusting having to talk that way: the attacks, court, police, solicitors. I felt like dirt. These men had pulled my life to pieces. What scum. I wish I'd never met either of them.

The doctor, a small quietly spoken lady, asked, "What do you want from me Zoe, how can I help?" She looked at me with a concerned expression.

"Well, I've now been summoned to Crown Court and family court on the same day, and I can't physically do both, obviously. I need a doctor's note to explain this to the court." I looked at her with a wry smile.

She shook her head. "I can't give you that because if I did it would be like giving students a pass out from exams."

I look back at her dumbfounded. Students! Exams! It was hardly the same. I was horrified. I started to cry again, tears streaming down my face. I felt humiliated.

"I CAN'T GO TO BOTH; can't you see what is happening here? I'm being abused at every turn. I'm being asked to do something impossible. If I had a doctor's note, they would take it seriously. The courts won't listen to me, what am I meant to do?"

I just sat with my head in hands. I thought, *I'm not leaving without the note, so she needs to start writing*. I just sat there.

I look up at her, praying she had an ounce of empathy. "I can't keep doing this, why is this happening to me? How many more things are going to happen to me? This whole year has been one disaster and catastrophe after another. I don't deserve this. I am a good person!" I bowed my head again.

"Ok Zoe, I will give you the note but please call the court and tell them." She started writing out the form. I had a glimmer of relief but I would have to wait to see if they would adjourn the case. They might disregard the doctor's note anyway.

"I have written to my MP about this, and once this is all over, I will be shouting from the rooftops the injustice of all of this. I don't deserve any of it. I'm a good mother and a good person." I left the consultation room.

Another hurdle climbed. It was never ending.

Every small victory felt like a step forward. This is the way I dealt with all of this. I sent the doctor's note to Mr Hawley to send on to the court. I also called the Crown Court. I was making sure I covered all angles even if no-one else was.

I spoke with someone on the front desk. They told me to turn up for the Crown Court hearing as they were the higher court, then they would speak to the prosecuting barrister on my arrival to arrange an adjournment in family court, if this had not been done so already with the doctor's note.

This sounds like a sensible approach, I thought. *I'm sure the family court hearing will not go ahead if this is advised by a Crown Court official*. A glimmer of hope.

So that's what I did.

Finally, the trial day came round. This was now a year and two months after the attack. I had been through the mill. Literally my entire life had become a constant battle: constant family court hearings, witness intimidation, being threatened with arrest for sending three messages, trying to get back into work, the victim blaming, the video statements for the police, the constant meetings around my case with MPs, advocates, charities, the huge media storm, the other victims of Smith. The realisation that I had been with someone known to the police who had done this before.

I could not think straight. I was in a complete state of anxiety. I was shaking and I had not slept properly. I took the kids to school in my tracksuit and when I got home I started to get myself prepared for court. I had already chosen my outfit, a black dress with white lapels and thick black tights with little flat pumps. I wore very minimal make-up.

I posted a very sombre selfie on Facebook. I needed the support of my followers. A lot of eyes and ears were on the case. [Head up, shoulders back.] That saying stayed with me throughout. All my new followers sent messages of support on Facebook; they were rooting for me. Validating me. Sending strength.

It really helped to have such an outpouring of support from all of my friends, old and new. It kept me going through the hard days. Old school friends got in touch, new friends who were victims/survivors of domestic violence, people from all over the world who were watching my case and waiting to see what the outcome was. It kept me strong knowing I had the support of others, I had my followers, believers, and those who understood domestic abuse and what this does to your life in the flick of an eye.

My case was high profile. The media were waiting to hear the outcome of the trial; there had been so many headlines over the last 12 or so months.

'I survived an 8-hour attack at the hands of my ex-boyfriend'

'Brave mum of two who survived boyfriend's brutal meat cleaver attack'

'Thug who battered his girlfriend in an eight-hour attack'

'My stalker ex almost killed me – and my 999-call failed'

'Victim of savage domestic violence in Coventry dragged through family court'

'Zoe Dronfield thought she had the perfect boyfriend – until he stabbed her as she slept'

'Domestic abuse victim Zoe Dronfield speaks out after police interview her over claims she harassed her attacker's family'

I always knew when an article had gone in as I would have a flurry of friend requests and messages of well wishes on social media. I have to say that kept me going.

I had meetings set up after the court case where I would speak on the news at the top of the court steps to read out the verdict. I was hopeful it would be the right one. Smith had tortured me to within an inch of my life, using a meat cleaver and an eight-inch knife. The headlines were horrific. However, when I spoke to the press, I was open; I had no shame. I wanted to be clear that I did not blame myself and I wanted to make that clear to everyone else. I refused to be held responsible for what that maniac did to me.

One of my mantras throughout this ordeal was "I am not ashamed; the shame lies solely with my perpetrator".

When my story first broke in my local news, my phone blew up. I had journalists contacting me for comments. I would often hear updates on the case from the journalists first which was frustrating and very scary. The police are slow, and information was dripped through the system at a snail's pace. No-one gave a thought that a victim's life was on hold while waiting for the trial and finding out about appeals by media is unforgiveable, not to mention extremely dangerous.

I would have expected there to be one liaison contact that supported the victim. There was not. I was left to navigate everything myself. Most victims would not have the strength. I was dealing with different agencies all needing different things. I had to change my face depending on what professional I was talking to; when social care wanted to meet me, I had to be a strong mother, held together and family orientated. In the criminal arena I had to be a weak victim deserving of justice and in family court well who knows, that is a kangaroo court and if it was up to Judge W I would have been burnt at the stake, I'm sure.

I was lucky, and looking back I see what a strong network of friends I had around me. I was supported by an advocate from the domestic abuse charity Refuge in the criminal case with Smith. The same advocate supported me through family court and Laura Richards, the founder of Paladin National Stalking Advocacy Service, had been amazing when dealing with the witness intimidation and the ongoing stalking by Smith. My friends were all amazing too; even friends I had not seen in years since school all sent well wishes and watched my story unfold, offering support along the way. This was all invaluable.

Waiting for that court date was the worst. My life had been on hold. It had taken over 12 months to get to this day and it had been quite a rollercoaster.

Right, breathe!

Here we go.

This is it.

I wondered if I'd see Smith. I wondered if I would be cross-examined in front of him. *That would be hard,* I thought to myself. I had asked the DC to ask for special measures however I would not know until I arrived at court if they were granted. Special measures meant I would give my evidence from behind a screen. So not in view of the defendant, Smith, or the public gallery.

The DC in charge of the case picked me up from my house. "You ready?" she said, looking at me and clenching her fists up in front of her as if to show support.

The DC had been great throughout the whole process. She had always shown empathy without losing her professionalism. She stood by me. She knew the truth. She knew that I was not lying. She also answered my millions of questions about the law and always made me feel at ease as much as humanly possible.

It was not her fault the system was flawed. She would often empathise with me when I told her how broken the system was. I would talk to her about the law, how it is not on the side of the victim and the offender seems to get all the rights. She understood. It made me wonder, who oversees this whole process, as no-one had any ownership over the entire process. When the DC found out I was interviewed for harassment she was shocked. She was doing her best with the system she had; so are most professionals but it is just not good enough. Everyone should be responsible for calling out injustice and broken processes.

I arranged for my therapist Mr Kilmurry from DK Hypnotherapy and my close friend Jodi to meet me at the court for moral support. I'm sure the DC drove me to ensure I turned up. Many domestic abuse victims back out and this would have meant Smith would walk for almost murdering me and leaving my children motherless; there was no way I was going to let that happen. It also meant I would arrive earlier than anyone else and could use a separate entrance to enter the court building so I wouldn't bump into the Smith family.

My dad was not able to come to the court. The court room was situated on different levels. As he is disabled the court building had no access for him to sit in the public gallery which was the only viewing option unless he was on the court floor which they suggested, sitting alongside the barristers and in direct view of Smith. I did not want this, and the Smith family would no doubt be in the public gallery too. I did not want to put my dad through that, to be sitting by that family who denied Smith's abuse of women and had enabled his behaviour for years.

I walked up the steps. My heart was pounding and my hands were sweating.

I remember telling the DC, "I'll write a book one day you know." I'm not sure if she believed me or not. She always said how brave and strong I was. I didn't feel like it at the time. I suppose I did not have much choice. The DC clearly dealt with cases like mine all the time. You'd think she would be desensitised by it, or lack empathy, but quite the opposite. She was professional, humane, caring.

Smith's original charge was attempted murder, however this had since been reduced to a lesser charge. The DC explained why: "The Crown Prosecution Service (CPS) often do this if they are more confident to secure a sentence on a lesser charge." For me it seemed truly unbelievable. He wanted me dead. The knives, the continued assault, cleaning the knives in the bath, calling my friends pretending to be me, cutting his wrists saying "We are going together babe" is not really the act of someone innocent or not intent on murder, is it?

The DC had warned me before that this would happen which gave me time to understand this decision. I researched both charges to try and understand this. The prosecution would find it harder to prove beyond reasonable doubt the 'intent' to murder as Smith and I had been in a relationship. I know, crazy right! The new lower charge was Grievous Bodily Harm with Intent (GBH Section 18). This is the most serious form of assault short of attempted murder. Both attempted murder and GBH with Intent carry a life sentence. Attempted murder requires a demonstration of the intent to murder, and this is where the CPS's decision came to reduce to GBH s18. I suppose it was the right decision to get the right sentencing result.

The CPS did not want the case thrown out on a technicality; Smith had made the 999 call so his defence could potentially argue he did not actually want me dead. That's my interpretation anyway; I'm not a lawyer but with my practical head on I expect this is why this decision was made.

The DC and I were met at the top of the stairs inside the building by an older lady. The building was mainly glass and very echoey. She ushered us through a door then into a side room which was called Special Victims Unit. This is a unit within the court run by volunteers who are there to support vulnerable victims while you wait to be called.

"Hi, Zoe, isn't it?" One of the volunteers guided me through to a room where Jodi and Mr Kilmurry were already waiting. It felt totally surreal. The room we were going to be in for the next two weeks was tiny and felt claustrophobic; it had no windows and no natural light. It was like a tiny doctor's waiting room. A few comfy chairs, an old-fashioned box TV in the corner, a couple of old magazines on the table.

The volunteer gave me a sheet of paper that set out expectations of the day. Apparently I was lucky to have the room to keep me safe; this is one of the special measures put in place for vulnerable victims. At least I did not have to wait in the public building as I could have bumped into Smith's family, who would no doubt be there. It allowed me to keep my composure and not get too overwhelmed.

The trial had been set for two weeks. This meant I had to attend every day until I was called to the witness stand. I had been pre-warned to take drinks and snacks as I could be in there a long time. I hugged Jodi and we sat down. We just looked at each other in disbelief. The DC stepped into the room. "He might actually plead guilty with a bit of luck, and we can all go home. Offenders often wait to find out if the victim has turned up for the trial. Then when they realise you are going ahead with it, they plead guilty. The judge can give them some lenience if they do this," she explained.

"Bloody joke the way it works to be honest, how can you get leniency when you have dragged everyone to court? I bet he won't." I just knew he wanted his day in court plus he had convinced himself of his own lies.

The way criminal court works here in the UK and in my case with Smith is I am the victim and witness, therefore I do not have the opportunity to see any of the court documents as it's the Crown's case and not mine personally. I had no idea how they would position the case. Smith was the defendant; this meant he must defend the allegations and charges against him. The case was owned by the Crown Prosecution Service (CPS). The CPS prosecutes criminal cases that have been investigated by the police and other investigative organisations in England and Wales. The CPS is independent and they make their own decisions independently of the police and government. So, the police build the case with statements, crime scene pictures and witness testimony and it goes to the CPS to decide on the charge and if in fact it should go to court. So, the case against Smith is the Crown vs Smith as opposed to a case I would bring myself.

The duty of the CPS is to make sure that the right person is prosecuted for the right offence, and to bring offenders to justice wherever possible. My witness testimony, my previous police statements and other witness statements like the police officers attending and ambulance staff would all be used to build the case but I didn't get to see the case files or meet the prosecuting barrister of the trial until the day of the trial and even then, she just checked in.

The prosecuting barrister bustled into the little waiting room dragging a case of files behind her. "Hi Zoe, I am the prosecuting barrister, I'd just like to let you know that I have just heard that Smith is still pleading not guilty, so we are going ahead with the case, ok?" She was a petite lady. She looked so young, fresh out of law school, dressed fully robed in the court gowns which seemed to drown her, and she had the standard court wig on too. It was quite unnerving to be honest; she looked like she had only just finished university. I hoped she was going to be able to deal with him. She looked very flustered and rushed.

It was clear that Smith wanted his day in court. It was unbelievable he was still pleading not guilty. However before answering the prosecuting barrister there was one thing I still needed to get cleared up as I was also meant to be in family court for a hearing for the enforcement application submitted by Moran. This was not just any old hearing; Moran wanted to slap me with penalties - it was serious.

"Yes, that's fine, however there is one thing." I began telling the prosecutor my predicament. "I have been summoned to family court for an enforcement hearing around my daughter." I looked at her, shaking my head. "Would you be able to contact family court in Coventry please and ask them to have it adjourned as I'm obviously here at Crown Court putting a murderer away?"

She looked at me with no emotion and started to act even more flustered. "Oh, you'll have to attend that then," she responded. I was utterly shocked by this reaction. She seemed naïve. That was a 'throw your hands in the air and give up' response. I was not impressed, and this further sent me into a spiral.

"No!" I immediately responded. I looked at her in disbelief. "Can't you just call them to say I'm here; how can I be in two places at once? Surely this is the Crown Court and if they hear from you then they will adjourn? This is what they advised. What would happen to Smith if I didn't go ahead? No! We are all here. It's been over a year, why don't the courts talk to each other, what the hell is going on!" At this point I was so angry I couldn't help my outburst.

"What kind of fucking topsy turvy world is this?! I'm here putting a dangerous man behind bars and you won't just make a phone call to the family court, what the fuck am I supposed to do, give up on my daughter or let a monster free?!"

At this point I just broke down and started to cry out of sheer frustration. You know the cry when you can barely catch your breath? It was like that. I don't think I had released emotion like that for a while.

This is the problem with the system. Who owns this problem? No-one. It was a hot potato. It was down to me. It wasn't up to the prosecuting barrister to sort family court; all she cared about was Smith's case. It wasn't up to the DC either. So, it was down to me to liaise with a court and tell them I could not attend. Doesn't look good, does it? I was crying and it was a very uncomfortable atmosphere in the room. Neither Jodi nor Mr Kilmurry had seen me this way ever before.

It was like common sense had completely flown out of the window.

"I'm sorry but I just don't understand, this is a joke." I'm crying. My chest is tight. I feel like the room is spinning. "Oh Zo." Jodi is trying to console me. I was in a no-win situation.

"Are you going to be able to stand, Zoe?" The barrister was starting to get agitated that her case was about to fall apart.

"YES! I'll be standing, I'm here aren't I! I'll call the family court then and hopefully someone there has an ounce of decency or discretion to not hold a hearing without me!" I was visibly shaking, tears pouring down my face.

The barrister looked shocked at my outburst and demeanour. I did not care.

I knew the doctor's note had been sent to family court in Coventry by my solicitor; it's just I am thorough and wanted to cover all angles. It was serious and the courts had said the prosecuting barrister would do this, but she was not being helpful at all. I wanted the prosecuting barrister to make the call as it would have looked so much better than me making the call. It infuriated me she did not see the importance of this although she looked too young to have children, so probably had no idea or empathy for my situation. I just did not want Moran using my absence against me. Which he would and to not turn up to an enforcement hearing, I thought, would look like his lies about me being awkward with contact were true.

"Don't worry, I'll get my composure together, do you think I'm going to let that bastard get away with this?! I wouldn't be in this situation with Sofia if he hadn't attacked me, now I'm being presented as a bad mother because of his evil attack. It's not fair and he needs to be behind bars. He will do it again. He has done it before. Do you realise he's done this before?! Over and over again. You'll have this on the police reports, hopefully this is part of your case?!"

I snapped again. I couldn't take any more.

I was almost shouting at her.

The barrister looked at me blankly. "As long as you are ok to stand, Zoe." She clearly could not comment on the case.

"Yes! I'll be fine." I was so angry. How was any of this fair?

I made the telephone call from the reception desk to the family court and advised the staff on the front desk that I was at Crown Court for a serious case and would not be attending the hearing in Coventry. I also explained I had sent in a doctor's note.

They said the case would go ahead anyway as it was on the list.

I felt sick.

That meant I would not have any input in the hearing. Another breach of my human rights. Article 6 of the Human Rights Act protects your rights to a fair trial. I was furious, however I knew I had a legal standing, not that it gave me any reassurance whatsoever given the level of failings and incompetence I was dealing with throughout the entire process.

There is a real lack of emotion in the court process; you are almost dehumanised. Everyone seems too busy, too important to even acknowledge the very people they are fighting for. You feel like an insignificant pawn in a game of chess with zero control over the process and you just want it to end.

I would not wish this system on anyone. It was not so much the criminal proceedings as I knew what I had to do there. It was family court that was the worst; I was so disempowered. I felt respected in the criminal court; people asked if I was ok. They understood this was a difficult process. In family court it could not have been further from that. They were rude and disrespectful; you are treated like a criminal and you feel judged. In family court you feel like you are guilty and must prove your innocence. It is an absolute contrast.

The family court hearing that went ahead without me meant I was now slapped with an enforcement order, meaning if I breached the order by not sticking to the terms, I was threatened with the punishment of having my assets seized or prison. Seems reasonable, doesn't it? Utter craziness.

A couple of days passed and it was now day 3 of the trial. The court volunteer came into the room and said it was my time to go through. I'd been called. I had no idea what to expect, how I'd be treated by the defence. I was just going to tell the truth. That's all I had to do. It's easy when you are not a liar because it's all there. Nothing to hide. I had an IDVA (Independent Domestic Violence Advocate) from Refuge who could support and sit alongside me in court. She couldn't speak but she was there for support. It helped knowing she would be there.

Jodi had gone into the public gallery the day before to listen to some of the trial. She said Smith was bouncing around the defendant's box and banging on the window to his mum and dad in the public gallery which was the next room to the defendant box. She said she could see the guards telling him to sit down. He was shouting and gesturing with his hands, "Call me" to his mum, and banging on the glass. Not the actions of someone innocent really, were they? He was confident, flippant and aggressive even in the court room.

Mr Kilmurry also sat in on one of the days, only for a short time but long enough to see Smith on the stand. Apparently he was crying. Crocodile tears. He knew what he had done. Was he crying for me? I think not. It was an attempt to get empathy from the jury.

The IDVA and I were directed down a back corridor of the courts to a small holding room where we waited for another five minutes before being called into the court room.

I walk into the court room with its vast, high ceilings, very spaced out. The witness stand where I was positioned was a little wooden box, which felt like a church altar. I could not be seen by Smith or the public. The judge was higher than the rest of the room and to my right. He looked at me and immediately looked horrified. Maybe he had a daughter, maybe he just did not expect me to look the way I did; he would have only seen the injury pictures. But then I followed the judge's eyeline and he was clearly looking at Smith who must have been in a box directly opposite the judge. He gave him an angry glance. I could not see Smith; he was somewhere to my left next to the public gallery where no-one could see me either. The jury were directly in front me. There were 13 people in the jury; I could see them all and they could see me. I could feel their eyes staring at me. They were a mix of male and female, young and old. I glanced over but I was embarrassed. I did not hold anyone's gaze. I just looked down at my hands or at the judge.

Below the jury and in the centre of the room in a pit area and looking up to the judge the barristers were sitting with their legal helpers. There were papers everywhere. My barrister the Crown Prosecutor was nearest to me, although she was still quite far, and the room felt huge. I felt so tiny. I looked at her hoping she would be good enough. She seemed smaller in the court room. Did she care enough about me after my outburst earlier about family court? The defence barrister was next to her, a rather plump white middle-aged man. *How clichéd*, I thought to myself. I took it in. I wondered what Smith was doing. I wondered what he looked like. I shuddered. What on earth was going through his mind?

"Take a seat Miss Dronfield," the judge directed me. I was told to read the court oath.

Then my barrister spoke first. She asked me to describe where I lived.

"I live in a four-bedroom detached house in Coventry, it's a nice area where I live."

And then I described my work; I explained that I work in IT and provide IT solutions for companies to do criminal background checks on their staff.

I was then asked to describe in my own words what had happened on the evening of the attack, so I did.

I explained that Smith and I had met to talk about his previous actions, smashing my door and not leaving me alone when I asked him to. I talked about how we were fine and the evening was pleasant, however I was still cross at him about smashing my door. He had embarrassed me in front of the neighbours and caused the damage in front of my daughter. I then explained that I went to bed leaving Smith downstairs. As I began to talk about the attack, my voice started to crack, I felt a tightness in my chest and I was somehow taken back to the first day I came around in the hospital. It was surreal and I began to cry.

"I don't know why he did this to me." My voice was quiet. It was the first time I had ever felt any emotion over the attack. Up until this point I had been driven by anger and numbness.

My barrister then asked if she could present me with a folder which contained scenes of the attack. The folder was passed to me by one of the court ushers and I began turning the pages. I had not seen any of these pictures before.

They were photographs taken of various things. My injuries. I turned the page and saw a photo of Smith and his superficial wounds. They looked like scratches to his wrists and neck. Then I turned the page again...

It was my lovely bedroom.

I recognised it but it was completely covered in blood. All over the bed, down the walls. You could see where I had held the bannisters. There were streaks and splattering of blood everywhere ... so much blood. My white sheets utterly saturated. This was the scene of my attempted murder.

I was studying the picture; my laptop was open at the end of the bed on my chaise longue. Why did he have the laptop open while I was dying on the bed? The room looked a mess, not how I live. I am very particular; everything has a place. There was stuff everywhere. I couldn't quite believe the amount of blood, my blood.

I froze on that page, studying every inch of my bedroom. The blood was everywhere. Was I on the bed with blood gushing from me, or had I got up and moved around?

For a moment I forgot I was in court, everyone looking at me. I burst into tears and put my hands over my mouth and stared at the page. I didn't have much recollection of the night, but the feelings all came flooding back. I started to shake.

I turned the page again; there were pictures of the bathroom and the bath half-filled with bloody water where he had attempted to clean the knives. There was an eight-inch knife in the bath.

Was I unconscious on the bed when he was doing this? Was this the act of someone with no intent? Did he think I was already dead when cleaning the knives, cleaning the scene and weapons of his hand and fingerprints?

I felt so cold. My mouth was dry. I looked up at the jury briefly. They were all looking at me. I just bowed my head. It was mortifying.

"Take your time Miss Dronfield, have some water." The judge was so nice. The jury were given the pictures at the same time, and I could see one man glaring at Smith the entire time. He looked furious; he was really snarling at him.

I had a sip of water. I took a deep breath in and out. I tried to compose myself. *Come on Zoe*, I thought to myself. *Switch on your practical head.* I wondered what Smith was doing while we are all looking at what he had done. I wondered if he had remorse or even cared. Is he proud that he acts like this? So many questions were flooding through my mind.

The judge stood down my barrister. It was now time for the defence barrister to cross-examine me. "So you had been drinking, Miss Dronfield, on the night in question?"

I sat up straight at this point. What was he trying to suggest? "Yes," I calmly replied in a kind of nonchalant manner.

So what? Here we go! I thought to myself. This is where they try to push the blame on me, discredit me or make it look as if I somehow deserved this and Smith was a victim.

I looked at him, confused. *My injuries speak for themselves, don't they?* I was thinking and shaking my head.

How can he do this job? I'm looking at a defence barrister, a plump middle-aged, red-faced white man. He probably has children of his own, a wife or girlfriend, maybe a daughter. How could he defend such a monster?

He continued, "And you got angry when Mr Smith came up the stairs? You, Miss Dronfield, were standing on the bed brandishing a knife." He was waving his arms doing a swooshing movement as if with a knife in his hands.

I let out a sarcastic snigger. I couldn't help it. It was utterly absurd what he was suggesting and the way he looked.

"That is not true," I responded with a hint of sarcasm and rolled my eyes as if it was the most ridiculous thing I had ever heard. He looked like a complete prat for even saying that. I was 5 foot 2 and 8 stone; Smith is 15 stone and 6 foot tall and the hand gestures, well, they were something else.

It was a pantomime.

"I have no idea why Smith did this to me, I really don't. I have told you what I remember and the injuries speak for themselves, don't they?" I kept my composure. My voice was clear and direct.

"No more questions, Your Honour."

I was done. I was not up there long. I suppose they had heard enough from me. There was not much to say. I could only remember snippets, but the pictures told a thousand words.

Thank goodness that was out of the way. Now all I had to do was wait for the verdict.

The jury were now out for deliberation...

RED FLAGS & REFLECTION

I later researched this whole process of going through the criminal court and family court concurrently and why the courts' attitudes are so different and disjointed. I came across a study by Marianne Hester. It was like a light bulb moment, a complete validation of the absurdities I was dealing with.

Marianne is a professor, internationally recognised for her research on domestic violence and in her case study she explains about the three planets: the domestic violence planet, the child protection planet, the child contact planet. I read this research when I read all the other books and information I have come across on this subject with my head nodding and saying out loud "Oh my god!" Why is this not taught to those in these professions? It is absolutely what happens.

She outlines the three planets as follows.

The domestic violence planet

On this planet, domestic violence is considered a crime. The father's behaviour is recognised by the police and other agencies as being abusive to the mother, so he could be prosecuted for a criminal or public order offence. He might also have a restraining or protective order taken out against him. At the same time, support agencies provide protection and refuge for the mother. The civil and criminal laws provide intervention and support mechanisms, and on this planet the focus is on violent male partners who need to be contained and controlled in some way in order to ensure that the women and children are safe.

The child protection planet

When children are living with a mother who is experiencing domestic violence, another planet becomes involved where a different set of professionals live. Here, social workers reside alongside the National Society for the Prevention of Cruelty to Children – those who have a statutory duty to protect children – so this planet has a different population and consequently a different set of laws. Here public law deals with child protection and the approach is very different from that on the domestic violence planet. On the child protection planet, the emphasis is on the welfare of the child and its carer.

In order to protect the children, social workers are likely to insist that the mother removes herself and her children from the violent relationship. If she does not do so, it is she who is seen as 'failing to protect' and the children may then be removed into the care of the local authority. This puts the mother in a very difficult position and makes it more difficult for her to contact social services; thus the children remain vulnerable to abuse from the father. On the child protection planet, therefore, despite professionals identifying that the threat of violence comes from the man, it is the mother who is seen as responsible for dealing with the consequences and the violent man effectively disappears from the picture.

The child contact planet

On this planet there is yet another population because a different set of professionals reside here, governed by private, not public, law. The Children and Family Court Advisory and Support Service has tended to place less emphasis on child protection and more on the idea that children should have two parents. In this context, an abusive father may still be deemed a 'good enough' father, who should at least have contact with, if not custody or residence of, his child post-separation. So the mother who has tried to protect the child from his violent behaviour by calling in the police and supporting his prosecution on the domestic violence planet, and by leaving him as instructed on the child protection planet, is now ordered to allow contact between her violent partner and children, leaving her confused and fearing yet again for the safety of her children."

(Professor Marianne Hester, The Three Planet Model, 2009, http://www.bristol.ac.uk/news/2009/6703.html)

So you see this is a self-perpetuating cycle that a mother and victim of domestic violence cannot win in any planet. There is no desirable outcome. It is this injustice merry-go-round that compels me to continue my campaigning, to raise awareness. To educate those who put women in this impossible scenario. The practices, because they are so disjointed, are barbaric; they feel utterly inhumane.

At least understanding this information made me more powerful in the situations I found myself in. With this understanding I could challenge the system from a position of knowledge and truth. This is very hard to argue against. I would often find myself talking to professionals who would suddenly look from a different perspective when I explained the contradictions.

Because it was true. You are completely and utterly in a no-win situation. This is what must change.

Preparation, being organised and understanding processes, was extremely important for me. When going through this entire journey I needed to maintain an element of control over what was happening in my life at this time. I felt as if I was shoved into a system, on a conveyor belt with no way to get off. I never asked to be a victim nor did I want to have to deal with the constant attacks but they kept on coming, so I only did what I know best and fought back.

To keep my sanity I made sure I looked after myself first, getting enough sleep where I could. It was difficult and I had to remind my subconscious that I was safe. Smith could not attack me in my sleep again. I would lie in bed, the very same bed he attacked me in, and would think over and over: *he will not win, I will have no fear*.

In addition to self-care, I made sure I knew all about the criminal court process before stepping into that witness box. This is something I would advise anyone going through our justice system. It is a daunting process, however I found the criminal court much more empathic to my situation than the family 'justice' system.

If you can, speak to as many people as you can about what to expect. I even had a tour of the court room before the court date, so I had an idea what to expect. I spoke with the charities supporting me and other survivors about their experience of criminal court. Like I keep saying, knowledge is power, and the key to keeping yourself sane.

Being prepared is key. There will always be something to throw you off course. It's not an everyday situation and things can happen that blow up your day. For me at this time it was the two dates being the same for the different courts. It was bizarre. No professional wanted to help or could help. It made no sense.

In this chapter I was angry; I spent a lot of time 'furious', however I channelled this into fighting in both courts – my superpower was activated. And being prepared allowed me to stay focused and positive.

How would you prepare yourself for court?

CHAPTER 19:

The Verdict and My Growth Game

After giving evidence I went back to the victim support suite to wait for the verdict. I would not hear the jury read the verdict myself as I was still in special measures, so I had to just sit and wait to be told.

That was a long wait.

It felt like forever since the jury had gone out to deliberate. My palms were sweaty, and sitting in the waiting room we had spent all week in, it felt like the walls were closing in. I could hear the clock ticking as we sat just looking at each other and shrugging. Jodi was still with me. We just kept looking at each other. Jodi was reassuring me that of course Smith would be found guilty. I kept second guessing it; I had heard too many horror stories. Often the abuser of women with a more terrible story than mine gets to walk free with a community service order. That would be scary.

My heart was in my stomach. My mind was racing.

What am I going to do if they say "Not guilty"!? I was thinking the worst.

I tried to stay positive and focused, but it was hard not to at least prepare myself for the worst. The jury are human; how could they possibly think he was not guilty? There was no-one else there and I had not inflicted all those injuries on myself, as much as Smith wanted to convince people I did.

His story changed many times throughout the course of the trial according to various sources, from I fell down the stairs, to I was standing on the bed brandishing a knife, Smith was helping me as I fell, and it was self-defence as I was attacking him. Surely they would see the truth, but it only takes an element of doubt.

My actual memory of what happened was hazy, so my evidence was short and more emotion than fact as I kept crying and saying "I don't know why he did this to me". That was the truth; I still at this point could not understand why Smith had hurt me this way. It made no sense at all, however it had crossed my mind that Smith may have spiked my drink with something. Just the way it all played out was strange. He was so calm. Why was I so drowsy? How come I had zero memory of the attack and how all those injuries were inflicted?

If they found him not guilty, he would be able to walk out of the building, and I would no longer have access to special measures, support or protection. That's it. I would be vulnerable again.

I thought about that for a moment. So what if someone is truly guilty of a crime but they get off on a technicality? This must happen a lot, I thought.

Imagine being the victim of a physical attack and the person walked free and you had to face them outside the court. Good heavens. I started to panic.

Think positive! I told myself.

All of a sudden, the DC appeared at the door with a great big grin on her face. I let out a huge breath of air as if I had been holding it for hours.

"Guilty, Zoe."

"Oh wow." I felt numb, odd and a bit confused as to how I should react.

"Ok well good. Now what, how long will he get?" I asked, feeling quite sick. I also felt sorry for him. Yes, I am human and not an arsehole. I felt sorry for him; I thought what a waste of his life. I know what he did was utterly abhorrent, but I could not help but wonder why he had turned out that way.

"We have to wait for sentencing, that will be another hearing Zoe," said the DC. I felt confused.

"And how long will that be?"

"The judge has ordered psychological testing of Smith before he makes his decision. He will also find out about the others now, Zoe. Let's hope they give him what he deserves." I nodded. In a court case the judge will only ever have information around the offence on trial so any historic offending of perpetrators is always kept from the court until the verdict has been reached in the live case. This can often be an awful situation if the jury have found a perpetrator not guilty to then discover after the case that actually they have manipulated them and have a history of domestic abuse or stalking. This is why I campaign today to have serial perpetrators put on a register so the dots can be joined, but more about that later.

I was comforted that justice was served. Jodi had jumped up and was hugging me. "Good, the bastard!"

I didn't know whether to laugh or cry. It was a bittersweet feeling. I was still numb.

Justice had been served on Smith, however my life had been turned upside down. I was still fighting for my daughter. My son was in counselling. And I had to deal with visits from a social worker. Some scary information had come to light about Smith in the counsellor's sessions with Cameron. Smith had taken him to his friends' houses after school; he was either made to wait in the car alone for hours or one time he was told by Smith to play PlayStation games with his friend, and there was a big dog there. Cameron was scared of dogs. Smith bribed Cameron with a present so he would not tell me this happened. Cameron also said how Smith would drive really fast, scaring him. This made me sick to my stomach. I had gone back to work at this point, but I had changed jobs thinking a fresh start would be good; in the process I had come up against victim blaming and other vindictive people who took my victim status as a weakness. It was difficult having to justify myself constantly.

Lots of questions were running through my mind. I wondered what Smith was doing when the verdict came through. I was told he cried. What had happened to him that made him treat women this way? I wonder if he consciously thought about the damage he caused in people's lives, not just mine but all of the women who came forward.

Why was he so messed up?

There was more to Smith, much more that I clearly never knew.

We left the court through the rear entrance, and the DC dropped me home.

So, that was it.

Smith was guilty.

Twelve long months passed by before the day of sentencing. In that time, I was meant to just get on with my life. It was difficult. I struggled with everything I had been through. Why me, why was I being attacked by two men? I looked into myself a lot. There was no way this would define me, and I was determined to make change for the future for other women and my own children. The whole thing had made me so angry at the system.

Dealing with the attack was one thing – that I had got over physically. I still have scars. I have a scar to my face under my chin, my right eye socket is damaged and dented, my left hand has not recovered complete use however due to my sheer determination and refusal to accept my hand would not work, it is probably 80% recovered. I cannot grip properly; the back of my hand is numb and I cannot point as my tendons are severed. I have the occasional nightmare and am triggered by many things: hearing other stories, the broken system, but I channel this and it keeps me focussed on creating change. All I felt was pity for Smith. He had destroyed his own life, and for what? But the family courts allowing Moran to abuse me legally, that I could not forgive.

As soon as I received the date for sentencing, I asked some of my friends if they would come with me. I wanted to sit and hear with my own ears how long Smith had got. The only thing is I would have to sit in the public gallery. They could not offer special measures for the sentencing. The police did not want me to go. They advised against it, saying it would not look good.

I disagreed.

I needed closure.

I HAD to be there.

None of my friends could come. Everyone by this point had long since moved on with their lives, of course. Their worlds had not stopped turning even though my life felt like it was on pause waiting for this day. I did not blame them, but I was going anyway, even if I had to go alone.

I contacted Carmen, Smith's police officer ex. We had been in touch after the court case. We could not speak before as we did not want to prejudice the case. She told me some of things she had endured at the hands of Smith, and it was harrowing: rape, serious injuries caused by jumping from a window to escape him, assaults, burglary, false imprisonment, witness intimidation, threats to kill and harassment. It was just awful. Carmen agreed to go to the sentencing too. In a way it vindicated her as well. After all these years she also had closure. She had gone through hell dealing with Smith all those years before my ordeal. The victim blaming back then, 10 years prior to my attack, was rife and Carmen being a police officer, well she was vilified for being a victim of domestic abuse. The system treated her with contempt as 'she should know better'.

For me it was just proof that it can happen to anyone. Domestic abuse has no social class, no financial class, no ethnicity. It crosses every boundary. It can literally happen to anyone.

I had arranged to meet Carmen at the court building. I drove there alone. Mr Kilmurry knew about the date. I told him I was going with friends. He found out I was going alone and kept ringing and ringing in the morning, worried that I should not be attending alone. For me it was an absolute must. I showed no fear. And it was a twos up to Smith's family who had disgustingly tried to have me arrested.

Head up, shoulders back.

Mr Kilmurry rang me, and by now I was already in the car on my way. "Zoe, do you want me to come with you? You can't go alone. Maybe just wait to hear."

"I'm already on my way, I'm in the car." I did not want him there either.

"I'll meet you there," he said, concerned that I was doing the right thing.

One thing is for sure, if I make a decision, I stick to it and I was going, and I did not want to walk in with another male. Therapist or not.

I raised my voice down the phone. "Don't you dare! Thanks for the offer but I am going alone. It sends a message. I'm not scared of him or his family. How dare they try and make me feel like I am in the wrong. I'm a good person. He is the criminal."

"Ok Zoe, you know best." By now Mr Kilmurry knew there was no talking to me. I had a very strong mindset, and he knew there was no way of changing it once I was utterly adamant I was going.

I pulled up at the front of the court. I parked in one of the spaces directly outside and thought to myself, *This is it. I will finally get to know how long I am safe for.* I glanced around to see if I could see anyone that could possibly be Smith's family.

The day before I had a conversation with a local media company. They wanted to film me speaking at the top of the court steps once the sentencing had been passed. The journalist met me before going in.

"Hi Zoe, how are you feeling?" he asked kindly.

"A bit nervous. I'm just worried about his family or friends being here, to be honest. Sick they would even support what he did."

"So bad Zoe, hopefully the judge sees sense. We will be set up at the bottom of these steps when you come out. Have you prepared something?"

"Yes, for either way," I said, rolling my eyes, trying to make light of it.

I walked through the court doors. This time without special measures, or anyone with me.

"Head up, shoulders back," I whispered to myself.

The court staff directed me where to go and I had to walk along a corridor and go up in a glass lift. There were barristers passing me with bundles, and I could see every door open and close. I was on high alert. I reached the waiting room. As I walked through the doors, I saw Carmen and her mum standing by the window directly ahead at the back of the room.

Then I looked to my right and there they were, all of Smith's family. The mum, the dad, the uncle and a few faces I had never seen before. I just glared at them.

What the fuck are they doing here! I thought to myself, hands clammy, heart pounding.

Vile they could even contemplate supporting him. If my son ever behaved in that way, I would not be able to look at him again. I would be embarrassed, ashamed. In that moment it became clear. They are like him and that is why he is the way he is. Do they think he is innocent? Have they not seen the pictures? I was furious. It said more about them though. Who supports a women beater? Someone with zero morals, that's who.

I just looked straight ahead and smiled at Carmen and her mum even though my adrenalin was off the scale. I was so mad the Smith family had turned up mob-handed. What a bunch of bullies.

As I reached Carmen, the Smith family all left the room. It was a very odd response to my arrival. I just thought they were pathetic, if I'm honest. Carmen introduced me to her mum. She hugged me and thanked me for seeing this through. I almost cried. This was justice for her daughter too. She had watched how Smith nearly destroyed Carmen. Her as a person, emotionally, physically, as a mother and her career in the police.

He deserves this, I thought to myself. All those fond memories with Smith disappeared at that moment and I felt glad I had fought my way to this point. Smith was a serial offender. He had attacked and frightened women over his lifetime from school age. He was now going to get his just desserts, hopefully.

The court usher suddenly came into the room and asked us to move to the court room public gallery, a small room where you sit behind a glass window peering into the court room. It felt like a small goldfish bowl. We could see what was happening on the floor of the court, the judge, the jury, the barristers.

Smith was in the box next to the public gallery so we could not see him or he see us as the glass between was frosted. In a kind of a way I wanted to see his face. I wanted to see if he was sorry but actually it was for the best I did not. Who knows what that would have done?

I had not set eyes on Smith since the night of the attack, over a year before. As Carmen, her mum and I walked into the small room, all of Smith's family were already in there. I did not even look in their direction. I sat down next to Carmen's mum who sat in between Carmen and me.

The judge started. He outlined the case and what Smith had been found guilty of. It was hard to focus. Smith's mum was snarling over in our direction in a whispering voice. I could not quite make out what she was saying but I heard the word 'liar'. I could not believe it, that this woman could sit there and hurl abuse in our direction. I was appalled.

What was wrong with her? Had she no shame whatsoever? Her son was the abuser; did she think we were somehow to blame for our own abuse? She was as deluded as him, and this was clearly where his entitlement had come from. Why was she not ashamed? I know I would be if it was my son. I understood she was there to stand by him but sneering at his victims was so low. I felt sorry for her. It was a lack of intelligence.

We just ignored her. *How embarrassing*, I thought to myself. I thought about my mother for a moment, and it made me realise how lucky I had been as a child really to have had such strong and non-toxic people around me. My family were not perfect but there was no doubt in my mind, had I had done something so bad they would not have been supporting me.

The judge continued. He said he wanted to read the victim statement. As he began, I started to panic.

They were not my words. What was he reading?

He was talking about the victim being held down, with a knife to the throat, after he had kicked her around on the floor because she had said his parents obviously did not realise they had bred a monster. It was then that I realised he was reading Carmen's statement. The prosecutor was obviously making the point that Smith is a serial offender by reading a previous victim impact statement. This is not normal practice, however. It's proof and a case in point really that offenders of this type of crime often go on to repeat offend at extremely high rates.

Laura Richards has done extensive research on serial perpetrators:

- 1 in 12 rape inside and outside the home ('Getting away with it', Laura Richards, 2004, http://paladinservice.co.uk/wp-content/uploads/2013/07/Getting-Away-with-It.pdf)
- She has profiled 30 perpetrators who killed 38 women and 8 children and seriously harmed 58 women and 13 children (https://www.laurarichards.co.uk/domestic-abusers-should-be-treated-like-terrorists/)

The Domestic Abuse, Stalking and Honour Based Violence (DASH) Risk Identification, Assessment and Management Model was implemented across all police services in the UK from March 2009, having been accredited by ACPO Council, now known as National Police Chief Council (NPCC). The model was further developed from the SPECSS+ model in London by Laura Richards, who worked in partnership with Safe Lives. https://www.dashriskchecklist.co.uk/

One study by Women's Aid (April 2016 to March 2019) of 96 cases of domestic abuse recorded by the police found that men are significantly more likely to be repeat perpetrators and significantly more likely than women to use physical violence, threats and harassment. In a six-year tracking period the majority of recorded male perpetrators (83%) had at least two incidents of recorded abuse, with many having a lot more than two and one man having 52 repeat incidents (https://www.womensaid.org.uk/information-support/what-is-domestic-abuse/domestic-abuse-is-a-gendered-crime/).

As the judge continued to read out Carmen's ordeal, I felt lucky to have not been stuck in an ongoing relationship with Smith. At least my attack was quick, over with. It sent shivers down my spine. She had been trying to shake him off for months and Carmen is a police officer!

All this time the police knew what this man was capable of but they somehow made me feel stupid for reporting him. They made me feel like he had done nothing wrong. What about his history?!

That was a complete failure in their duty in my mind.

The judge cleared his throat. "So, I am going to read out the sentence now, please in the public gallery I do not want shouting out or any commotion," he warned.

I thought, *Wow that's interesting, he has given that warning*. We sat with bated breath.

He addressed Smith first. "Smith, I have no doubt you are a good father to your daughter, however you are also a violent man who cannot take no for answer. Not content with just stamping all over Miss Dronfield's head and disfiguring her, you then proceeded to take a knife to her face. You are looking at a long custodial sentence."

I could not breathe; the air was thick. I could feel Smith's mother's eyes boring into my head. She was glaring at me from the side; I could see her with my peripheral vision. How could she do that?

"I sentence you to 10 years in prison, with 4 further years on licence. You will also receive 6 months for criminal damage to Miss Dronfield's door and 6 months for witness intimidation to run concurrently. On completion of the 10 years, you will be required to go in front of a parole board to establish whether you are deemed safe for release. Court dismissed."

I looked at Carmen with no expression. We got up and walked out before the Smith family. I was so pleased. I felt that justice had been served. It seemed like a lengthy sentence in comparison to those I had read and heard of, with similar injuries. I felt like all my public work had been worthwhile. It was so important to me to not be silent. I had not done anything wrong. I never ever in my wildest nightmares thought Smith would hurt me but here I was.

As I walked out of the court room the press were waiting and I gave my speech.

It was over, finally. I had 10 years of peace ahead.

Or so I thought.

RED FLAGS & REFLECTION

Families of abusers can continue abuse by proxy. The Smith family turning up at court like that, mob-handed, what message were they trying to send me with this behaviour? I understood they wanted to support their son, but the mum, dad, uncle, auntie and the milkman all in attendance...

I was there alone.

My father was in a wheelchair and could not attend and my mother died when I was six. There was no-one there holding my hand. Yet I was the one who was brutally attacked by their 15 stone 6 foot tall son.

Why do we give abusive men such a barrage of sympathy from people, and we weirdly and almost naturally look at the victim to take some blame? I find this shocking and odd, but you see it everywhere. There is no wonder abusive men have so much entitlement when they get far more support than their victims.

Being abusive is a conscious decision, never forget that!

I absolutely 100% will not accept any blame or shame for what happened to me and if you feel that I should own some of the responsibility, please walk on by. I know what happened that night and it should never have been this way.

I never asked for nor wanted the whole ordeal I was thrown into, however I would like to wish them all the best. To Smith, Moran, their families, the family court judge who ripped my daughter away from her loving mother and brother, the rude family solicitors; to the domestic abuse advocate at West Midlands Police who came to my house and said in a very condescending manner "It does happen to people like you, you know!"; to the police officer who called me to threaten me with arrest for harassment when I was asking that the intimidation towards me by Smith from prison should stop; to the school headmistress who happily sided with my daughter's father because she wrongly thought he paid for her schooling (I did; she just wanted her fees); to the police officers who joked on a callout to my house and said that I needed to get a 'nice' boyfriend; to the officers that took my 999 calls only to not bother to check the history of Smith and mark me as standard risk; to the doctor who wanted to refuse to give me a doctor's note...

I am sorry!

Sorry that you live your life in fear of standing up for what is right.

Sorry you have no integrity in your job.

Sorry you feel the need to use someone else's weakness to cover up for your own and I am sorry that you probably won't even know the damage or impact you had on my life at that time and therefore will not learn from your mistakes.

I am sorry.

The ignorance of others is the evil among us.

Be conscious.

Be aware.

Have empathy.

Even though I regret what happened to me, having been through such an ordeal has opened my eyes to good and evil in the world. I was naively tiptoeing through life when I was set upon by two men, however I lived to tell the tale and I hope that my story inspires you to not just accept things that happen in life.

Use your voice.

Do what you can to be brave, no matter how small. Every achievement you gain swells your power.

And if something feels wrong, it probably is. Trust your gut.

I continue to support women and girls. I will always campaign and lobby to make change for the future. I am compelled.

We owe it to our children.

After an emotional ordeal such as a court case, how you would ground yourself? Now self-care is important, but what would you do to stay strong emotionally?

CHAPTER 20:

My Growth Game – You Can Do It Too!

You don't have to be defined by something that has happened to you. It is up to you how you frame it.

Me, I refuse to be a victim.

I was a victim at the time, however I refused to stay there.

I survived. I thrived.

Once I recognised I was a victim of abuse, that's when I woke up.

There was no way I was going to be downtrodden by these men and I was going to come back stronger and wiser in every way.

And now I conquer.

How?

I consider myself to be a pretty tough warrior given everything I have been through, and I have always been a positive person. Even in a bad situation I can usually find a positive way to look at what has happened and why. Clearly that has been a benefit given the many circumstances I have found myself in. I don't dwell on things or sit feeling sorry for myself and I channel anger in a positive way.

Many of us have a story, some worse than others. What I have noticed of others throughout my life is that those who succeed and come out of the other side of something terrible are those who don't stay in the victimhood and find a way to deal with whatever happened to them in order to move on. It's not an easy journey and you may sometimes want to give up and think 'why me' but staying should not be an option. Be kinder to yourself.

I hold no shame for what happened to me. Saddened yes, angry yes but it's a healthy anger. However, shame or guilt, no!

The shame solely sits on the shoulders of both abusers and throughout this journey my number one focus was my mindset.

I needed clarity of thought, and I found this in educating myself. I needed to focus, and I found this in time management, boundaries, and my end goal. I needed strength; I found this in fitness and self-care. I also surrounded myself with people who supported my growth, would validate my experiences, and understood the process I was going through.

And that has driven me to achieve things I never thought possible and get involved in some amazing projects and campaigns through which I have met some absolutely incredible people, extraordinary survivors. We are united by a grief, an understanding we never wanted or asked for. These are amazing campaigners and tenacious professionals, and my journey has taught me there are some tremendous people in this world who fight to make the world a better place for others.

So, I thank all of those who knocked me down because if it were not for this terrible ordeal I would not be where I am, so the very thing that was meant to break me, made me!

I have a newfound super strength on top of my superpower. An ability to grow after adversity, and I wanted to share this journey with you, which is why I wrote this book.

Here are some of things I have been involved in, achieved, and continue to fight for to this day...

Campaigning and law change

Maximum sentences extended for stalking

In 2017, we successfully campaigned to have the maximum prison sentences for stalking doubled from 5 to 10 years. This campaign was spearheaded by Laura Richards (founder of Paladin National Stalking Advocacy Service) and was a direct result of the case involving GP Dr Eleanor Aston who had been stalked for years by a previous patient at her practice.

https://www.gov.uk/government/news/maximum-sentence-for-stalking-to-double

https://www.legislation.gov.uk/ukpga/2012/9/part/7/crossheading/stalking/enacted

The perpetrator carried out a seven-year reign of terror against Eleanor and her family, making their lives a living hell with his persistent and incessant stalking behaviours. The judge in Dr Aston's case was so incensed by the fact he could only hand down a maximum 5-year sentence that he told her she should speak to her MP to have these sentences lengthened.

https://www.gloucestershirelive.co.uk/news/cheltenham-news/jailed-gloucestershire-stalker-raymond-knight-2961309

Smart judge, although that campaign took years to see any change in the law as do most, and the result will sadly not help Dr Aston and her family who have now left the country to start a new life outside of the UK.

The singer Lily Allen also joined this campaign following her own trauma and this gave it further media coverage. She too had been a victim of a horrific incident where the perpetrator managed to gain access to her property while Lily and her children were asleep. She was not injured, however it's the mental scars she will carry with her through this ordeal which are palpable.

https://www.theguardian.com/music/2016/apr/16/lily-allen-stalked-singer-police

Domestic abuse and stalking

Serial Domestic Abusers and Stalkers Register #serialregisterneeded
Another prominent campaign I have been involved in with Laura Richards and John Clough (father of Jane Clough) is to include serial perpetrators of domestic abuse and stalking on the Violent and Sex Offenders Register (ViSOR), meaning they would be tracked and monitored by police – proactive policing.

This was again driven by the work of Laura Richards who was trained by world leaders as a criminal behavioural analyst at the Behavioural Analysis Unit, National Centre for the Analysis of Violent Crime at the FBI and New Scotland Yard. Laura has an in-depth knowledge around this subject, having applied her psychology degrees to analysing violent crime from a behavioural and preventative perspective. On reading her work this makes total sense and most people think this type of monitoring already exists in our police forces, but it does not.

Tracking and monitoring serial offenders in this way would move away from the current police process of dealing with incidents in isolation, as they did with mine. Had this been in place prior to my attack, Smith would have most definitely been on the register, it's unlikely I would have met him, and it may well have reduced or stopped his offending. This campaign is still ongoing (2021) however following lots of debates across both houses in Parliament we have had confirmation from the government that they will introduce a super database in 2022. We continue to fight for these changes, and I remain close to the changes.

As Laura wrote in the petition update, "A huge win for this campaign happened on 15 December 2021, when a new national police framework to tackle violence against women was announced, with little fanfare or media focus". https://news.npcc.police.uk/releases/violent-men-who-harm-women-warned-that-police-are-increasing-action-against-them

It includes a strand to relentlessly pursue perpetrators, manage the most dangerous and prolific perpetrators, and better use of police powers to protect women and girls and to manage and disrupt perpetrators.

This is exactly what we have been asking police to do using a national approach. Laura Richards has produced overwhelming and compelling evidence over the years including many cases where women and children have been murdered as well as survivors such as myself and families speaking out, and many MPs and Peers in both Houses raising questions, tabling debates and yet still the government had resisted, until this time.

Our petition at time of print has almost 267,000 signatures who support our calls for serial domestic abusers and stalkers to be proactively monitored, identified, assessed and managed just like sex offenders. https://www.change.org/p/priti-patel-focus-on-serial-perpetrators-and-stalkers-who-abuse-multiple-women

We know that perpetrators go from partner to partner; they travel and move and try to fly under the radar. They use power and control tactics on partners, family members, the police and others.

They are the most dangerous of perpetrators yet there has been no proactive approach, problem solving or join up by police - until December 2021.

It's about time the tables were turned on these violent men. They should be the ones to live in fear and feel under threat and pressure - not women and girls.

The relentless pursuit of perpetrators is the most important part of the new national strategy, in my opinion. Perpetrators need to know that the police are proactively coming after them and that they will be held accountable for their behaviour.

Family court – Domestic abuse

Women's Aid - safe child contact #childfirst

In 2017 we saw a huge win for the Women's Aid 'Child First' Campaign in making child contact safer. I campaigned alongside Women's Aid and Claire Throssell MBE, who despite her horrifying story continues to fight to this day for change for the sake of her sons and for the sake of others. I talked about her case earlier in the book. Polly Neate, the CEO of Women's Aid at the time, MP Jess Phillips (Chair of Violence Against Women and Girls APPG), MP Peter Kyle, Claire and I delivered the petition to Number 10 demanding change. Following this campaign, they introduced Practice Direction 12j.

https://www.examinerlive.co.uk/news/local-news/barnsley-mum-claire-throssell-whose-19540476

https://www.womensaid.org.uk/twenty-child-homicides-child-first-goes-downing-street/

Practice Direction 12j

"This Practice Direction applies to any family proceedings in the family court or the high court under the relevant parts of the Children Act 1989 or the relevant parts of the Adoption and Children Act 2002 in which an application is made for a child arrangements order, or in which any question arises about where a child should live, or about contact between a child and a parent or other family member, where the court considers that an order should be made.

"The purpose of this Practice Direction is to set out what the family court or the high court is required to do in any case in which it is alleged or admitted, or there is other reason to believe, that the child or a party has experienced domestic abuse perpetrated by another party or that there is a risk of such abuse."

https://www.judiciary.uk/wp-content/uploads/2017/09/presidents-circular-domestic-abuse-pd12j-substituted-pd-20170914.pdf

I Want My Mummy (IWMM) Facebook campaigning page #openfamilycourt

My lobby group have an ongoing campaign to #openfamilycourt and I have worked alongside many organisations and campaigners over the years to push to have the family court opened to scrutiny. Currently family court proceedings are held in secret. This in my view is outdated and dangerous. Anything held in secret can harbour abuse and is open to corruption, something that has been cited a lot over the years. I raised this with the then MP of Coventry South, MP Jim Cunningham, and we had several meetings to discuss how the family court could change. Jim even tabled two Early Day Motions in the House of Commons on my behalf. These atrocities still continue today and must change.

https://www.change.org/p/prime-minister-boris-johnson-voice-of-the-child-culture-change-within-the-family-court-openfamilycourt

Domestic abuse

Landmark Domestic Abuse Act

Over the years there have been many campaigns relating to domestic abuse and stalking. Finally, in the Queen's speech in 2019 she announced that there would be legislation to protect the victims of domestic abuse. This was a huge step forward for us as a country in recognising this heinous crime and a chance for campaigners to contribute to the new Domestic Abuse Act which would eventually get Royal Assent on the 30th April 2021.

https://www.legislation.gov.uk/ukpga/2021/17/contents/enacted

This was our chance to really make a change, however each campaign must go through both the House of Lords and House of Commons before it gains Royal Assent. MPs debate the changes and what will be included. Some of what we called for was included, however there is still more to do.

These are the key elements which were included in the Act:

- A legal definition of domestic abuse which recognises children as victims in their own right.
- A Domestic Abuse Commissioner to stand up for survivors and life-saving domestic abuse services.
- A legal duty on councils to fund support for survivors in 'safe accommodation'.
- New protections in the family and civil courts for survivors – including a ban on abusers from cross-examining their victims, and a guarantee that survivors can access special measures (including separate waiting rooms, entrances and exits and screens).
- New criminal offences – including post-separation coercive control, non-fatal strangulation, threats to disclose private sexual images.
- A ban on abusers using a defence of 'rough sex'.
- A guarantee that all survivors will be in priority need for housing and will keep a secure tenancy in social housing if they need to escape an abuser.
- A ban on GPs for charging for medical evidence of domestic abuse, including for legal aid.
- A duty on the government to issue a code of practice on how data is shared between the public services survivors report to (such as the police) and immigration enforcement.

Coercive Control Act

Laura Richards spearheaded a successful campaign on behalf of Paladin (NSAS) with Women's Aid. This was the shortest, most successful campaign in Parliamentary history. It took 12 months to convince government it was needed using the victim's voice – women's voices and overwhelming evidence for change. In December 2012 the new law was announced.

Silent 999 calls – press 55

In April 2019 I joined a campaign to raise awareness around silent 999 calls. In my case I had called the police from my landline after the attack by Smith. The call never connected, however had it connected to the police it is a myth that the police would have turned up. I also believed this to be true. This is not the case, however had I used a mobile phone which the majority of people have these days and hit '55', that would have triggered a response. My involvement was to ensure this information was shared; it's no good having a service that no-one knows about.

Ask ANI

In January 2021 the government launched a new scheme called 'Ask ANI' through our network of pharmacists.

The Ask for ANI scheme allows those at risk or suffering from abuse to discreetly signal that they need help and access to support. By asking for ANI, a trained pharmacy worker will offer a private space where they can establish if the victim needs to speak to the police or would like help to access support services such as national or local domestic abuse helplines.

This was another awareness campaign.

Ask for Angela

Ask for Angela is the name of a campaign in England which started in 2016 that is used by bars and other venues to keep people safe from sexual assault by using a codeword to identify when they are in danger or are in an uncomfortable situation. When an establishment uses this programme, a person who believes themselves to be in danger can ask for Angela, a fictitious member of staff. The staff will then help the person get home discreetly and safely by either escorting them to a different room, calling them a taxi and escorting them to it, or by asking the other party member to leave the establishment.

Charity work

I have run charity events including a Valentine's ball, 'Love doesn't have to hurt'. I ran a half marathon in Coventry for survivors of domestic abuse and I did a walk for Refuge in London where I met the A-List actress Helena Bonham Carter. I regularly collect and give to local shelters and charities and in September 2015 I was appointed as a trustee/director of Paladin, the National Stalking Advocacy service. It is an independent trauma-led charity that advocates on behalf of victims with police and other agencies. I was invited as a 'Local Hero' to open a new Asda store in Coventry. https://zoedronfield.wordpress.com/2014/10/08/local-hero-opening-asda-daventry-road-coventry/

My contributions

I have contributed to articles in various publications including *Policing Insight* and *Metro News*. I have also contributed to a BBC *Holby City* storyline/script.

My campaigning and story have been featured in media outlets including TV (Sky News, BBC News, ITV News, GB News, Judge Rinder's Crime Stories), newspapers and magazines (the Independent, the Guardian, Daily Express, Metro, the Telegraph, the Financial Times, the Sun, the Mirror, Cosmopolitan, New Magazine, That's Life, Coventry Telegraph, CCChat Magazine, Vice News, Express, The Times, iNews, the Daily Mail, the Observer), podcasts (CCC Chat podcast, Domestic Abuse - The Cutting Edge, Crime Analyst - Laura Richard, Real Crime Profile, JUSTICE with Lady Edwina Grosvenor) and radio (BBC Coventry & Warwickshire, Heart FM, BBC Radio 5 Live, Planet Radio, Hillz FM), Radio 4's 'The Archers'.

And not all of this was just in the UK. I have featured in news and magazines globally - in Australia, Hong Kong, Japan, Canada and America.

Vice News (Broadly website): Together with Sirin Kale (Journalist at Vice), Zing Tsjeng (Editor at Vice), and Laura Richards (Founder of Paladin National Stalking Advocacy Service) we ran a campaign called #unfollowme which looked across Freedom of Information (FOI) police reports for stalking and domestic abuse. https://www.vicemediagroup.com/wp-content/uploads/2019/09/PRESS-RELEASE_-Broadly-FOI-Investigation-UK-Universities-4_9_19.pdf.

'Unfollow Me' was focussed on serial domestic abusers and stalkers launched across Broadly.vice.com in the summer of 2018 with an in-depth editorial and video series examining the dangers and realities of serial stalkers and domestic violence; from an exclusive YouGov survey gauging the public's opinions towards stalking and domestic violence related crimes in the UK, to a first-person piece from a young stalking survivor, as well as original short films about the lives and deaths of victims Alice Ruggles and Meera Dalal. This campaign was nominated for a BAFTA Award!

In February 2018 the Ministry of Justice invited me to become a committee member for the Victim & Witness Engagement Group, giving feedback around court reform in the UK. I continue to sit on this group today.

I have spoken at many conferences and events, telling my story to inspire and educate others. These have included college students, universities, a Police Crime Commissioner event, charity conferences and the first victim-led conference organised by Rachel Williams called Stand up to Domestic Abuse #sutda. Rachel was shot by her ex-husband Darren Williams after asking him for a divorce; her son Jack then killed himself just six weeks later.

I have also been lucky to be nominated for some great awards. I am humbled even to be a nominee.

- West Midlands Police – The Bob Jones Community Award – Jan 2017 (shortlist)
- Pride of Coventry – Most Inspiring Person and Local Hero – Apr 2016 (shortlist)
- CRN Women in Tech Awards – Role Model of the Year – July 2021 (shortlist)

Fighting on

You may be wondering what happened to Smith. Since being incarcerated in prison, he has appealed twice, the first time in January 2016 to have the charge thrown out using my hypnotherapy treatment as a reason. This was not granted. It beggars belief that this was even given time in court as my injuries spoke for themselves.

Then Smith appealed again in May 2017 to have his sentence reduced on the basis that it was too lengthy; this again was not granted. Both applications for leave to appeal were denied. I was not informed of this formally and only found out through the media.

Then in August 2019 after serving just five years of his prison sentence, someone in our probation service thought it a good idea to move Smith into open prison conditions without even considering me, the victim, my family, or any of his other victims.

Two police officers turned up at my house one weekend telling me that they were 'considering' moving Smith to open conditions. I just played along with their narrative that prisoners need to be rehabilitated, however after they left I wrote to Justice Minister Robert Buckland who gave me a very helpful chronological view of Smith's movement. He had already been placed in open conditions!

I was furious. They had put me and my family at risk.

My legal team issued proceedings for a judicial review against the Secretary of State for Justice and Her Majesty's Prison and Probation Service for their decision to release a dangerous serial perpetrator of domestic abuse into an open prison which would likely allow him day release near my home.

On serving the court papers for the judicial review, Smith was immediately moved back to closed conditions, so we had no need to proceed.

Throughout 2020 and 2021 Smith attempted to gain early release through the parole board - Covid first delayed this decision early in that year, then in August 2021 I was informed that the Parole Board had made the decision to keep him inside with his next parole due in July 2022. Something very odd was said in this correspondence: that Smith had decided to stay behind bars to work on himself. This statement struck me as another form of manipulation that managed to make its way to me. This was not Smith's decision, however he was making it seem so and even managed to get this into a letter sent to me.

And herein lies the problem: most within the system do not really understand the inherent manipulation of predators. Every year I have had to fight to reverse something, halt the progress of appeals or have been on the receiving end of more legal abuse or stalking.

This has to stop.

We must put the rights of the victim at the heart of any decisions around a perpetrator. Currently the system focuses largely on the perpetrators and their human rights.

What about the victims of these crimes? Don't they matter anymore? Don't they deserve to feel safe? What about their human rights? Or do we just disregard victims once their perpetrator has served their time?

After all we never chose to be a victim, did we?

After everything I maintain that mindset is everything and, in the end, it was my **Mind Over Manipulators**. I consider myself to be a winner every day. Because every day includes an achievement, no matter how big or small. I position my day that way.

What next?

I will continue to carry out my work as a campaigner and provide mentorship for other women looking to thrive and conquer after abuse and provide social housing to support the housing shortage in the UK, focusing on victims of domestic abuse and stalking.

You can get in touch with me at:
Facebook: search 'Zoe Dronfield'
Twitter: @ZDronfield
LinkedIn: Zoe Dronfield
Email: info@zoedronfield.com

I am available for conferences, after dinner inspirational speeches, educational talks, and media interviews.

Resources

Recommended reading

Lundy Bancroft, *Why Does He Do That? Inside the Minds of Angry and Controlling Men*

Rhonda Byrne, *The Secret*

Rhonda Byrne, *The Power*

Pat Craven, *Living with the Dominator*

Melanie Tonia Evans's blog, https://blog.melanietoniaevans.com/

Professor Marianne Hester, 'The Three Planet Model', 19 September 2009, available at http://www.bristol.ac.uk/news/2009/6703.html

Peace, *Psychopath Free: Recovering from Emotionally Abusive Relationships with Narcissists, Sociopaths, & Other Toxic People*

Tina Swithin, *Divorcing a Narcissist: Advice from the Battlefield*

Marney Thompson, *Providing a Safe Haven: An attachment informed approach to grief*, January 2019, available at: https://bcacc.ca/wp-content/uploads/2019/01/Providing-a-Safe-Haven-An-Attachment-Informed-Approach-to-Grief-Counselling-Marney-Thompson-Winter-2018.pdf

Lenore E. Walker, 'The Cycle of Abuse', 1979, https://en.wikipedia.org/wiki/Cycle_of_abuse

Women's Aid Forum, https://survivorsforum.womensaid.org.uk/

Organisations that can help

Paladin National Stalking Advocacy Service 0203 866 4107
https://paladinservice.co.uk/contact-links/
Support for high-risk victims of stalking

National Stalking Helpline run by Suzy Lamplugh Trust 0808 802 0300
https://www.suzylamplugh.org/pages/category/national-stalking-helpline
Support for all victims of stalking

Women's Aid
https://www.womensaid.org.uk/
Women's Aid is a grassroots federation working together to provide life-saving services and build a future where domestic violence is not tolerated.

National Domestic Abuse Helpline run by Women's Aid and Refuge for women experiencing domestic abuse, their family, friend and callers on their behalf
https://www.nationaldahelpline.org.uk/

LGBT+ Domestic Abuse Helpline 0800 999 5428
https://galop.org.uk/domesticabuse/

Northern Ireland: Domestic and Sexual Abuse Helpline 0808 802 1414
Online live chat
help@dsahelpline.org

Scotland: Domestic Abuse and Forced Marriage Helpline 0800 027 1234
Online live chat
helpline@sdafmh.org.uk

Wales: Live Fear Free 0808 80 10 800
Online live chat
Text info@livefearfreehelpline.wales

Victim Support 0808 16 89 111
Live chat https://www.victimsupport.org.uk/help-and-support/get-help/support-near-you/live-chat/
Support for victims of crime

Broken Rainbow National Helpline 0300 999 5428 / 0800 999 5428
www.brokenrainbow.org.uk
Domestic violence helpline for all LGBT communities, their family, friends and callers on their behalf

Karma Nirvana 0800 5999 247
www.karmanirvana.org.uk
For those experiencing honour-based abuse and forced marriage

Revenge Porn Helpline 0345 6000 459
www.revengepornhelpline.org.uk
Supporting all adults (over 18) whose intimate images and videos have been shared without their consent, or under the threat that they will

Men's Advice Line 0808 801 0327
www.mensadviceline.org.uk
Advice and support for men experiencing domestic abuse

ManKind Initiative 01823 334244
www.mankind.org.uk
Advice and support for men experiencing domestic abuse

Respect 0808 802 4040
www.respectphoneline.org.uk
Help for domestic violence perpetrators

About the Author

Zoe Dronfield is a survivor of a high-profile domestic violence attack, having been tortured and held for over eight hours. Although she escaped with her life, she was then subjected to a justice system that she describes as broken.

Using her 20+ years of professional experience working across the public sector, health, law enforcement and local government, advising on technology and services that support government policy, and having run a child protection agency, she can see clearly where the system is failing, so is compelled to make a difference.

A regular commentator in the media, Zoe is a campaigner for the rights of women, victims of domestic abuse and stalking. She has made fundamental changes in both the criminal and family justice system by using her own experiences to highlight failings and has changed legislation to close loopholes.

Zoe is also on the Trust Board of Paladin National Stalking Advocacy Service, the first trauma informed service for high-risk victims of stalking, and sits on the Victim and Witness Engagement Group at the Ministry of Justice with an input into court reform.

Zoe has even incorporated her keen interest in property to help others and owns a property portfolio in her home city Coventry, where she works with local charities to house victims of abuse and homelessness.

You can visit Zoe online at www.zoedronfield.com or on social media:
Facebook: search 'Zoe Dronfield'
Twitter @ZDronfield
LinkedIn Zoe Dronfield

Baroness Jan Royall, Patron for Paladin National Stalking Advocacy Service, speaking at the Houses of Parliament

Zoe at West Midlands Police's Diamond Awards

Zoe at the Pride of Coventry Awards with the Winner of Pride of Coventry 2016, Reece Dry

Zoe (second from right) at Judge Rinder filming with (left to right) Wayne Griffin, Carmen Chicarella and David Kilmurry

Zoe being interviewed at home

Zoe being interviewed

Zoe (far left, front) at a SUTDA (Stand Up to Domestic Abuse) event with other survivors

It's everywhere: Zoe holds up a Dutch magazine in Ibiza displaying a domestic abuse story (the cover line reads: Sorry, I won't ever do it again)

Zoe in a West Midlands Police Diamond Award brochure – always the nominee, never the winner!

Zoe is interviewed outside No. 10 Downing Street for the Serial Register Campaign

Zoe outside the Houses of Parliament for a family court protest

Zoe speaking at a SUTDA event

Zoe speaking at a Paladin conference for Police Crime Commissioners

Zoe outside No. 10 Downing Street with John Clough MBE (father of Jane) and Laura Richards of Paladin National Stalking Advocacy Service

Zoe speaking at Twitter headquarters

Zoe speaking at Twitter headquarters

Zoe with (from left) MP Jess Phillips, Claire Throssell and Polly Neate in support of the Child First campaign

Zoe with campaigner Claire Throssell, MP Peter Kyle, MP Jess Phillips and then CEO of Women's Aid Polly Neate outside No. 10 Downing Street as part of the Child First campaign

Zoe speaking at a West Midlands Police event

Zoe with Coventry Lord Mayor office's Cllr Michael Antony Hammon attending the Pride of Coventry Awards lunch event

Zoe with actress Helena Bonham Carter listening to speeches at the Walk4Refuge event in London

Zoe with Jo Brand at the Refuge – 45 years commemoration at the Houses of Parliament

Zoe with John Bercow, then Speaker of the House at the Houses of Parliament

Zoe with MP Jess Phillips in 2016

Zoe with Pete Townshend at the Refuge – 45 Years commemoration, Houses of Parliament

Zoe with the Domestic Abuse Commissioner Nicole Jacobs (second from left) along with policy makers, campaigners and survivors

Zoe (second from right) with others at the House of Lords Unfollow Me campaign in November 2018

Zoe with survivors and Helena Bonham Carter at the Walk4Refuge event in London

Printed in Great Britain
by Amazon